Foxfire
STORY

Foxfire

STORY

Oral Tradition
in Southern Appalachia

Edited by

T. J. Smith

ANCHOR BOOKS
A Division of Penguin Random House LLC
New York

AN ANCHOR BOOKS ORIGINAL, APRIL 2020

The Foxfire Fund, Inc.
PO Box 541
Mountain City, GA 30562-0541
706-746-5828
www.foxfire.org

Library of Congress Cataloging-in-Publication Data
Names: Smith, T. J., 1977– editor. | Foxfire Fund, other.
Title: Foxfire story : oral tradition in Southern Appalachia /
Edited by T. J. Smith.
Description: New York : Anchor Books, A Division of Penguin
Random House LLC, 2020.
Identifiers: LCCN 2019029608 (print) | LCCN 2019029609 (ebook)
Subjects: LCSH: Folklore—Appalachian Region, Southern. |
Oral tradition—Appalachian Region, Southern. | Ethnology—
Appalachian Region, Southern. | Folklorists—Appalachian Region,
Southern.
Classification: LCC GR108.15 .F69 2020 (print) | LCC GR108.15 (ebook) |
DDC 398.20975—dc23
LC record available at https://lccn.loc.gov/2019029608

**Anchor Books Trade Paperback ISBN: 978-0-525-43631-7
eBook ISBN: 978-0-525-43632-4**

Book design by Nick Alguire

www.anchorbooks.com

Printed in the United States of America
10   9   8   7   6   5   4   3   2   1

This book is dedicated to the contacts and students who have passed away over Foxfire's fifty-plus years.

Your legacy still glows.

CONTENTS

ACKNOWLEDGMENTS

I would be remiss to not first acknowledge the hundred or so folks who make every *Foxfire* book happen. Without the students, without the contacts, these books would never come into being. Period. You can find their names throughout this and every *Foxfire* book and also listed in the back of each book. They are responsible for creating and growing this incredible experiment.

Additionally, I want to thank my editor/liaison at Anchor Books, Tom Pold, for his work leading me through my first *Foxfire* book. Tom and his team have been great partners to Foxfire, and we are very thankful for all of their hard work.

Finally, I want to thank the members of the Foxfire staff, namely Barry Stiles (curator), Kami Ahrens (assistant curator), Jessica Parker (donor relations), Bridgett Gladney (sales and marketing), Jan Vonk (finance and administration), and our summer graduate interns, Jen England and Walker Boswell—all who assisted in this book's creation.

FOREWORD

by John A. Burrison

I'm thinking back to 1966, a bit more than half a century ago. A lot was going on in the world then, not all of it good—like the Vietnam War. But 1966 was a good year for folklore research in Georgia, a state that had seen little exploration of its people's traditional way of life. That was the year that a young teacher named Eliot Wigginton began the Foxfire program at the Rabun Gap–Nacoochee School in the mountains of Rabun County as an alternative to the routine English high school curriculum. An experiment in "experiential education," the students were sent out armed with tape recorders, notebooks, and cameras to interview and document older mountaineers—in some cases the students' grandparents—about their memories of growing up in the area and their continuing craft, storytelling, and other traditional practices.

As some of you know, the main idea was to engage the students in literacy not just as an academic exercise but as a publication project in which they could take pride. The first issues of *The Foxfire Magazine* were a modest mix of oral history, folklore, and creative writing, but, much to everyone's surprise, the program blossomed into a national phenomenon, with other schools adopting the Foxfire learning model and adapting it to their own situations. The magazine spun off a book series (the present volume being the latest), a play and movie, and a museum. The timing was right: many Americans were fed up with a diet of mass culture and the urban rat race, and Foxfire fueled their desire to get back to the land and "live off the grid" by providing detailed instructions from the mouths of mountaineers who had been doing so for generations.

Now, here's where I come in. In 1966 I came to Georgia with a graduate folklore degree from the University of Pennsylvania to develop and teach a folklore curriculum in the English Department at Georgia State University in Atlanta. While an undergraduate journalism major at Penn State I'd stumbled into a course on folk ballads taught by Samuel Bayard, a Harvard-trained folklorist who had collected folk songs and instrumental music along the Pennsylvania–West Virginia border—the upper reaches of Southern Appalachia. As a participant in America's folk music "revival," which reached its height of popularity in the 1960s, I was introduced by Professor Bayard to a more serious perspective on folk songs and an appreciation of the mountain people who grew up with them as an integral part of their lives. I mined the library for publications on Appalachian folklore, and was especially impressed by Allen Eaton's 1937 *Handicrafts of the Southern Highlands*—not so much for Eaton's history of mountain crafts and efforts to make them economically viable in the early twentieth century, but by the accompanying portraits of traditional craftspeople taken by New York photographer Doris Ulmann, which cut through hillbilly stereotypes to reveal the souls of a proud people whose inherited hand skills were carrying them safely through the depths of the Depression. Given my interest in the traditional culture of Appalachia that continued to grow in graduate school, imagine my good fortune when I was offered the opportunity to move to Georgia, a state whose uplands were a virtual terra incognita when it came to folklore research.

Since my early fieldwork was concentrated in those North Georgia uplands, it was only natural that my path and that of Foxfire would cross. In early 1967 I met Eliot Wigginton while visiting Rabun County to investigate and acquire crafts as curator of a planned exhibit for a newly formed organization called Georgia Mountain Arts. At the time, "Wig" was enjoying the hospitality of Mary Hambidge at her hand-weaving center not far from where he was teaching (his students later built him a house on Foxfire's Black Rock Mountain property). He presented me with a copy of the first number of *Foxfire Magazine*, and I was soon a subscriber and supporter of the program, impressed by the documentation his students were doing in their corner of North Georgia and adjacent North Carolina, at the same time my students were engaged in folklore fieldwork throughout the state. Between our two programs a cooperative relationship developed; I served on the Foxfire Advisory Board from 1974 to 1978 and later coordinated a three-hundred-page feature on Southern folk pottery for the *Foxfire 8* book (1984). Then in 2002 a Georgia State undergraduate English major who'd grown up in the Georgia mountains, T. J. Smith, took my Folklore and Literature course and "caught fire" to the subject; after minoring in folklore with me, he went on to earn his PhD in folklore at the University of Louisiana at Lafayette. It took a while for T. J. to find the right job fit, but in 2017 he was hired as executive director of Foxfire—where he put together this book!

The Foxfire magazines and books are perhaps best known for their descriptions of Appalachian material folk culture, often detailed enough, for example, that readers could follow the plans for a traditional log cabin and actually build one. But other types of folk-cultural expression also are abundant in the Foxfire archives, with the present book featuring oral traditions—stories, songs, riddles, sayings, folk beliefs, and folk speech, as well as accounts of pranks and customs such as

Christmas "serenading"—recorded by the students (with a few nonstudent contributions) over a span of several decades. The stories fall into two basic categories: traditional legends and folktales learned by the tellers from family or neighbors, and personal experience accounts that incorporate the narrators' community worldview—including supernatural beliefs—as well as something of their personal life histories. Older folk stories include Stanley Hicks's "Jack and the Giants," a good example of an Appalachian "Jack tale" with European roots; Lloyd Arneach's "Listening for the Little People," representing Cherokee Indian fairy lore; and Don Patterson's legends based on mountaineers' once-prevalent belief in witchcraft. These examples all appear in "The Tellers" section, where seven individuals forge their identities as storytellers with their diverse repertoires. Altogether, a very human portrait of Appalachian culture is painted, parallel to, but also departing from, what historians and sociologists have written about the region.

While this book provides plenty of enjoyable reading, it also offers a glimpse of the changes the region has experienced— for better and worse—since the early twentieth century. Life in the mountains now is not the same as it was fifty years ago when the first Foxfire students ventured out for good material to publish; the older generation has since passed on. Were it not for the dedication of those early students and their teachers, as well as those of today who are still producing the magazine, our knowledge of a very special culture would be much the poorer.

INTRODUCTION

Chances are if you've picked up this book, you have some idea of what Foxfire is. Over the past fifty-plus years, twelve volumes of the Foxfire book series, and ten additional titles, we've amassed quite a following. However, should you be a new reader, someone drawn to this title for reasons beyond familiarity with our organization, then allow me to briefly share with you the Foxfire story.

In short, Foxfire is a classroom-based, student-led, high school journalism project that far exceeded anyone's expectations. It was a project that began in response to a stagnant education system and is a shining example of what can happen when teachers let go of methods that don't work and students take ownership of their own learning. That is exactly what happened in a small, shared public-private school in extreme northeast Georgia in 1966, when students in a high school English class were encouraged by their teacher to go out into their communities and talk to people about life and survival in the Southern Appalachian mountains.

After collecting a dozen or so interviews from locals in the community, the students were asked what they might like to do with the information. Their response: Start a magazine. So, these high school kids went out and sold advertising, found a printer-for-hire, taught themselves how to glue-up layout sheets, and, in the spring of 1967, they published the first *Foxfire Magazine*. We've been in continuous publication ever since. The magazine eventually found a national audience, and the students were then invited by E. P. Dutton (now part of Penguin Random House) to put together a book—an anthology of the best articles from the magazine. That first book, published in 1972, sold half a million copies in just six months, bringing more national attention to the program and earning the students and this organization many accolades . . . and, a first for them, royalties.

Arie Carpenter with students

In 1973, the students, already working on a second Foxfire book, were charged with deciding how to best use their newfound revenues. They decided to spend the money, in part, on the creation of a museum and classroom site, for which they purchased fifty acres and began the process of relocating log structures from around Southern Appalachia to be repurposed as exhibit spaces for artifacts, learning spaces for classes, and office space for the rapidly growing magazine program. Today, nearly fifty years later, that part of the project has grown to 110 acres, some thirty-one log structures, and a museum and heritage center that includes active traditional arts demonstrators, artists, and instructors.

We still have high school students exploring their community and their region. Every year, our Foxfire Fellows—high-school-aged students from throughout Rabun County—spend their summers at the museum and heritage center. During the eight weeks of the fellowship, these young people learn and develop skills in interviewing, writing, photography, electronic layout and design, documentary filmmaking, and podcasting. Additionally, each student apprentices in a heritage skill, such as blacksmithing, weaving, broom making, woodstove cooking, and the like. After the summer, they dedicate hours after school and on weekends to putting together two double issues (Fall/Winter and Spring/Summer) of *The Foxfire Magazine*. It is a very special experience for them, to say the least. Likewise, it is a very special experience for me.

Folks like to toss around the term "dream job" when talking about their professional lives. It's not a term I've ever liked because it suggests something unattainable or otherworldly—something that doesn't exist in reality, but only in dreams. Previously, I'd had some really great jobs, but none of them was anything I'd place in the same dimensional plane as where I'm able to fly through the clouds and shoot lasers out of my fists. Then I was hired as Foxfire's executive director, and I finally understood "dream job." Now knowing what Foxfire is, I think you can see why.

I am a folklorist. Defining what that means is a rabbit hole into which I could easily get lost. Stripped down, folklorists explore the relationships between groups and their traditions. A "group" can be as nuanced as, say, a community or as strictly defined as a family. The traditions, or folklore, of those groups is the stuff they share in common. So, a folk group (family, friends, coworkers, community, etc.) is a group of people, and the traditions they share is what constitutes "folklore." Folklore can be pared down to specific types, such as material culture, foodways, music, belief and religion, and, the focus of this book, narrative.

A while back, I was interviewed by a graduate student, Dylan Harris, doing research in the Foxfire archive. The topic of our conversation was storytelling—storytelling in the general sense, but also in the larger context of narrative, its role in the human condition, and as a folkloric genre. It just so happens that this interview took place around the same time that I was piecing together the contents of this book, the topics of story and narrative very much fresh in my mind.

It is a rare occasion when I get to put on my folklorist hat and chat about folklore things. I relish these opportunities. I especially love discussing something so meaningful as the way people use story and narrative to negotiate reality. While I absolutely love material culture, I do not think there is anything as important to our understanding of ourselves as the study of how we frame our existence through story and narrative.

The archive at Foxfire is full of stories. It's a remarkable repository. I have great fun pulling folders of interview transcripts, often losing myself in story when I'm supposed to be looking for something else. For instance, I may go to the archive with the intention of finding information on smokehouses and processes for curing pork but end up getting roped into a series of "painter" (panther) stories (a specific type of animal tale) and lose a good hour just mesmerized by the narratives. In moments like that, I recall the stories I heard as a kid growing up in the South (first in middle Georgia and later right here in the Northeast Georgia mountains) from grandparents and neighbors, and I feel reconnected to my family and to this community. That's the power of story. That's what I've come to realize over the years—that the narrative impulse and our attraction to story can teach us so much about the human condition. It's a revelation I first came to in a university classroom in Atlanta, Georgia.

The class was John Burrison's Folklore and Literature—an introductory course examining connections between oral tradition and literature. John did an incredible job of placing his students firmly in the context of the folklore he presented. He is a pretty good storyteller in his own right, and can still thrill a room of twenty-first-century twentysomething college students with a traditional tale like "The Golden Arm" or a literary folktale, such as "The Monkey's Paw." Beyond his examples of story in prose, he often brought in a portable turntable and played for us various versions of folk ballads, another genre of folk narrative, covering the spectrum from beautifully simple, field-recorded renditions of standards like "Barbara Allen" to the studio-produced sounds of the electric folk revival group Steeleye Span. Likewise, there were recordings of great storytellers like Ray Hicks, whose performances of Jack tales (see page xxvi) were raucously fun and melodic. We also explored jokes, anecdotes, jests, and the oral traditions of children. In every case, I found the narratives to be thrilling, haunting, hilarious, tragic, entertaining—indelibly human.

This brings me back to my conversation with Dylan Harris. I don't think there is anything quite as intimate or grounding as the ways in which we use narrative in our day-to-day lives and in the grander storytelling contexts we encounter. In our preliterate history, humankind used narrative, in story and song, to make sense of the world. The purveyors of this art were as important as chieftains and kings. They were the keepers of the historical record, keepers of laws and customs, keepers of a group's beliefs and of its heroes. They were the documentarians of their specific folk groups. But narrative was not a verbal art reserved for a select few. Narrative was found in songs sung by mothers to their children or by laborers in the fields. Narrative bloomed around family fires and around the fires of war parties, in mead halls and at the feast day tables. In each context, narrative was all at once a mode of entertainment, a means of reestablishing familial and tribal ties, a device for educating the listeners on community rules, and a way to control behavior. Or, as folklorist William Bascom more succinctly put it, the functions of folklore, including folk narrative, were/are to entertain, validate, educate, and control. And while we today feel far removed from our preliterate, oral-tradition-centered ancestors, and though we rarely think of it in the contexts I've alluded to here, folk narrative remains very much alive and just as important today.

As we love to do around here, I want to pull out a portion of the transcript from my interview with Dylan because I think it's a good conversation about story and narrative and a solid summary of how the stories in our archive—from which we've put together this book—came to be:

Dylan: I am curious how you conceptualize storytelling . . . maybe in your own work but also here at Foxfire.

T. J.: I think, in terms of Foxfire: What is the role of storytelling in community? Because that's really where the stories out of the archive are built from, and, you know, think about the context in which the students are gathering this information. First of all, you have these students—high school students— who are interviewing members of their immediate community. They're insiders; they already have a connection with these people. Later, in the organizational, programmatic history of Foxfire, that changed a little bit . . . but at least from the onset it was really about connecting students with their community through the process of going and sitting down and having a conversation. In those conversations, stories came up. And stories came up because stories are a part of a conversational process for people because it's built into their customs and traditions. You use stories as a mode of illustration, to illustrate a particular point. You use story to connect. You use story to do all these different things, and it is not this isolated verbal art that takes place in a vacuum. It generally takes place in a larger context—a conversation, a barbecue, a church meeting, or a family gathering or something like that. The idea of a storytelling context—a formal storytelling context—is not a new one, but, for this community, it is something different.

Like, if you want to go way back, we can go back to medieval times—Anglo-Saxon, Germanic . . . —I am also a bit of a medievalist, so . . . studying the works of King Alfred or studying Beowulf or something like that. In those societies you had these people called scops [pronounced shōp] who were storytellers. And that was a very important role because, as with a lot of civilizations at that time period and before, words had magic . . . words had power . . . and the ability to craft story was seen as a high art. It was [some of] the only art. It was a preliterate society; these people as individuals carried with them the history of everything in their stories. Then literate society comes into play, and that doesn't mean we stop telling stories . . . but the context changes. It evolves. They still had telling stories around the fire, at the pub, or something like that . . . so still a storytelling context, but, again, not like "tonight we're going to have stories at the pub" . . . right? It was just something that came about naturally. And, that's still where we kind of are now with storytelling . . . where we've been for the past five hundred years. There's these little things that happen in the context of—you know, there's this really great, I think it was a Pat Mire documentary about Louisiana that he did . . . You know it was a bunch of Cajun, Louisiana folklorists talking about storytelling . . . He illustrates, you know, there's a group of men standing around; they've got something on the grill; they're drinking beers, and one of them says: "Have you heard the one about . . . ?" and that starts this process. They're passing the time; they're telling stories, but they're also solidifying their membership in that particular group. "Yeah, we've all heard these stories a thousand times, but we're going to tell them again to each other anyway because we're in this social context, and this is a way of reaffirming our membership." So, that's what I mean by the context for storytelling. It's not, you know, the scop with the fire—"gather round, children"—or that kind of thing.

So, with Foxfire, these kids are going out and doing these interviews. They're sitting down and talking with somebody about a particular topic maybe that's come up, . . . and in order to illustrate their point, the interviewee launches into a story. And, then there's also the context in which the students become cognizant that—whether they're told by their teachers or come to this by themselves—that people have stories to tell, and they go into an interview saying: "Do you have any stories about 'blah,' or do you know any good ghost stories, Aunt Arie?" And then they are controlling the context and shifting those people to that context. But, I think it starts with those early interviews where they didn't go in with any preconceived notions of what they would find . . . but they found things, and they would go back for second, third, fourth, and fifth interviews to narrow in on a particular thing. And then whoever the publisher was, or the teachers, would focus the students' attention on a particular thing. "Can you get a section on ghost stories in the newest book?" And so, the kids go out and collect ghost stories.

*

It's the storytelling contexts, *where* we use narrative and *when*, that make many of the stories in our collection so important. Putting someone on the spot to tell a story can yield fair results, but presenting stories in the context of a larger conversation is truly the magic of storytelling. It is in that situation that we get to see how story works for the individual—the teller—as a tool for communicating, a vehicle by which to best illustrate their intention. So, while several of the stories in our archive were collected through a more formalized "ask," there are also a great many that came to be recorded in an organic context—conversationally and without prompting.

To help with your own understanding of story, reflect on some regular family or social gathering—this could be Sunday dinner at Grandma's or a yearly family reunion, an annual professional conference, or getting together with your neighbors every year for the Super Bowl. Regardless of the specific context, just reflect on that kind of gathering and then think about the kinds of stories that come up. For instance, in my family we always get together at my uncle's house for Thanksgiving. This has been a family tradition for as long as I can remember. And, in the context of that gathering, there are inevitably those moments—either amongst small groups (the kids table) or with the whole tribe together—that one person or another says something along the lines of "Y'all remember when . . ." Thus, it begins.

Special family gatherings are a great illustration of how storytelling still functions in our hypermodern lives. Part of the reason is that these gatherings are often the only time of year we see our extended family. We come together with aunts and uncles, cousins, and others with whom we haven't spoken in a year or longer. Yeah, they're blood, but beyond that, where's the connection? Here's where storytelling comes into play. Here's where those family tales that you've heard a hundred times or better are retold again for no other reason than to remind everyone in the room that "hey, we're familiar here—we have history, we are connected." The stories we tell this year are the same stories we tell practically every year, but they're *our* stories. They are the narrative glue that hold us all together. Shared stories equate to shared membership in a folk group—be it our family, friend group, church, school, the office. Stories help to remind us of our membership in the groups of which we are a part and tie us to the other members of those groups.

This is just one example, one context, in which story and

narrative still operate in our lives. There are many other ways and contexts. I think of how parents will use a story/anecdote from their childhood to illustrate a point to their children, equating experiences to provide guidance. I think of how jokes and riddles still thrive among children as an entertainment and a means of pushing the boundaries of language and taboo. I remember, very clearly, how urban legends and "folk rules" govern college campuses (how long *does* one wait for a late professor?). All of these are ways in which story and narrative remain a relevant presence in our culture. I also want to recognize that I'm discussing this topic through a Western/American lens. This discussion is very much limited in scope, which brings us to this book.

What's in a Story?

The contents of this book run the gamut of oral tradition genres and include, as well, a few literary works. We've also included some performance genres that possess some narrative element, including songs and stories about pranks and serenading. Much of what is printed here was originally published in *The Foxfire Magazine*; however, there is also a great deal of material that has never before been seen by anyone outside of those few of us who have access to the Foxfire archive. The remarkable thing about all of it is that, even after publishing more than twenty books over the course of the organization's fifty-year history, we still have so much wonderful, rich material that has not made it into the public eye. This just speaks to the volume of material Foxfire students have collected over the years.

From that material, we've gathered a thorough sampling of various oral traditions. We begin with a collection of "mountain speech"—folk speech or vernacular from the region. This glossary of terms has been added to act as both a guide to some of the speech you'll encounter in the stories and as a glimpse into the colorful, poetic language of Southern Appalachia. Building on that language, the next chapter covers some of the region's more colorful proverbs and colloquialisms. As with the glossary of mountain speech, our aim is to provide you with a foundation of phrasing that you'll encounter throughout this collection.

From these foundational chapters, we plop you right into legends, ranging from stories that teach us about place to hair-curling tales of the supernatural. Of all the genres covered in this book, legend is probably the most relevant to our present age. We find that folks, especially young people, still like to share legends, popularized now as "urban legends," whenever opportunities for storytelling arise. The collection of legends herein represents a blend of traditional stories as well as more modern "urban legends," such as those popularized in contemporary film and television. Legends are distinguished from other types of oral tradition in that they are accounts of events or circumstances believed to be true by the storyteller and his or her audience. They can be historical, but today tend toward the supernatural. You may recognize some of the motifs—it seems that every town has a legend about a ghostly prom queen who appears on a bridge on a certain night of the year or one about a pair of star-crossed lovers leaping to their deaths from some high point near town. This is the stuff of campfire gatherings, the tales best accompanied by a flashlight held just below the chin.

We then move from legends to another traditional folk narrative genre, the folktale. Up until just about the time Foxfire students began interviewing people in the 1960s, folktales still played a significant role as entertainment for Southern Appalachian communities. While people aren't spinning yarns like this much anymore, the folktale played a very important role in the construction of the larger American mythos. For the Southern Appalachian region, the folktale gave birth to a great many of the characters and caricatures—for better or worse—that have become fixtures of a larger Appalachian identity. The folktale form itself, best popularized by the brothers Grimm in Germany, generally consists of coming-of-age stories that feature a young hero or heroine overcoming a great challenge through generosity, cleverness, intellect, or some similar trait. These kinds of tales were perfect for young audiences, at times instructive or containing a moral lesson. In the Southern Appalachian region, there might not have been a more popular series of folktales than that of the "Jack tale," named for the tale's central hero, a trickster figure who uses his cunning and wit to get out of any number of sticky situations. Jack is often found facing off with ne'er-do-well authority figures or even the devil himself.

Another well-established folktale type from this region is the jocular tale or jest. Narrative jokes such as these have been a popular form of entertainment for centuries, from Elizabethan England onward. Ranging from exaggerated tales of strength and cunning to more bawdy humor, jocular tales are enjoyed by audiences of varying ages. Humorous stories around hunting and fishing are the most common, along with stories involving the art of making (and drinking) moonshine whiskey. Tales of compromised preachers are another motif that we find with some frequency in Southern Appalachia.

While our archive is replete with these specific genres of verbal art, the majority of this kind of folklore was collected in the first two decades of the magazine program. All across the country, the frequency of these forms begins to fall off by the mid-1980s and decreases exponentially from that point forward. These kinds of stories today are more or less relegated to formal storytelling festivals.

One oral tradition form that we have no shortage of is the anecdote. Of all the genres that fall under the heading of "verbal art," the anecdote is by far the most accessible and most abundant, not only in this particular region, but throughout the United States. Anecdotes, or memorates, are the stories we build from our experiences.

These are the stories of us. They are the narrative snapshots of our most memorable moments—moments we experience as individuals, as families, as communities, and, yes, as a nation. When I think about anecdotes, I think of them as the purest product of our (human) narrative impulse. Anecdotes are the stories about ourselves we have come to value, so much so that we care enough to share them with those around us. These are the stories we tell our children and grandchildren. These are the stories about the most remarkable and affecting events in our lives, told as a means to bridge new relationships and to strengthen old ones.

It may come as no surprise that anecdotes make up the bulk of the stories in the Foxfire archive. Our magazine articles over the past twenty-five years or so have been predominantly of the biographical sort. In those interviews, in which we asked contacts to talk about their lives, folks shared the stories of their most memorable experiences. These included stories about their families, their communities, their occupations, and their hobbies. In the study of an individual, these tales can tell us about that person's life, specifically his or her values, world-view, and activities. A collected anthology of such stories from different individuals connected by a common geography can help us form an ethnographic picture of a community—its shared values, worldview, and traditions. In short, anecdotes are a wonderful example of the narrative impulse and what we can learn from it.

Stories, specifically anecdotal stories, often arise collectively, from significant events that impact a community. Many communities throughout the United States have experienced some kind of great and/or terrible event that lives on in a sort of collective memory. Folks living along coastal waters may share stories about bad storms, a town's folk history may contain a collection of memorates about a particularly bad fire or period of lawlessness, or an isolated rural community may remember well the impact of something like a mining disaster or a flood. Much in the same way we have a collective memory of national stories around events such as the political assassinations of the 1960s, the explosion of the shuttle *Challenger*, or the events of 9/11, so too do small communities possess a collective memory of stories around events that changed those communities forever.

We round out the first section of the book with three genres that more closely skirt the line between oral tradition and performance. Under the larger definition of folklore, or folk tradition, folklorists define performance as an aesthetically marked mode of communication. It's communication with flair. The purpose of folk performance is not just the transfer of information, but also to entertain and color that information with all manner of performative tools like inflection, facial expressions, body movements, melody, and the like. The difficulty in presenting performance in the context of a book such as this is that performance relies on human interaction between performer and audience. What I'm driving at is that while I hope you appreciate reading the contents of this book, I encourage you to seek out opportunities to experience these genres as live performance.

The first of these chapters is on songs. In the context of the larger folk song genre, the folk ballad has played an indelible role in the storytelling tradition of this region. As a holdover from the Old World, some songs stretching back five hundred years or more, this form provides us with insight into closely held worldviews that traveled with the area's first European settlers. The folk ballad was a versatile folk song form most popular in England and Scotland among the peasantry. Folk ballad narrative themes ranged from cautionary tales of the supernatural to accounts of current events.

For the common people who learned and performed them, folk ballads were at once a means of underscoring community values and sharing the latest news. With the advent of the printing press in the fifteenth century, the broadside ballad (so-called for the long pieces of paper on which they were printed) exploded in popularity and became *the* means of sharing current events throughout the English and Scottish countryside among the laboring class. Upon their arrival to the Americas, English and Scottish settlers maintained the tradition, creating new ballads as broadsides or as purely oral compositions. In the centuries that followed their arrival, as they moved through the North American continent, settlers and their descendants continued to use the folk ballad as a means of recording events and communicating their worldview. In Southern Appalachia, the form continued on well into modernity, and we've shared a sampling of that tradition in the chapter on songs.

Work songs were another popular holdover from the Old World, found not only in Europe, but in West Africa as well, and we've included a popular work song or chant connected to the task of churning butter. White settlers and African slaves alike carried with them to the region work songs and chants that were used as a means of making work pass faster and, in some instances, as a way to maintain a rhythm to the work itself. In the process of collecting information on the butter churning song, we came to learn that it was utilized by members of white and black communities throughout Georgia, which is an interesting glimpse into how folk traditions diffused among even segregated communities that shared common geographical space. There are many books on the topic of American folk songs and their Old World antecedents, too many great ones to list here. If you have an interest in learning more, I urge you to visit your local library or spend some time researching the topic on the Internet. It won't take long to find yourself deep in the rabbit hole of folk song traditions.

Following our chapter on songs, we get into a bit of humor with pranks and jests. Jests are, more or less, jokes, but less formulaic. Those included in this chapter are more in line with humorous anecdotes but do possess something like a punch line at the end. Humor in storytelling is an important component in the Southern Appalachian oral tradition. Folks enjoy getting a laugh, so most carry with them a humorous anecdote or two to share should the opportunity arise.

Our proclivity toward humor can also manifest itself in forms of play. The prank is one such form. Before beginning this project, I really had no idea that pranks and similar kinds of folk play or performance were so prevalent in Southern Appalachia. But a substantial article in *The Foxfire Magazine* set me right. It appears that folks around here love a good prank. What was especially surprising was reading the accounts of a very special kind of prank known as "serenading."

As a grad student in southwest Louisiana, I had the honor of witnessing (and participating in) one of the best examples of how folk groups use performance and play. Throughout the rural communities of Acadiana, the francophone region of Louisiana that stretches across the southern portion of the state, from just west of New Orleans to the Texas border, folks participate in the annual Mardi Gras celebration in a very distinct way. When most people think of Mardi Gras, they think of New Orleans and Bourbon Street, but the activities associated with these rural Mardi Gras, or *courir*, is something altogether different. The courir is a begging ritual that entails community members dressed in playful costumes and masks, traveling house to house, engaging in a highly performative play that involves pranks, song, dance, and ritualistic begging, all in the interest of coming together as a community to feast and reconnect. As it is also deeply connected to their Christian faith, participants in the courir view this performance as sacred and a preparation for the somber, contemplative, and faith-affirming Lenten season of fasting. The rural Mardi Gras is also an incredible example of an Old World tradition (dating back to the Renaissance) brought over by immigrant groups to the New World and maintained, in part, due to the relative isolation of these communities and their insulation from the larger homogenous American popular culture.

In Southern Appalachia, serenading also takes the form of

a highly performative play that includes ritualistic begging and that also came over with immigrating communities from Europe. In England, Ireland, and Scotland, the mumming tradition was—and still is—a Christmastime or Epiphany tradition that, like the rural Mardi Gras, involves costumed and masked members of a community traveling house to house, rousing their neighbors (albeit in the evening as opposed to the morning or day as in Mardi Gras), and performing a somewhat-formal play (in the dramatic sense). In portions of Southern Appalachia, mumming turned into *serenading* and, though it lost some of its Old World elements—specifically a more formal, dramatic play—became a regular Christmastime performance ritual. The costuming was less intricate and not always required, generally involving various forms of cross-dressing among the young men and women and other attempts to conceal their identities. But as with its European ancestor, the goal of this play was similar in that there was an expectation the serenaders would be invited in by the targeted households to have some food and drink. Like its Louisiana and Old World counterparts, serenading was also a ritual that strengthened community bonds and broke up the monotony of the cold winter months.

Finally, we conclude the first section with a chapter on folk belief, perhaps better known by the pejorative "superstition." Of all the genres covered here, folk belief is the hardest to ascribe a genre label. Is it religion? Is it performance? Or, if we unpack it further, is it a form of sympathetic magic? Folk belief is, in fact, all of these things, but I'm lumping it in with the other performance genres because of folk belief's reliance on the believer to act (perform) a certain way in a certain situation to increase the probability of a desired effect. I am also placing it here because ritualistic characteristics of folk belief as ritual also depend on performative elements.

I want to underscore my use of the term "folk belief" as opposed to "superstition." The main issue is that the term "superstition" suggests something that is "backward," "silly," or "primitive." When we hear the term "superstition" we associate it with the illogical or farcical as opposed to something of value. To those who hold on to folk beliefs, these customary behaviors are very valuable and very much a real part of their lives. They believe in the correlations between the folk practice associated with the belief and a desired outcome.

There are two primary types of folk belief: the magical and the empirical. The first acknowledges supernatural elements at work in the universe as observed by the believer, whereas the second is based more on observation and experience absent of any supernatural or mysterious influence. While I wish things were as neat and tidy as that, there are (as with all folklore) gray areas in how we define folk belief where the line between the magical and the empirical gets blurry. An example of one such folk belief is planting crops or a garden by the signs of the zodiac. In the chapter on folk belief, I use this as an example of the empirical, but, depending on perspective, one could also place it in the realm of magical beliefs. Planting by the signs is a belief that maintains its value through observable experience and is applied, most often, in a way that is very much a practical science for those who follow it; however, there are those who have come to practice this belief by way of its connection to their faith and their interpretation of biblical texts, which contain elements of the supernatural.

In either case, this practice and those like it are not carried out because the practitioners are simpleminded or primitive (as the term "superstitious" would suggest), but because they have experienced positive results from behaving in this way. No folk tradition carries forward that does not have value.

The Tellers

Whereas the first section of this book focuses on genre, our second section centers on the people at the core of Foxfire's success as a repository for Southern Appalachian culture. These chapters are a study of seven distinct storytellers from our archive, spanning a half century of interviews. The challenge was deciding which tellers to feature. As you might imagine, there are quite a few remarkable individuals possessing a repertoire of great Southern Appalachian storytelling. Our primary goal is to ensure that we've captured stories from each of the five decades that Foxfire has been collecting and to present a diversity of voices. As such, the tellers included in this section of the book are a good representation of the evolution of storytelling in Southern Appalachia over Foxfire's lifetime and feature stories that span a timeline reaching back as far as pre-European exploration and settlement of the area.

One Last Note

For more than fifty years, the formula for Foxfire's success has boiled down to the curiosity of young people to learn more about their communities and the willingness of those communities to share their knowledge. Dating back to those first interviews in 1966–67, Foxfire has recorded some three thousand hours of interviews on a broad range of topics that encompass the folk culture and history of Southern Appalachia. The intimate relationships between these students and their contacts have translated into one of the best repositories of authentic, unfiltered information about life in Southern Appalachia from the post-frontier, post–Civil War communities of the late nineteenth century to today's modern landscape.

It should be noted, however, that as thorough an archive as we possess here, it lacks a complete picture of the region, specifically a substantial cache of information from communities of color, which include indigenous peoples, African Americans, and newer immigrant groups, such as those from Mexico and Latin America, Asia, and the Middle East.

However, with time, and with ever-changing, ever-diversifying racial and ethnic demographics in the region, our opportunities to dig deeper into the full Southern Appalachian experience are increasing. This is an exciting prospect for all of us involved in the program, and we are encouraged by what the next fifty years holds for us and for our ability to continue our mission as a preservation and interpretive organization representing this remarkable part of the world.

Foxfire
STORY

PROLOGUE

It's hard to believe, but in all the volumes of the Foxfire book series, and all the companion books to that series, we have never published Foxfire's very first article—an interview with retired sheriff Luther Rickman about the Clayton Bank robbery that occurred in 1934. We can't begin to figure out why, as it is one of the best examples of an anecdote in our collection. It's so good, in fact, that we selected it as one of two audio excerpts that visitors to the museum can listen to when they visit the Carnesville House, which serves as our archive building and holds *The Foxfire Magazine* office. As Foxfire's first recorded interview, one rooted in story and memory, we felt this would make a great introduction to this book focused on oral tradition.

The interview was conducted in March of 1967, just weeks before the very first issue of *The Foxfire Magazine* went to print. While the story itself is amazing, the audio is incredible and demonstrates just how often Sheriff Luther Rickman recounted the story of the bank robbery. His performance feels like someone giving a statement in court (as one might expect from a retired law enforcement officer), but what makes it grand are the instances where Sheriff Rickman gets stuck in his delivery, and his wife, who was present in the room during the interview, fills in the "script" without missing a beat and gets Sheriff Rickman back on track. Apparently, she had heard the story a time or two. If you ever get the chance to visit us at the museum, this really is worth a listen.

As an example of how collective memory, folk anecdotes, and oral history around an important community event can differ from person to person, we've also included an article from 1989 in which Huell Bramlett, a bystander who witnessed the same bank robbery, and who later helped identify one of the robbers, tells his version of events as he remembers them. The first major difference is the dates provided by the two men. Based on the historical record, Sheriff Rickman's date is incorrect. By his account, he is five days and two years off, which isn't all that strange, considering his age. To their credit, the students writing the 1989 article went to the local newspaper's archives to find the exact date, which corroborates Huell Bramlett's recollection. Also of interest is that Huell's tale is limited to his own involvement. For him, we go from the robbers heading to South Carolina to their being apprehended in Asheville, North Carolina, in just a few sentences, whereas with Sheriff Rickman, we see all the intricacies of their route from the bank to their capture with great detail. When you put those stories together, you get a powerful record of an event that was a remarkable one for the town of Clayton and Rabun County.

The Clayton Bank Robbery of 1936

An Interview with Sheriff Luther Rickman, Retired
As told to Perry Barrett, Bobby Bass, and Bill Selph

Luther Rickman was born in Dillard on March 20, 1889, raised in Dillard, and still lives there today. His grandfather settled here shortly after the Civil War, and it was for Jesse H. Rickman that Rickman's Creek was named. Luther still owns part of his grandfather's original property.

While still a boy, Luther Rickman helped grade the land and haul the foundation stones, driving mules to a slip pan, for the first building of this Rabun Gap–Nacoochee School. He attended school here on the first day it opened its doors.

He can remember wanting to be a sheriff from the time he was ten years old. At that time, he saw the old sheriff chase and arrest a man, and that night he went home and said, "Mama, quick as I'm old enough, I'm going to be sheriff." Her advice to him at that time was to start making friends now, for he would need lots of them to get elected to a job like that. He must have followed her advice, for at the age of twenty-two, on the first day of 1913, he found himself on duty as a deputy. Four years later, the first day of 1917 and the first day of Prohibition, he was made High Sheriff, a position he held for twenty-four years in Rabun County.

Having heard that he had a fine story about a bank robbery that he might agree to tell us, we went to visit him, tape recorder in hand, one evening in early March. This is the story he told, and we reproduce it here in his own words.

On August 26, 1936, I was gettin' a haircut in Roy Mize's barbershop and heard a gun fire. I ran out the door, and as I hit the sidewalk, Sanford Dixon hollered, "Sheriff Rickman! The bank's bein' robbed! They have just gone out of town in a black Ford." When that happened, I ran into the front of the bank, and Mr. T. A. Duckett, cashier, was comin' in at the back of the bank.

Miss Druilla Blakely was the only person in the bank when the robbers came in. "Hand over the cash, Miss Druilla" was what they said to her; "Hand over the cash." Just one man, and he had the gun on her, and when he called for the money she screamed and run out at the back of the bank like a bullet—just went a-flyin'.

She ran into the back of Dover and Green's Drug Store and

screamed, "Doctor Dover, the bank's bein' robbed!" Doctor
Dover walked out at the front door, and as he hit the sidewalk,
one of the robbers with a small machine gun said, "Big boy, git
back in thar," and shot down near his feet. Doctor Dover said
he felt of himself to see if he'd been shot! Now listen. When
that gun fired, that disturbed the man that was a-gettin' the
money, and he only got 1,830 and some dollars and ran out the
door and jumped in the automobile—and left.

From that Fred Derrick ran into the bank and said to me,
"Sheriff Rickman, we'll get some guns and ammunition," and
ran to Reeves Hardware and began to jerk down guns and ammunition, and from that I deputized two men and jumped in
a little old Ford and started south in the direction the robbers
had went. And a man hollered at me, said, "Sheriff Rickman,
nails in the road!" Well, there was four cars off the road with
their tires punctured. They was tar-paper nails, the kind with
the big heads, and so about half of 'em was standing up. One
of the robbers had ordered fifty pounds of them from Greeneville, Tennessee. They had the back glass out of the car and was
sittin' with their backs to the front of the car. They strode them
out as they went, and careful—didya ever see Santa Claus sittin'
up here in town a-throwin' out candy? Like that. And just on
one side. I took the wrong side of the road and dodged the nails,
and when I did, the nails lasted from Clayton to Tiger, Georgia.
A little below Tiger. They made 'em last until they turned off
on the Eastman Road.

I went on from Tiger to Cornelia, Georgia; and when I got
in Cornelia, I got a message that this car had turned on the
Eastman Road. Now, where the Eastman Road empties into
the Wolf Creek Road they was some county men a-workin'—
scrapin' it was what they was a-doin'. And they had got their
road machine balanced on a rock and was blockin' the road.
Well, the robbers came a-flyin' up Wolf Creek and met that
road machine and hollered at these two men to move that thing!
And one of the county employees said, "Don't be in too big a

hurry." And about that time one of the robbers stuck a machine gun out the window and told him, says, "Move it!" And the boys both said, "Yes sir, we'll get it off as quick as we can!" And did. And they went on.

I got back from Cornelia and traced that car on the Eastman Road to Wolf Creek Road through the Bennie Gap to the War-woman Road, and from there east to Pine Mountain, turned north and went to Highlands, and from there over into Transylvania County, North Carolina, into a sawmill camp where these robbers had a hideout. From there the robbers spent the night, and they never divided their money until they got into the hideout. One of the robbers told me later that there they divided this money equally between five.

The next morning, they left out early in a brown Ford that they had left there on the way to do the robbery. And that night they had a wreck in Old Fort, North Carolina, and wrecked this brown Ford. Well, a man drove past where they was wrecked and saw a man standin' in the road with his face bleeding; and the gentleman that was driving the car asked if there was anything he could do for him, and the man told him, "Yes, get me to a hospital." At that instant, one of the robbers came up with a machine gun and told him to get back up that road. And walked him and his boy at least two hundred yards up the road and told them to keep going. Then they all got in this high-powered car and lit out. Well, they went six or eight miles and had a blowout. So, they put on the spare and went on and by George, had another blowout. So, they abandoned it and I found it on an old mountain road.

From that, I went from there to Spruce Pine, North Carolina, and got some information. When I got this information, I began to trace the robbers. But first, from Old Fort, I called Charlotte, North Carolina, and found out who this brown Ford's tag was issued to. Where this car was wrecked there was machine gun shells; there was some .32-cartridge shells to high-powered steel jacket gun and rifle shells, and seems like some bedding. From that, I learned who this car belonged to—whose name the car tag was issued in. When that happened, I went to where this car had been traded to the Ford people and found that Zade Sprinkle had bought this automobile, and from that I went into Greeneville, Tennessee, and got close on the robbers but didn't catch 'em. They separated there, I was told later by one of the robbers.

When some of the robbers went on in the direction of Virginia, Zade Sprinkle stayed in Johnson City, Tennessee, for a night or two and then came back in the direction of Asheville and wrecked his automobile—ran into a telephone pole. The sheriff's office at Marion, North Carolina, arrested Zade and called me and told me that they had Zade Sprinkle, the man I had told them to look out for and had gave the description of buying this Ford car.

When that happened, I went to the sheriff at Marion, North Carolina, and I took two witnesses with me—the same two men that had the road machine stalled. I told the men that for them not to say that he was the man or he wasn't when they brought him down out of the jail, but if he was the man to just look at me and wink. And they both did that and I walked up and shook hands with Zade Sprinkle. When I did, I told him, I said, "Zade, I came to discuss our bank robbery."

He said, "Sheriff Rickman, I've not been feelin' good and I'd rather not discuss it." I said, "Sheriff, carry him back and lock him up and I'll just stay over until tomorrow and talk with Zade." Well, when I done that, he started back and got back near the elevator and says, "I have had some experience with Sheriff Rickman before, and I'm a-gonna tell you the truth. I want'a talk to you and Sheriff Rickman alone." And we went into the back of the jail and he upped and told me about all of the men except one he said he didn't know—a man by the name of Slim—and that they divided the money at this camp where they spent the night over in Transylvania County. And from there they had warrants for him for takin' that car from the gentleman from Charlotte when they wrecked at Old Fort, North Carolina. And he served his term sentence, and then I went and got him and brought him to Rabun County. He was tried and sentenced there in our Superior Court and sent to the penitentiary. He was sent sometime in the August term of court—I don't remember the date he went—and had a heart attack—two severe heart attacks—and was pardoned by the governor of Georgia. All the other men was caught except for Slim.

Curious about something we had heard him say earlier, we then asked Sheriff Rickman if he would mind telling us what the previous experience was that he had had with Zade Sprinkle:

I had reason to serve papers on him two years earlier. I heard he was hidin' at Jabe's Roadhouse, so I went and asked Jabe if he was there, and Jabe said, "Yes, Sheriff Rickman, in the second room at the head of the steps on the left."

I walked up and knocked on the door, and Zade said, "Who's there?" I said, "Sheriff Rickman; open the door, Zade," and he jumped up in his sock feet, opened the door, and made this statement: "One telephone call too many." And I said to him, "Zade, where's your pistol?" And he said, "Under my pillow," and that's what made me be in sympathy with him. He might have made me a-done somethin' that I wouldn't have wanted to do under any consideration. And he might'a got me first; you can't tell.

And when that happened, he asked me, "Sheriff Rickman, are y'gointa put me in jail?" I said, "No, not necessarily, Zade. If I can get a-hold-a the sheriff at Asheville, I'll not putcha in jail at all."

Zade and myself came down in the office, called the sheriff from Cannon's Camp, and in less than two hours he drove up in his automobile with a bloodhound and two deputies and came in and shook hands with Zade, and told one of his men to go back and get those credentials.

Whenever he came in, he had handcuffs and leg irons, and I told him, I said, "Don't put them leg irons on Zade. He's been nice to me, and here's his pistol. I got it from under his pillow."

When that happened, the sheriff said this to me: that I didn't know him as he did; and I told him rather than see Zade have the leg irons put on, that I would drive him to Asheville myself. And the sheriff didn't put the leg irons on him. And he got there with him, too.

The Clayton Bank Robbery of 1934

by Erin Smith, Kelly Cook, and Aubrey Eubank

. . . Kelly Cook and I told Mike Cook, our Foxfire teacher, about this story, and he was ready to send us to interview Huell Bramlett on the spot. Mike got really excited because there had never been an interview about this bank robbery since students interviewed Luther Rickman, a witness, in 1967 for the first issue of Foxfire. *Another reason why he got so excited was that there has never been an account of this robbery printed in* Foxfire *from a bystander's point of view. The first interview was not with a bystander, but with Luther Rickman, the sheriff of Rabun County at the time of the bank robbery.*

Erin Smith

The Rickman interview was Foxfire's *very first interview. It was printed in volume 1, number 1, and reprinted in the Spring [1986] 20th Anniversary issue. Here are a few facts that Huell left out. The amount of money that was taken was about $1,830. The robber's name was Zade Sprinkle. There* *were some others, but Zade was the leader of the pack. The exact date was August 21, 1934.*

Kelly Cook

This robbery took place in 1934, to the best of my knowledge and abilities to tell it. I was going to school in the tenth grade at Clayton High School [Rabun County High School]. My principal and teacher, Mr. Reynolds, he had an asthma attack, and he wanted me to drive him up to the drug store. The drug store was by the bank at that time. I drove his car up there with him, and he got out and went in the drugstore. While he was in there, I heard shooting in the bank. I didn't know what was going on. I found out later that it was Dr. Dover that was in there when it was happening. He was a prominent doctor there at that time and an official of the bank. But anyway, the gun shots were shooting at the floor and we still did not know what was going on.

The officers of Rabun County were not around at that time. So, Mr. Reynolds came out with his medicine that he got in the drugstore, and he got in the car. I started to back out. This other man that was with the robber was sitting in the car next to ours and he pointed his pistol over at us and said, "Pull back up in there and don't move." I still did not know what was going on and I was scared, too, I guess. At that time the robber came out with the money in the bag. I do not know whether it was a paper bag, a sack, or what. He got in the car, and the robber began driving.

They took off down 441 South to the Boggs Mountain Road, but when they [the robbers] took off, I was sitting in Mr. Reynolds's car. I could see some kind of machine gun in the back of the car. I did not know exactly what it was, but the evidence [later presented in court] said it was a machine gun. Anyway, they strewed roofing tacks in the road so the people that were chasing them could pick up the tacks and puncture their tires, and that would delay their capture.

Naturally, the Rabun County Law, Sheriff Rickman and Harley McCall, had time to get there, and they were chasing the robbers. Anyway, they went across Boggs Mountain Road, and the county crew workmen that worked on the road were there scraping the road, and something happened, and they could not get their equipment out right then. Those two robbers told the workmen to move immediately. So, they did; they moved it, and they went on and proceeded into South Carolina.

In North Carolina, the police officers were alerted. At that time, there weren't any radios, I don't think, or any kind of equipment that they could get ahold of any other officers and let them know what was going on. So, they were apprehended in Asheville, North Carolina. So, this one robber—I don't know what happened to the other one that was with him—they put him in jail at Asheville.

Then they appointed me to go and verify him after they had found out that I had seen the robber who came out of the bank with the money, to see if it was him. So, this man didn't have any hair, and he was a fat, chunky fella. And I had to verify him. When I verified him, Sheriff Rickman and Harley McCall got him to come on out, and Sheriff Rickman called this man's name and said, "Get in the backseat with me. I'm not gonna put no handcuffs on you. If you do anything or try to run, I'll shoot you."

So, he came on to Clayton Jail, and finally he had a trial. When he had trial, he told Sheriff Rickman, he said, "Sheriff Rickman, I'm glad you wasn't in there 'cause I was in there after that money and me or you, one would have died. . . ." That's all.

THE STORIES

Chapter One

MOUNTAIN SPEECH

Any piece of verbal art—be it a joke or a folktale or an anecdote—is the sum of its parts. The foundational part of that sum is language. We could make analogies about houses or engines or some such here, but we think most folks can visualize the ways words come together to create ideas. In school, we learned vocabulary through weekly word lists. In the formal structure of our schooling, we learned about nouns and how they work, verbs and how they work, the function of adjectives, whatever the heck it is that adverbs do. Some, if not most, of us were even amazed by words and, at times, confounded by them. We struggled with the idea that there were rules, yet exceptions to those rules, for how words operate in our language. And, no doubt, we also came to understand that there were words we used—some of our very first words, words handed down to us from the most trusted sources, our friends and families—that weren't recognized as "real" words in our schoolbooks.

Those words, most often those of our grandparents and neighbors and immediate community, make up something we call "vernacular." In the United States, we have distinct vernacular regions that possess varying and colorful words for everything under the sun—from toilets to soft drinks. For its

Harley Carpenter

part, there might not be a more colorful vernacular than that of the Southern Appalachians. As is the case with many rich, verbal cultures, Southern Appalachia is chock-full of wonderful words—some widely recognized, some not so much—used in everyday speech. Caricatured in the media, the Southern Appalachian vernacular is often ignorantly characterized as "backward." In context, these words are poetic and full of wit. What's more, they are necessary to fully experience the region's oral tradition.

Here, we provide a glossary of terms collected by Foxfire students in the early days of *The Foxfire Magazine*. Let this serve as a reference as you make your way through the stories, tales, jokes, and songs herein.

all-overs: chills or nervousness
ambure (amber): snuff or tobacco juice
bad: to indicate excessive interest in something, as in "He was awful bad to get into the whiskey."

battlin' stick (also, "punchin' stick"): used to beat dirt out of clothes before washing them in an iron pot

biddy (also, "doody" or "diddle"): young chicken

big eye: unable to sleep, insomnia

blue-john: milk without cream

branch: small stream

britches: harness for a mule

broadcast: scatter over, as in broadcasting manure over a garden

can-house: smokehouse or storage area for meats and canned goods

catty-whompus: something lopsided; hanging or sitting crooked

cellar: a room at ground level (not necessarily under the house) used for storage of canned foods, potatoes, etc.

cent: bit, as in "don't care a cent for," meaning, "I don't mind it a bit"

chinquapin: money; change, as in dimes, quarters, etc.

choke-rag: necktie

chunk: small; as in, "I was just a chunk of a boy"

clodhoppers: boots or heavy shoes

commodities (also, "mullicans"): foods given to individuals by the government

confidence (verb): to trust; as in, "Can I confidence you?"

cornfield beans: beans that grow up cornstalks

counterpin (also, "counterpane"): bedspread

country Cadillac: pickup truck

crawdad: crayfish

crossways [of each other]: to be in disagreement; to disagree

discomfit: to inconvenience someone; to put someone out in any way

dodger (also, "turn of bread"): a cooked pan of cornbread

dog-irons (also, "fire dogs"): the two irons used to support wood in the fireplace

donie: a young girl; a young woman

doublebait [that]: request to have something repeated

dough-sop: bread soaked in gravy

fireboard: the mantel above the fireplace

fist-and-skull [fight]: bad fight

fleshy: fat

flint rock: quartz

fogeyism: something considered nonsense or superstitious

galouses: suspenders

gee-whiz: a type of plow

git-fiddle: term for guitar in the context of old-time string music

glib: active; young acting, as in "She's pretty glib to be as old as she is"

go-devil: a maul; a wood-splitting tool

gooseneck: a garden hoe

grabble: to harvest young potatoes

haints: ghosts or spirits

hard: bad, as in "I'm awful hard to remember names"

haul-off: to act; make an action, as in "I'm going to haul-off and take these books to the library."

heart dropsy: down at heart; to not have the will or spirit to forward an action

hearthrock: a large rock at floor level that extends out in front of the fireplace, acting as a hearth

hissy: a fit; acting very upset, as in "She had a hissy because I dropped the bread"

holp: past tense of "help"

jack beans: lima beans

kindlin': small pieces of dry wood used to start a fire

larrupin': to taste very good

latchpin: safety pin

loaded for bear: to mean business; overloaded, or loaded to the top

lobberin': to go wandering

long sweetenin': honey

mean'ness: as in, "lowdown meanness"; getting into trouble or mischief

meetin': a church service, as in "goin' to meetin'"

mink-mink: rabbit

nary: not any, none, and the like, as in "I didn't see nary a one."

no rate: spread around, as in "Don't no rate it!"

no such a (also, "no such of a"): as in "I never seen no such a thing in my life."

noted fact: a proven fact; disreputable fact

painter: panther

pianner (also, "pie-anna"): piano

piazza (also, "pie-azzer"): a front porch

poke: a brown paper sack

pokin' stick: a fire poker; a stick used to stir coals in a fire

pole axe: hatchet

poppin' [one's teeth]: to be angry

poppycock: an "unnecessary" gathering, as in a dance party or similar social event

quietus: to make someone back down or give up an argument

rheumatism medicine: moonshine

ride a broom: to sweep a floor

roastin' ears: ears of unshucked corn

rudimentals: a portmanteau of "rudiments" and "fundamentals"

sallet: turnip greens

sawmill gravy: gravy made with cornmeal instead of flour

short sweetenin': sorghum

slick foot: to not be able to sleep at night

smooth your feathers: a command, meaning "comb your hair"

snake feeder: a dragon fly

soak-toddie: biscuits soaked in coffee, eaten for breakfast

spittin' fire: to be angry; to express anger

splatterment: a mess or a fight, as in "You've never seen such a splatterment in all your life."

switchell: a drink made from vinegar and honey

thumpin' gizzard: one who appears heartless; someone who does evil things

tote: to carry

undoes: to upset someone

up your trotter: to fall or slip to the ground

vittles (also, rations): food

wag: to carry something

wasper: a wasp or hornet

weathercock: a weathervane

whatnots: three-cornered shelves

whenever: when, as in "He was there whenever I went."

whet-rock: whetstone; a stone used to sharpen knives

white tops: daisies

witches foot: a peace sign

yankee dime: a kiss

young sprouts (also, "tads"): young boys

Chapter Two

PROVERBS & SAYIN'S

If you'll allow it, we'd like to carry over the grade-school analogy from the previous chapter. In grade school we learn words and their functions and how they come together to form ideas, or sentences. In oral traditions, a culture's vernacular comes together in the same way to give us some of the most fundamental pieces of the verbal art puzzle. Colloquial expressions, or "sayings," are a great example of the colorful way in which a folk group negotiates the world. Through these sayings, we can learn a great deal about cultural communities—everything from how they may relate to the natural world ("hollow as a gourd") to the occupations that make up their economies ("Sharp as a pegging awl"). These expressions are very much rooted in place and connected to all the ways in which people pass their time on the earth.

The next step up from the colloquial expression is the proverb. You will undoubtedly recognize some of these even if you're not from Southern Appalachia. Many of the proverbs that pop up in our regional ethnographic collection have their roots in the Old World and show up wherever immigrants to the New World landed and put down roots. Proverbs have an uncanny way of simplifying the world in commonsense terms (no doubt why they are so often used by our grandparents when we are small). Like any verbal art form of any merit, proverbs are full of great wit and often appear as a clever turn of phrase.

Expressions

One of Foxfire's aims since its founding has been to record patterns of speech that are distinctive in the mountain regions. The following is a sample of the material that we have gathered from the northern portion of Rabun County and the southern portion of Macon County, North Carolina. All were recorded in an area about fifteen miles in diameter, and all are ones that we have heard personally and so we know to be authentic. Underscoring, where it occurs, indicates voice emphasis.

Most typical among the many people we have talked with, and heard with great frequency even among students in high school and grade school, are expressions like the following:

- "the first" or "number one" for "a single one" as in "I went looking, but I didn't see the <u>first</u> sang plant." "He didn't give me dollar <u>number one</u> for all that work I did yesterday."
- "caution" in reference to something to marvel at, often in jest, as in "It's a <u>caution</u> all right," or, "He's a caution, <u>he</u> is."
- "care" for "mind" as in "I don't care to tell you," which actually means "I don't mind telling you at all." Similarly, "I don't care for you to do it" means "I don't mind if you do it." "I don't care for him to come around" means "I don't mind if he comes around whenever he wants to."
- Inversion of word order is frequent. "Ever I saw," for example, is a common usage for "I ever saw," as in "Hit beat ary locust that <u>ever I saw</u> for splittin'."

- "the like of" for "as many as" or "as much as"—recently a man was talking to us about a huge still he ran across, and he exclaimed, "I never have seen the like of mash boxes since God made me in this world!"
- "directly" for "soon," and "fairs up" for "clears up" (as in weather). One example: "If it fairs (pronounced *fars*) up a little directly, I may want you to go help me move the sheep."

A people with strong roots in the land will naturally use descriptive figures of speech that reflect this background. Some that we hear frequently are the following:

- "fine as frog's hair"
- "mean as a snake"
- "silly as a goose"
- "fast as greased lightning"
- "nigh as a pea" (meaning very close to)
- "hollow as a gourd"
- "slick as a butterbean"
- "white as a snowball"
- "steep as a horse's face"
- "tender as your eyeball"
- "tough as a pine knot."
- When one is invited to dinner, the host sometimes says, "It may not fill you up, but it'll keep you from going hungry." If there is no food in the house, he may say, "I'd sit up with you all night before I'd see you go to bed hungry."

Other expressions are heard much less frequently, or are even once-in-a-lifetime comments, but they still ring of the mountains and their people. Such expressions or quotations that we have recorded are like the following:

- "He doesn't do enough work to break the Sabbath."
- "He's so deaf, he can't hear a clap a'thunder."
- "devilish as a cocked gun"
- "straight as a rifle barrel"
- "slick as a ribbon"
- "Ask and you'll always have welcome."
- "She hung on to them like Grant hung around Richmond."
- "A road's got to go somewhere, and us boys has just naturally got t'follow."
- "Jesse James used to rob you with a gun. They do it with a <u>lead</u> pencil now."
- "Everything that grows was put here for a reason, and our job's t'find out what it's here for."
- "When that morning glory sticks its head up in the mornin' and smiles, you just know it's goin' t'take a <u>heck</u> of a frost t'put it down."
- A man who used to use a turkey call well said to us, "I could <u>really</u> tread a chunk."
- If something has a strong, unpleasant scent, some say, "It smells like a buzzard on a gut wagon." If it has a strong scent, some say, "It has a good, loud scent."
- One man who was talking to us said, after having been interrupted, "Now, let's see. What was I a'strikin' for there?"
- Another, when talking to us of a stubborn relative, said, "You'd do just as good to tell that stump there to get up and <u>walk</u> as to ask <u>her</u> to do anything."
- And another told of a friend he knew who, when caught in a white lie or a practical joke, would look sheepish and "take a bad case of the dry grins."

This list, obviously, is far from being complete. In fact, it will probably never be complete. Things are said every day that would make good additions, but we just don't happen to be in the right place to hear them. As we find more, however, and as space allows, this list will be continued.

Old-Time Expressions

A list of expressions using "as" was given to the first quarter Foxfire class. Each student took one home to be completed by an older relative, such as a grandfather or grandmother. We wanted to collect as many old-time expressions used by the people of our Appalachian area as we could. Each student returned his or her paper to Kin Hamilton so she could collate the information.

The results are as shown:

Black as
  the ace of spades
  a coal fire
  coal
  tar
  soot
  night

Blue as
  the sky
  indigo
  three rainy days

Green as
  a gourd
  grass

White as
  a ghost
  a sheet
  a new blanket of snow
  snow

Yellow as
  a pumpkin
  gold
  butter
  daisies

Mean as
  the dickens
  the devil a grizzly
  a hornet
  a poison snake
  a striped snake
  sin

Loud as
  a firecracker
  thunder
  Gabriel's trumpet

Quiet as
  the night
  the dawn
  a mouse
  a church mouse
  a graveyard
  church on Sunday
  snow

Rough as
  a cob
  a corncob
  a wildcat den
  sandpaper
  pig iron

Smooth as
  a baby's butt
  a flatiron
  silk
  glass

Flat as
  an anvil
  a rock
  a fritter
  a board
  a pancake
  a hoecake

  a creek bottom
  a tabletop

Sharp as
  a razor
  a pin
  a knife
  a tack
  a briar
  a needle
  a pegging awl

Wild as
  a buck
  a boar
  a panther
  an Indian

Easy as
  pie
  homemade pie
  falling off a log

Hard as
  a rock
  a brick
  a board
  glass
  nails
  ram's horns

Poor as
  a snake
  a church mouse
  a whippoorwill

Job's turkey
gully dirt
dirt

Rich as
the dickens
a king
a pine knot
cream
silk
can be
gold

Tight as
a miser
a banjo head
a banjo string
a drum
a tick
the bark on a sapling
the bark on a tree
leather
Dick's hatband

Loose as
a goose
a tooth
sows' ears

Short as
a midget
a rabbit's tail
a stump
a minute

Tall as
a tree
a pine
a giant
a beanpole
a ten-foot pole

Slick as
a button
a mole
a whistle
a rock
a greased pig
an eel
a ribbon
a butterbean
a diamond
glass
grease
oil
ice

Good as
an angel
gold

Bad as
the devil
a bull
a bear
a wolf
can be
sin
bad money
gar broth

Fat as
a hog
a pig
a bear
a cow
a horse
an elephant
lard

Thin as
a rail
a razor
a shadow
a skeleton
a hair
a toothpick
a beanpole
a stick
paper
ice
water

Stout as
a mule
a bull
a tree trunk
a stump
a horse
an ox
Samson

Weak as
a kitten
a baby
water

Old as
the hills
time
Methuselah

Young as
a spring chicken
a filly
a newborn calf

Ugly as
a duck
a mud fence
mud
sin
homemade sin

Pretty as
a picture
a flower
a peach
a speckled pup
a rose
pink

Stingy as
the devil
Scrooge

Lucky as
a leprechaun
a horseshoe
a charm
a four-leaf clover

a rabbit's foot
number seven

Useless as
  a leprechaun
  an old worn-out shoe
  a wooden nickel
  a hole in the wall
  a sow with a side saddle
  a saddle pocket on a hog
  tits on a boar hog
  can be

Thick as
  molasses
  syrup
  mud
  blood
  mush
  tar
  thieves
  fiddlers in hell

High as
  the sky
  a cat's back
  a mountain
  a kite
  the trees
  a Georgia pine
  a Maypole

Low as
  a snake
  a snake's belly

the ground
dirt

Dry as
  the desert
  a stick
  a chip
  a bone
  a whistle
  a powder house
  cotton
  dust

Wet as
  a drowned rat
  a wet hen
  water
  rain

Tough as
  a mule
  a pine knot
  a shoestring
  a maul
  leather
  whit leather
  shoe leather
  nails

Sure as
  a fleeting arrow
  a risin'
  a boil
  the world
  the sun's going to rise

rain
stars in heaven
can be
shooting
sin
fire
gold
thunder

Sweet as
sugar
sugar candy
honey
syrup

Sour as
a crab apple
a lemon
a pickle
a persimmon
kraut

Hollow as
a log
a stump
a dead tree
a gourd
a straw
a jug

Full as
a tick
a jug
a drum
a bucket

Fine as
a fiddle
a frog's hair
a dog's hair
a baby's hair
a feather
silk
salt
sand
fizzle dust

Dumb as
a mule
a cow
a wedge
an ox
a donkey
a jackass
a doorknob

Sore as
a boil
a risin'
a mad hornet sting

Silly as
a goose
a clown
a loon

Lazy as
a dog
a jackass
a mule
a knot on a log

a hog
an old hound dog

Busy as
  a bee
  a bee in a tar bucket
  a beaver

Mad as
  a hornet
  the devil
  a bull
  a dog
  a setting hen
  a wet hen
  a puffed toad

Happy as
  a lark
  a dead pig in the sunshine
  a mule eating oats

Scared as
  a rabbit
  a cat
  the dickens

Cold as
  a well digger's pocketbook
  a well digger's butt
  a witch's titty
  blue blazes

Hot as
  a poker

a hen laying in a wood
  basket
fire
hell
blue blazes
red pepper

Tender as
  a bird's eye
  your eye
  a baby
  a baby's butt
  a feather bed
  the bottom of your feet
  marrow

Straight as
  a pin
  an arrow
  a string
  a fence post
  a stick
  a board
  a rifle barrel

Crooked as
  a stick
  a dog's hind leg
  a snake
  a black snake

Steep as
  a mountain
  a horse's face

the hills
a cliff

Limp as
a rag
a dishrag
a wet noodle
a leaf
Raggedy Ann

Fair as
a maiden
a lady
a clear day
a princess
a lily
the day
the sunshine
the morning
the weather
the sky
flowers

Tired as
a mule
a dog
a working horse
a horse after plowing

Deaf as
a post
a doornail
a doorknob

Thirsty as
a dog
a man in the desert
a sponge
an ox
a goat

Hungry as
a bear
a wolf
a horse

Queer (strange) as
a two-dollar bill
a three-dollar bill
an old sock
a gourd seed
the sun in a shower

Sneaky as
a black snake
a snake in the grass
a fox
a rat
a wolf
a suck-egg dog

Chapter Three

LEGENDS

The term "legend" gets tossed around a lot these days. We hear about sports legends (Michael Jordan), political legends (John F. Kennedy), legendary rock 'n' rollers (John Lennon), and even legendary failures (we won't name names for this one). Legends—real legends—are, in folkloric terms, accounts of events that, as far as the storyteller and audience are concerned, actually happened. They are "true" in the sense that they are believed. Whether or not there is any factual basis for these stories is of little consequence. For the people who tell them and those who hear and repeat them, legends play a substantial role in a community's identity.

The Foxfire archive is full of legends. From the time of the first interviews until now, students have always found someone eager to tell a legend or three to a willing listener. Granted, the number of legends has fallen off over the years, but we still find them now and again, nested in memory. The majority of our collection falls under two types: place legends and supernatural legends (with a smattering of animal legends here and there). This is in no way indicative of a larger pattern and probably says more about those collecting the stories (and our process) than about being proof of any kind of pattern or story census. Though, if we were to venture a guess (and if I may make some generalizations), old folks like to remind young people where they come from (place legends) and young people love hearing scary stories, especially those that have identifiable locations (supernatural legends). Whether or not there's anything to that theory is something else altogether.

What we've published here is just a sampling of what Foxfire has collected over the years. For those interested to read more, my recommendation would be to pick up *Foxfire 2* and read the section on "Boogers, Witches, and Haints," which is some thirty-eight pages of supernatural legends from Southern Appalachia, collected at a time when there were still a great many folks telling them. For now, enjoy these legends and what they tell us about these mountains and the folks who inhabit them.

Place Legends

Every community has its share of special geographic locations for which there may not be any official or government-applied designation but that have earned a name among community members. These places could be small water features such as lakes or ponds or could be a distinct land formation like a rock outcropping or a valley. With these place-names often come narratives that explain how the place came into existence and how it earned its name. What's really interesting is that, even in smaller communities, there may not always be consensus on these names and legends, which gives rise to variations and different perspectives. These variations can be due to cultural variations within a community or different groups within a community holding different values that come through in their folklore. This section provides some examples of place legends from the immediate communities surrounding Foxfire and demonstrates the kinds of variations that can arise within a community.

Tommie Shope (right)

Tommie Lee Shope shared his story
about how Buddy Gap Road got its name.

Buddy Gap Road

Let me just tell you how this road named Buddy Gap Road got its name. There was a neighbor of ours, and his name was Raleigh Burton Bradley. People nicknamed him "Bud." He inherited this piece of land from his dad. This mountain and gap called "Buddy Gap" was right in front of Bud's house that he and his dad built once Bud got the land. Raleigh Burton Bradley was the brother to my grandma Bradley, and Grandma later married David Shope. Anyhow, after Bud inherited the land his dad gave him, people started calling it the Buddy Gap Road. So, that is how it got its name. I think it is very interesting to have a mountain and road named after some of my good kinfolks. Another mountain that I can tell you about is called Allen Mountain. There was a man named William "Bill" Allen. He owned the lower end of this big mountain, so when people found out he owned the land, they started calling the mountain Allen Mountain. That is how that mountain got its name.

Billy Joe Stiles tells us how Wolffork got its name.

The Story of Wolffork Valley

When I was younger, I was told this story and I don't know how reliable it is, but this is the way it was related to me. There was some wolves coming down from the mountains, killing sheep and so forth around the place at the mouth of Wolffork Valley. Several men got together and they killed this great big wolf and everybody wanted to see it, so they strung him up in a tree, between the fork of a tree, and people came by and looked at him and admired the big wolf and went on. And, as time went along, they passed this tree, they simply referred to it as the Wolffork and from then on the Valley got its name—it was called Wolffork Valley. How reliable this is, I don't know. I've never seen a wolf in Wolffork Valley, but years ago there might have been.

Tim Vinson provided us another version of the same legend.

Well, a long time ago, where there wasn't many people living up on Wolffork, there was a bunch of wolves going around killing these children that was playing at night. So, all the men got together and hunted the wolves down and finally caught them. They killed 'em and cut their tails off and hung it on a forked stick at the head of the valley and they've called it Wolffork ever since.

Janie Taylor

Janie Taylor shared her version
of how Tiger, Georgia, got its name.

Tigers in Georgia

In the 1800s, British soldiers went over to fight the battle in India. While they were stationed there in service and fightin' this over in the foreign country of India, they heard many sounds, including the Bengal tiger. Now, this tiger has a terrible wail and a terrible scream and these soldiers from Britain learned to dread this sound because it meant danger. Well, when the war was over and the soldiers went back to England, then they migrated to the new world and so they came through South Carolina and round our mountains here in North Georgia. No sooner had they got here they heard this piercing screaming cry that [sounded] just like the tigers in old India and so, "let's just call it Tiger Mountain." Now, you and I know that it wasn't a tiger at all because they don't have this habitat, but instead it was a black panther—the panther that we know and fear so much. And, so, all the time it wasn't a tiger at all, but it was the cry and scream of the black panther that terrified these early settlers.

Doug Young tells us a legend he heard from
his father about an old man who lives in Tallulah Gorge.

The Hermit of Tallulah Gorge

This feller back in World War I, when they had the draft didn't want to go 'cause he was scared to go, I reckon. So he moved down in the gorge in a cave where he had a bunch of old goats. They've still got goats down there; but you don't ever see the old man because he stays up in the cave all of the time. He hardly ever comes out, but people said they've seen him once in a while and he wears old raggy clothes and stuff.

Lynn Phillips told a story about a "bottomless" hole.
Carroll Lee told her this story about his grandfather
Leander Ramey.

The Bottomless Hole

They say that down there on the Chattooga River at Bull Sluice, there's a big rock; where the falls are, it has no bottom. And one time this man went down there and picked up about a seventy-five-pound rock and jumped in and went down a long way and never hit the bottom. So he finally had to let go of the rock and come back up.

Billy Joe Stiles tells us a legend about Green Pond.
He says he's heard there is a bulldozer in there.

The Story of Green Pond

Up my way there's a rather interesting little place called Green Pond, and in the bottom of Green Pond there's supposed to be a bulldozer and several things like that.

Green Pond was made right after the turn of the century in early 1905, or something like that. At the time they didn't even have a bulldozer. What happened was they were blasting for rock. They'd get it out to put on the highway. Water seeped in and got on some old tools.

The only bulldozer in those days was mules. To my knowledge, there's no mules left in the bottom of Green Pond.

George Bowen tells us the legend that he has heard from
a lot of people about the "Frog Pond" in Rabun Gap. This is
the same pond that Mr. Stiles refers to as "Green Pond."

The Story of Frog Pond

Well, I just heard that there's a pond up there at Rabun Gap where there used to be a rock crusher. When they were paving a new road through there. And it's just real deep there and rain had filled it all up. They say there's two or three cranes in the bottom of it. But really nobody knows just how deep it is and it's on the side of the road going up on 441. That's about all I know about it.

Kirk Patterson heard this legend from his grandfather.

A Body in Fontana Dam

My grandfather told me that he used to work on the Fontana Dam. He said that when he was working over there, it was a long time ago. I don't know exactly what time of year it was, he said that they were working on pouring parts of the dam and that there was this man working over there with them and he fell off someway into the dam and they just buried him alive.

*Helen Craig told us about something
that happened when her father was helping
to pour the foundation for Rabun County Hospital.*

Foundation Burial

When I was little, my dad was telling me about when he was working at Rabun County Hospital, when it was first started. He helped lay the foundation. There was an old man there and he had a heart attack, or something, and they couldn't get to the ambulance and he was already dead so they just buried him in the foundation.

*In 1982, Ode Reeves shared his story
of how Auraria became "Knucklesville."*

Welcome to Knucklesville

They called Auraria "Knucklesville" because they had so many fights there. People skint their knuckles, you know. All they knowed back in them days was to fight with their fists. And they had a barroom there. They said they wasn't a rock down there that hadn't skinned somebody's head. That was a rough place to be.

There was two bullies that hung around down there. When a man came in there to get 'im a beer or a drink of liquor, those two'd have 'im dance for 'em. You know, pull out their pistols and say, "How about dancing for me?" or "How about buying me a drink?," one or the other. If you could buy 'em the drink, that was okay and if you couldn't, you'd have to dance for 'em.

There *was* somebody who challenged them, my uncle Terry Reeves said. There came a man a-riding up on a horse. Said he got off his horse and walked in [the bar]. Said they asked him, "Where you from?" Had to know all about him. Said he told them. Then he walked back out on the little porch that went in on. Then one of 'em said he'd see'd he had a gun on 'im, a cowboy. Asked him if he could shoot pretty well. The stranger said, "Well, I can do fairly well. I ain't the best, but throw up a silver dollar out there."

One of [the bullies] throwed it up and he shot it twice before it hit the ground. Said those bullies sat down and didn't bother that man no more. They didn't want no part of him. He got on his horse and rode off.

This part of the country is filled with stories of gold mining and prospecting. John Crisson shared with us his story of the first gold rush in our region.

The (Real) First Gold Rush

Actually, the first gold found in this part of the country was in North Carolina at the Reed Mine, not in Dahlonega. Dahlonega takes credit for it, but it's not true. There was a slave at the Reed Gold Mine in North Carolina who found a rock completely laced with gold. He carried it to the master, or whatever you want to call him. It was a beautiful rock, white quartz with all this yellow stuff running [in it]. He didn't even know what it was. He set it down in front of his door as a door prop. Back in the old days, they didn't have screens. They would prop the door open and use a rock or something to keep it from blowing shut. There was a man, a salesman, who came through and recognized it for what it was. The Reed Gold Mine was a rich mine, and it was in operation for years and years in North Carolina. It was before Dahlonega—something like nine years before the gold rush began in Lumpkin County.

Auraria, at one time, was the metropolis of the North Georgia area. There was ten thousand miners in that area at one time. Auraria has a lot of tradition behind it. There's some good mines around Auraria. The Briar Patch and some of the better mines of this nature are considered to be in the Auraria area. The gold belts in Georgia run right on through North Georgia, South Carolina, and as far as Virginia and Maryland.

John Crisson

The growth in Auraria began before Dahlonega did. Of course, when Lumpkin County became the county seat for the county, there were two communities. Dahlonega was known as Licklog before they decided it would become the county seat of Lumpkin County. They put salt out in those times to salt the deer to bring them in so they could be readily accessible to kill for food. Around this area, they salt the logs because the deer in most cases gets around a log or something and it'll [scratch for food], and it'll eat. They put this stuff on logs and so forth. The salt would dissolve and go into the bark and of course this attracted the wildlife and that's why they called it Licklog. There were a lot of deer up here. Again, this is what my grandfather said. When it was first recognized as the county seat, they called it Dahlonega. It means "Land of Yellow Meadow" in the Cherokee language. That's what I am told. I can't state that to be a fact. There was an election held [to determine the county seat], and Dahlonega won; however, Auraria was the original settlement. The buildings and everything are older than what we have here in Dahlonega. The people felt Dahlonega was more centrally located within the county and within the gold rush. That's the reason why they chose Dahlonega as the county seat for Lumpkin County. The first courthouse that was built there burned down, unfortunately. It was a log structure. Some of my ancestors helped construct that courthouse.

[From the] facts that I've gained through my ancestors, I think that there were white people here with the Indians before this gold strike was made. For instance, my great-grandfather's birth is recorded in North Carolina, when in fact, he was born at Ten Yard Branch Creek in 1818. The Indians were still here in this area. The Indians were north of the Chestatee River at this time, and then intrusions made by the miners in the Indian territory brought the federal troops in to keep [the prospectors] out. Most of the gold that was mined in this area was north of the Chestatee River. This was where the road went and everything was at. For instance, Benjamin Parks, who was the man that first discovered gold, had property right next to one of the main Cherokee villages up here. But his house is still standing. You wouldn't recognize it, but it's still there. The Indians themselves were friendly and they got along well together. Greed is what drove them out. They possessed the land the white man wanted.

I think it was the greed of gold. I think eventually it would have happened even without the gold rush. I think the gold rush just brought it on earlier. Eventually, they would have been forced out just as they had been forced out of their lands in the western states. The gold was what brought it about.

The earlier settlers had a few rowdy people. You will find that anywhere you go. Most of them were good, caring, honest, hardworking men—family men. They came from North Carolina, England, France, and all over the world. They came to the gold rush here. We had a mixture of cultures and people, but they lived well together. The only brawl that I am aware that ever happened—well, actually there were two—but the main one was down here at Battle Branch. They had some shooting down there. There were miners claiming different portions of this stream. They actually had some shoot-outs and some killings over here because the mines were exceedingly rich. In the only instance I know, I think six or eight men were killed. They just literally got their guns, and they would go western style, [and that's the way they settled their problems]. Fear of that did exist in some cases, but most cases there was a spirit of cooperation among them. They had another fight they called "The Shotgun Shoot" also in the Auraria area. The reason they called it "The Shotgun Shoot" is, here again, they had a dispute, and the men would take up the guns, and they guarded what was considered to be theirs with their guns. There were no shootings, but there were threats of it. Those were the only two cases I know of. They were men of dreams, but not like the ones we see out in the western states packing the six guns. I think most of them did pack some kind of weapon. They had to kill meat and stuff. The guns were not for the purposes of fighting off Indians. This didn't happen.

Like I say, it was a spirit of cooperation. They envisioned that this area would grow, and it did. They didn't just come here to leave here. Most of them settled here and they wanted to make it their homes. I think in this area you'll find people changing. The old-timers in and around this area here—even in Union County and everywhere else—[believed that] if a man's handshake wasn't no good, he was no good. They didn't just draw contracts between each other. There was land agreed upon and bought just with a handshake. That was it, and if word got out that your word was no good, you was no good. You were an outcast, more or less, among the people. No one had any respect for you. Now, this is the kind of people they were. Their word was their bond. You still have this with a lot of the older people up here today throughout this entire area. They won't even take a contract from you. If my word's no good and yours is no good, we can't do business. They still have a lot of that. I think it's good.

I think what people use for a stereotype for miners and prospectors is what they see in the western movies. We had a lot of these people up here, but they were not one of these types. They didn't use a burro. They walked. I bet you there's not a ground up here that's on this mineral belt that, at one time or another, hasn't been covered by a prospector.

"Knucklesville" wasn't just a rowdy town.
It was also the site of a major gold mining operation,
as we learned from Amy Trammel in 1978.

Mining in Auraria

You're talking about an old place that was fast on the move 150 years ago. It was in 1828 when it all began. Six miles south of Dahlonega, Georgia, in Lumpkin County on highway 9E, one can find a little lost town of Auraria, the place often called the ghost town. Many years ago, thousands trotted the streets going to and fro in the big gold rush days. It is now almost a forgotten place. Here near the foothills of the old Blue Ridge Mountains. Today, all the older generations have all been gone. Very

few now live to tell the story of the remaining facts that gold
was the motive for the history of Auraria in Lumpkin County,
the county created in 1832. Most all the old landmarks around
Auraria are gone forever from the sight of the old gold rush
town, but the earth remains the same forever. The only town
where the people kind of revered the dirt. And I don't think it
should be left to completely fade away. I think someday in the
future [the town] will return to claim its own. It's too much of
an old historical landmark to remain buried in the past. Who
knows. Maybe someday Auraria's history might hit the front
pages again. That yellow stuff called gold that so long ago lured
men from all walks of life, across the seas, through jungles and
deserts, could someday again draw the diggers to their promised land. Echoes of the wild rushing when Auraria hustled and
grew to one of the big cities in Georgia has long since faded
away. It's probably the nearest thing to a genuine old ghost
town to this side of nowhere.

   Gold had been found and mining going on a long time in
other places before gold was found by the white man here in
what was called the Indian nation. Over and over this story has
been told, how Mr. Benjamin Parks was the first white man to
discover gold in Cherokee land. Then, like now, you can't keep
a secret about gold. Mr. Parks just had to tell it, and the news
spread. And the fortune seekers came in like a swarm of bees.
They didn't settle in the place where Mr. Parks first found gold,
but worked the streams to the nearby point between the Chestatee and Etowah Rivers.

   America's first gold rush was in 1828. Soon the place had
so many people, it could be called a town, and the first to be
reared up as a mining town in the United States. By 1838, it had
been given the name Auraria, Georgia. In Latin, that means
gold. And the town was then at its highest peak. It had the
first of everything a mining town had. It was a town before
Lumpkin County was created. Then new ideas in business let

men come along, and since a new courthouse had already been built in another place named Dahlonega, poverty took over and Dahlonega went up and Auraria went down. But no one can tell the exact things the old-timers really did. All we can say is stories told on down through the years. It would be hard to go back 150 years and tell what they did then, but there was no question about it—it was the gold that drew the people to the area from everywhere.

Supernatural Legends

May Justus shared with us her perspective on how phosphorescent natural phenomena (like foxfire) may have contributed to the creation of local legends.

Foxfire

I think the phosphorescence in wood is akin to this that accumulates in the slime of ponds, and then there's a thing that some of the ghost stories and the old haint stories, you know, that they had. They'd be walking along and they'd see this mysterious ball that would bob up and down, bob up and down, bob up and down, and made from the phosphorescent gases that way, and that's where the graveyard and the stories about ghosts on battlefields, you see, it all comes from a form of decomposition. That what it is—it's the gases that form. And sometimes, maybe, when they didn't bury their bodies too well, or something, that there'd be cracks down in the grave, you know, and the coffins weren't very well built, and the body might as well have been dumped in the ground—maybe sometimes in the battlefields, you know, they didn't bury the dead very carefully, and then later on, these things that they thought were ghosts over the battlefield was nothing in the world but this phospho-

rescence that came from the gases from the decomposing bodies. Doesn't sound nice to talk about it, but that's what it was.
And then that gave rise to all these legends that the ghosts were
walking over the battlefields, and the soldiers had risen from
their graves, you know, things of that kind. And that's all so
much that is legendary has its spark of truth in reality.

Allah Ramey shared with us a story about
a haunting light in the cemetery near her home.

Light in the Cemetery

I's just spending the night at Grandma Rhodes's. Whenever
Garnet Williams come up to see us one night and whenever
he got ready to leave, I don't know, I guess he's afraid that he
would see that light. So we stood on the porch and Grandpa
went to bed in the time of it. Garnet went out toward the cemetery, and Grandpa was looking out the window, and this light
come up out of the cemetery. Grandpa said, "Now if y'all want
to see that light in the cemetery, it's out there." And we went
out on the porch just to look. He came to that branch that
turns up to Maude Fishers [sic], and right there [the light] went
up. It was just as bright as any car light you've ever seen. You
could see the shadow of the leaves all up and down the porch,
and [Grandma Rhodes] said, "Garnet, why if you see anything,
why holler when you get out there." Garnet said he would. He
got down nearly to the cemetery and said, "I don't see nothing,
Mrs. Rhodes." And we just went on back in the house. And
boy, when that happened, the light come down the bank on
Garnet, and boy, he just run till he got home and he run again'
the door. Mrs. Williams said, "What'n the world's the matter?" She said he just run out o' breath.

But it won't cross water, though; it won't cross the branch;
it just went as far a Tom Roane's. Mama lived there for years

and she never did see it, but Gertrude did. It was a big light and there was a little one behind it.

One night Virge Burton had blood poison and they sent the Fisher boys down at Tom Roane's to call the doctor. They come down that road and that light got after them and they come back to Grandma Rhodes about twelve o'clock and got her to go past the cemetery with 'em. She lit the lamp and stuck a pin through the wick and they walked down past that cemetery, goin' to call the doctor. They saw it as they went on, but they never did see it no more.

Oh, they say a bunch of people seen that light. Papa said it was a mineral light. But it looked scary.

One night Ernest was a comin' to Grandma Rhodes to get his hair cut. He's gonna ride down there and put his horse in a stable and stay till the next morning and go on back home. When he come over the top of the hill at Tom Rich's, why he seen that light coming out of that cemetery. He thought it was the Greens a fox huntin'. So he got on up there even with the cemetery, and that mare started jumpin' up and down and wouldn't go no further. Ernest turned and went back down to Tom Rich's to get Fred Henry to come back with him. Ernest hadn't had nothing to drink or nothin', but they never seen it as they come back.

Papa said it was some kind of mineral in the ground, and when it got damp, why, it looked like a light.

Ricky Justus tells us about the old ghost house
at Wall's Mill. He said his grandparents lived in this house.

The Ghost at Wall's Mill

Well, my grandpa and grandma, back in the thirties, lived in the old ghost house up there at Wall's Mill. They gave it the name ghost house on account of they was a man killed hisself in the bedroom of the house. My grandma said after they move in there, she went in and found an old patched quilt or something to cover up with, for it was in the wintertime, and it was cold as blue blazes. She said she went in there and blood was just all over the walls and doors, and what was left of that old bed was rotten and falling all to pieces.

That night, my uncle and aunt, Ump and Grace, and one or two of their younguns had to spend the night. I forgot the reason. They spent the night and slept beside the bed where my grandpa and grandma slept. They made them a pallet in the floor beside the bed and slept on the floor. Along over in the morning about two or three o'clock, getting up toward daylight, they heard a racket that sounded just like a man walking around in bare feet—sock feet, you know—and those old rough pine floors and them boards a'crackin'.

Grandma said along about crack of daylight, they heard a man saying, "I want my house." She believes it, and it woke Uncle Ump up too—that man walking around pecking on the walls saying, "I want my house," and so Uncle Ump said, "Ah, God, if you wait till in the morning, I'll give the [damn] thing to you."

We collected this legend about a father who
killed his son because of the way he treated his mother.

The Bloodstains That Wouldn't Go Away

I've heard this story a many of times.

Well, you know over there where Tom Brown and Tee-Bone lives? That man shot his boy because he'd been drinking and been jumping on his mama. His daddy finally got tired of it and just shot him. The boy was eighteen years old. He shot him on the porch of that old store building, and right there, every time it rains, there will be a thing come up like oil. You know, how oil comes up in rain and beads? Blood comes up where that boy lay and died.

Frank Miller wondered if anyone had ever parked their car on level ground and had something strange like this happen.

The Car That Rolls on Level Ground

There's a place somewhere, I don't know where at, where you can park your car at night, and when you cut your lights off, something comes around and pecks at your windshield. You can put your emergency brake on or anything and your car will roll from a level place. It scares you, too, they say. But, it's never happened to me.

This legend was collected from Nancy Hunnicut, whose mother actually went to see the "unclaimed body," which was said to be in a wooden casket with a glass front, standing upright.

The Unclaimed Body

My mama told me about this man that died a real long, long time ago and nobody never claimed the body. So, they couldn't bury him. He's at the funeral home in Charlotte, North Carolina, around back where they park their ambulance and everything. They've got him in a wooden box with a rope tied around his waist and he's been there for a long time. So, his head hangs over and his face up against the glass and he's just like a piece of leather. They can't bury him, so he's still there.

*Helen Craig also told us about a house on
Hellcat Creek (Rabun County, Georgia) where she once
lived. She said it dripped blood from the faucets.*

The Faucet That Drips Blood

There was this couple and they got in a fight and his wife killed him and now, like late at midnight, you can go in there and turn the faucet on and it drips blood. It was in Mountain City on Hellcat Road, but they tore it down. I'm not sure that it would really happen because I never did get up and try it.

*How would you like to be looking up at a mountain
some night and see a light come gliding off? Ricky Hopkins
told us about his experience.*

The Glider Ghost of Glass Mountain

There used to be a boy that would fly off the mountain on a hang glider. He was killed out in Utah. On a full moon, you can see a light up on the cliffs. About twelve or twelve thirty you can see a light fly off the mountain and a 360 kite will land in the field down below there. Sometimes if he doesn't land there, it just keeps going till it's out of sight. I have seen the kite flying and the light, but it didn't scare me because I didn't know what it was. The last time I saw it was about the middle of last fall. He makes a screaming and squawking sound, but I don't know what it hollers like. When I saw it, we were supposed to have been coon hunting, me and these two friends of mine was up there. We were about polluted ya know, but we don't think our eyes was playing tricks on us.

Hailing from Scaly Mountain,
Lillie Billingsley shared with us her story of a booger man!

The Booger Man

I'll tell y'all a story about a man that liked to work in the whiskey, he drank whiskey, and he sold it. He was a bad old man. He looked like the booger man to me. He used to come by and he'd say to my daddy, "How about you trade me them two girls and let them come stay with me for a while?" My daddy would tell him, "No, they better stay here. We don't let them leave the house too much. They got too many chores to do." He looked like the booger man, and I believed that he WAS the booger man.

So, he came in one morning, about four o'clock, and his wife was making breakfast. He was drunk—pretty well drunk. He had a good old lady—I mean a good'n. Her name was Sis. Sis is what they called her. I don't know her real name. He come in mad about breakfast, I guess, and he jumped on the poor thang. She was rollin' her biscuits now, and he just walked up to her and knocked her brains out, I guess. He hit her in the head, and she fell. Well, he see'd that he killed her, and he didn't know what he was going to do with the body. He built a fire and drug her in the front room, the kitchen, and he put her in the fireplace and burned her. He crammed her head in, and then her shoulders, and then her whole body into the fire. She was a big old fat lady, and the grease run out of her, all down on the floor. It was just real bad, you know. And that grease is still on that floor, they tell me, but I don't know. I stopped by that house one time and Jim's sister said, "Lillie, that's where he killed her." It was bad he killed her—threw her in the fire, and he killed her. He tried to live with that, but he just couldn't. He knew he'd done such a bad thing to kill his wife. Well, anyway, he decided to confess what he'd done. He tried to live on through the years, but I reckon his conscience got so tore up that he only come out of that house to get the mail. He had to go over this little branch by his house, and him and his horse would get to that branch, and that horse would not go across that branch. He would finally have to get off the horse, and he would have to pull the horse across that little branch.

So, he just went crazy. When he got old, he went to live with his daughter. Well, he went crazy; he didn't know what he was doing. They finally had to strap him down to the bed. They said he would just holler and scream. They said he said that he could feel the flames of torment—that they was going to burn him up. Well, he died tied down, and he did confess that he killed her right before he died. They buried him out there behind that old schoolhouse. Now there are five or six graves out there behind that old schoolhouse. I even went to school in that little building. It wudn't as big as from this table to the wall [motioning with her hands]. Mary James was the teacher; she taught five or six of us out there. We walked to school back in them days; we didn't have no cars or nothing.

Lillie went on to share
this story of a witch who lived up on Scaly.

The Witch Deer

There is this other tale I can tell you about Scaly. This is a tale that my daddy told me. He told me that there was an old lady who lived not too long a-ways from us. Daddy said she was a witch, and my daddy said that she would turn herself into a deer. As the men went by to work, she'd see them coming, and she'd turn herself into a deer. And she'd be that deer coming around that field pickin' along like a deer would, you know. So, they got the guns, and they was going to shoot that deer. So, they went to work that morning, and she turned herself into a deer because she was a witch. I don't know anything about witches. They shot about three shots, and when they got back home, Dad said that they talked about it. One of them said, "Now, I'll tell you how we can do this. If it's a deer, we'll get it this way. We'll put some good stuff in the gun, and we'll get that old deer tomorrow." And the next morning they did [shoot the deer], and they went to work. That next evening as they come back from work, they went by that old lady's house. They went in and knocked on the door, and nobody come. They went on in, and she was lying in the fire. She fell in her fire and burned up. So, when they shot the deer, they had killed her, too.

*Oakley Justice shared with us
this tale of a terrifying encounter with an owl.*

The Haint Owl

One time, Dad sent me and Bob to Brye Darnell's after eight pounds of lard. It was dark by the time Brye got home and [after dark when we started back]. We came back by where Pete Lattimer's house is, up over that red hill and down a little ol' hollow and across the rail fence. There at the fence it was as dark as a stack of black cats. You couldn't see nothing. I was in front and carrying the lard, and just as we crossed that fence, an old screech owl came right down over our heads making the awfulest noise I've ever heard. And Bob screamed! He jumped away out in front of me and started running, and I got to trying to keep up with him. And that thing followed us to up here above Billy's. And every time that thing came right down over our heads, it would start making that noise and Bob would scream as loud as he could scream.

Dad had got worried about us and he was coming across another trail when he heard us running and Bob screaming, and it scared him. He didn't know what was wrong with us. We come around by the barn down there, and up the branch home and got there before Dad did. I knew all the time what it was but I reckon him running scared me, too. And we was really a-leaving here.

Oakley Justice (left)

Melissa Rogers gave us a scare
with a short collection of ghost stories from her youth.

The Headless Sheep

This happened on a cold, windy winter night, where a brother of mine was walking down a road at Hiawassee, Georgia. He had been to visit a girlfriend that night. He had a great big old German shepherd dog with him ever'where he went, and [that dog] would fight for him and do anything he told him to. He didn't have to speak to him but one time.

He stayed with his girlfriend till about midnight that night, and then he had about two miles to go down the road and up through and around the cemetery [to get home]. About a half mile before he got to the cemetery, he heard something coming behind him—the ground was all froze and it was real cold and the wind a-blowing—and he could hear its hooves a-cracking, and he said he was afraid to look back. But after a while it got closter and closter to him and he turned around to look back, and he saw this sheep a-coming and it didn't have no head. So, he said that he could hear it just as plain, and he told his dog to go get it and his dog only got closter and closter to him till he rubbed up ag'in his leg. He said that sheep come right on down to the side of him and he couldn't no way get that dog to move. The sheep passed on by him and went on down the road out of sight, but he could still hear its feet a-poppin' on the cold ground —just a regular-looking sheep, only it just didn't have no head.

Melissa Rogers

Head & Shoals

My mother and my daddy [at one time] lived in a house that was said to be haunted. [People said] that they had been some people that lived back several years before then that had killed a man there. They was two men and a woman killed this man there, and they cut his head off. And after they cut his head off, why, the woman kicked it over across the floor. They was some big shoals off below the end of the farm, and they took 'im and put 'im over there in the big shoals where the water flowed off.

"Mommy, Are You in the Bed?"

Well, anyway, this happened to my brother one night when he and my mother and my daddy lived in that old house. All the other children were married off and he was the only son still living at home. The house didn't have no inside bathroom, so he had to go outdoors to the bathroom, and it was real cold that night. There was a big long porch come all the way across the house, and when my brother got up and went to the door, he seen this woman sittin' on the banisters of the porch, and he thought it was Mommy. So, he went back into the house in a few minutes and stood [at the door] for a while, and directly Mommy called him from the bed and said, "H. P., what are you a-doin' up?"

He said, "Mommy, are you in the bed?"

And she said, "Yeah." Said, "What's the matter?"

He said, "Well, I thought that was you a-sittin' out there on the banister." Said, "There's this woman sittin' out there where you've got that quilt spread across the banisters."

And she said, "No, I've not been out." And she got up and they both went out on the porch and it wadn't there anymore.

But he said it looked just like Momma sittin' there with her apron on. The moon was kindly shining, and he couldn't tell how she was dressed, but . . .

And another time, when they didn't anybody live in the house, there some men a-comin' up the road from way down on a place they called Persimmon. They was a-ridin' around this little crooked road and it was gettin' just nearly dusky dark, and they seen a woman a-sittin' out there at the fence. They said when they got up close to her, why she got up and went towards the house. She had on a black dress trimmed in pink, and she sit down on the porch, and they rode on by and she was still sittin' on the porch, but they wadn't nobody lived there and hadn't in a pretty good long time.

The Baby in the Box

Well, now this is a true story I'm gonna tell. It's very true 'cause my mother and my older sister told me about it. This woman [they knew about] had had some girls, and they'd got messed up and had a couple of babies, but nobody never did know what went with the babies. After the others had done married, the younger one got like that.

One day, the thrashers come to help thrash the rye fields. The daddy and the thrashers went out and worked till twelve o'clock, and the momma fixed dinner that day and they come in to eat. [The younger daughter's name] was Ada, and her daddy asked her where she was at. Her momma said, "Ah, she's out around here somewhere." So, she went out on the porch and she hollered and hollered. "Oh, Ada! Ada! Come to dinner!" And she never did come ner nothin'.

And her daddy got ready to go back to the field and he said, "Well, I'm worried about her." Said, "This is not like her to not come when she's called."

So, they went on back to the field and worked a little while, and he got worried and he come back to the house and he got to looking. He called in the neighbors, and finally at last they went in an old building, what they used to call a smokehouse, which was made out of just old puncheon-like boards where they stored a lot of stuff. And her momma had took some old plank and stuck it up in the cracks and had Ada a-layin' up on it, and she'd had that baby and she'd died. They all came in there, and they was a-gettin' her out and was gonna take her in the house. That's what they used to do, you know. They'd take 'em in the house and lay 'em out on a table or the bed or something like that. They didn't take 'em to the funeral home 'cause they wadn't anything like that.

One woman in there said she heared something a-makin' an awful queer noise, and there was big boxes of all kinda stuff packed up in there, and that woman got to listening and she said, "Well, I hear something."

And the girl's mother said, "Aw, it's just probably a rat or something." Said, "They're all the time around here."

And she kept hearin' it, and she kept hearin' it. And after a while she got worried and she started a-huntin'. (See, they knew that they had to be something somewhere.)

And so, she got to huntin' in all them boxes, and that momma had a big box of quilts packed up, and way down about middle ways under them quilts, this neighbor woman found this little baby. And it had the corner of the quilt stuck in its mouth, and she was gonna smother it to death like she'd already done two more. She had 'em out in the garden, and she'd buried 'em under an apple tree in a corner of the garden. And that's what she was gonna do with that one as quick as it was dead.

And this neighbor woman, she took the baby home with her, and she kept it and raised it, and I seen her myself when she was grown and married—the one that she had in that box. My sister showed her to me when we was havin' a big dinner on the ground at church one day. And she said to me, she says, "There is the little girl that was found in the box."

And she's still alive. So, that girl lived and stayed on with this woman until she married. She's a good bit older than I am, but so far as I know, she's still livin'. And she lives at Hiawassee where my sister does.

[That woman that killed the babies] they said she was just almost like a witch because she could almost do anything she set her mind to. And the ones that was there when she died— she died at home—they said that they had to hold her in the bed, and that when she died, the clock stopped—the big winding clock on the wall. They said it stopped, dead stopped.

Legends about the Cherokee

This collection of stories and legends about the Cherokee was published in the Winter 1977 edition of The Foxfire Magazine. *The stories herein, perhaps better categorized as anecdotes or memorates, are of the sort shared among non-Cherokee in the area as told by three local men, Billy Joe Stiles, Joe Arrowood, and Lawton Brooks. These stories help to give us a glimpse into the nonindigenous perspective on their Native American neighbors.*

Billy Joe Stiles

The Indians were great walkers. They traveled a lot and traded a lot, and in this area you'll find that your arrowheads are made out of rocks that came from Tennessee, Ohio, probably as far north as New Hampshire and some of those states. And undoubtedly the Indians had to walk and trade and bring back to this area those types of stones.

When I was very small, I got my pants dusted many a time for picking up rocks, and my neighbors would give me all the arrowheads they found. And pretty soon I had an extensive collection that I kept until I was in the sixth grade. I left it at a building, and when I went back, it had departed company. I had three arrowheads left out of probably half a bushel. I lost two pipes, deer skinners, and things of this nature.

Then I started another collection. And I've lost three more collections since, leaving them where the public can see them, and it is a mistake. Now I still collect, still hunt, but I don't leave it where the public can consume it.

A good place to hunt arrowheads, in my opinion, is an open field, or along a stream bed where the gravel pits wash out. Also, sandbars are a real good place; especially in middle and south Georgia. This is ideal.

The Indians used a lot of arrows and things like this to kill the game. And they lived in houses around here—not in tepees like a lot of people think. They usually wore one feather in their headband. The Cherokees even had a good alphabet, which many Indian tribes of the time did not have.

The Indians hunted gold—they had gold. They made their own arrows, they preserved their own foods, things of this nature. And they got along quite well. I've heard it said that there were probably more Indians in this area then than there are white men now. I couldn't back that up, but I've heard that statement made by old people.

They were peaceful people. The female seemed to have control of the society, which is kind of shocking to us today. They had one woman who was in charge of wars and things like this, and I've heard the rumor that she lived at a place here in the county called Warwoman Dell. Really, she should be called the "Peacewoman" because she controlled the society's wars and so forth within the tribe. The rumor was that she would go into that area and look for a large quartz—or look into a large quartz she had that was the equivalent of a crystal ball—and get a message and then tell the men whether they should fight or not.

The men did most of the hunting, and the women did the cleaning, the preserving, the cooking, this type of thing.

There are mounds in this area, but whether they are Indian or not, we don't know. There are several there around Dillard. They lived all through this area along the Tennessee River. Large fish came up the river years ago. I've heard it said that once they killed a fish that weighed many pounds that had come up the Tennessee River. Of course now, with the dams and so forth on the river now, they can't come upstream anymore.

They trusted the white man to a great extent, and this may have been part of their downfall. The white men would trade the Indians out of practically anything they could. They took their land and forced them to leave this area, and all we have left is what they left behind in the form of arrowheads and pots and things of that nature. There are even rumors of buried treasure, but they have never been proved one way or the other.

Joe Arrowood

Joe Arrowood

There was a Cherokee Indian boy who worked with Grady Nicholson at the Timpken Roller Bearing plant in Canton, Ohio, in 1924. The boy's family lived in Cherokee, North Carolina, and Grady was from Hiawassee. And this Indian boy told Grady a story that his grandfather had told him about a pot of gold he hid on Grassy Branch. He'd hid it in a hole to hide it. And Grady told that Indian boy that he lived right below Grassy Branch.

And so, one time when Grady was home, he told his friend Ed Brown about the story, along with his cousin, a Brown man from Tennessee who was visiting him at the time. See, Ed and Grady were friends, and Ed lived where we took pictures of those tracks today. And Gordon Kirby, the man we visited at the rest home today, he found out about that story, too. He could have told us all about it if he'd been able. . . .

Anyway, when Grady went back to Ohio, Gordon and this Brown man from Tennessee decided to go look for the gold. I would have gone with them except I was only about thirteen at the time and I had to go to school. So, they buddied up and hunted about two weeks. They started at the cave on Grassy Branch and found some signs and tracked them, and one night they found the lid, but it was too dark to do anything about trying to get it off right then, so they agreed to meet at eight the next morning and pry it off and see what was in there.

So, Gordon went to meet that Brown man the next morning, and waited and waited for him, and he never showed. So, he went up the creek to where they'd found the lid, and it had been pried off, and whatever had been in the hole was gone. And Gordon never heard from that Brown man again.

Lawton Brooks

I heard my wife's daddy tell one. Her daddy was just a good-sized old boy there on Nantahala, and an Indian come to this man's place right next to them up there. He wanted to stay there a few days, and they let him stay. And he'd go off of a day and come back at night. He stayed there about a month, and he'd go every day.

And my wife's daddy's brother got suspicious about it, and he said he was going to watch and see what he was doing, and he got to following him. That Indian would go up a creek they called Winding Spring Creek, and every day he'd go up that same creek. The last time he went up there, the brother didn't go watch him that day, and the Indian never came back. They went up there to see about him, and they could see where he'd been digging and working and everything, but they never did see the Indian no more. He must have found what he wanted, and they never did hear no tale about him.

Lawton and Florence Brooks

They did find a tree up there that had marks on it—a big old tree with some rocks sitting beside it and some marks on a rock and a thing pointing, and they went and hunted and hunted but never could find anything. Old Man Burt said he went with his brother up there to see if they could find anything, but they never could find anything. That pointed that that Indian had found something, I bet you, because he would have come back, but he didn't come back. He didn't want anybody to know what he found.

There's a place here on the old road going toward Helen—towards Robertstown and down to Helen that way—on that old road going through what they call Indian Gap. And there was a grave there, but I don't know whether it was an Indian grave or not. But it was right on top of a mountain, and they was a grave there. I stopped and looked at the grave back when I was a boy. We'd go through there in a wagon. That's the way we had to go to Helen when I first went. The first time, we went with a mail boy. They had a gate up there on the mountain where you had to stop and pay a toll of twenty cents to get a buggy, wagon, or anything through. He wouldn't unlock the gate unless you gave him twenty cents. That was the way they made money to work out the roads with.

Where the grave was, there was a rock stuck up there, and the place was called Indian Grave Gap. The grave was right off the road right in the gap. I just stepped out there and looked at it.

I guess that old road's still there. I guess a fellow might could still travel it; I don't know whether he could or not. That's been a long time ago. And a fellow could still find that grave, I guess, if he could get to that old road. If somebody could walk the old road, they could probably find it. It was only a few feet off the road, so you ought to be able to find it.

Four or five years ago, a man came to the old housing project with a map of the creek that runs by it. He said it was an Indian map. Fred Williams was standing in the road when he stopped to look at it. He told Fred all about it and showed him the map. And he told the name of the hill above the housing project. They call it Prime Hill now, I think. But that ain't the name of it on the map he had. They never did see the man after that. There used to be a lot of Indians back in there. There was Indians all over this country, no joke about it, and plenty of them.

Chapter Four

FOLKTALES

In the parlance of folklorists, folktales are largely recognized by the communities in which they are told as being fictitious, entertainment-centered modes of verbal art. In simpler terms, storytelling communities use folktales as an enjoyable way of passing the time. Folktales are our hero tales, our bedtime stories, and, most recently, the stuff of Disney movies. Folktales are coming-of-age stories, often revolving around a young hero or heroine, who, though unremarkable at first, rises to the occasion and overcomes great obstacles. They are stories of rebirth, ingenuity, unmatched wit, and courage in the face of seemingly insurmountable odds. Folktales are often filled with magic and the fantastic. They are the stories that capture the imagination of our youth and remind us, as grown-ups, of something we lost along the way—the ability to wander without restraint.

For those of us who came of age in modern times, folktales were most likely introduced to us in print or on film, perhaps read aloud to us in our preschool classrooms or projected onto the big screens of our hometown theaters. There are few among us in this part of the world who can really recall folktales that existed within traditional folk contexts. However, in the earliest days of Foxfire, folktales were still present (albeit, very sparsely) in the Southern Appalachian communities where students conducted their interviews. The most abundant of these were the Jack tales, which center on the antics of a trickster character named Jack as he outsmarts his foes, which include everyone from law enforcement to the Devil himself.

Additionally, there was an abundance of animal folktales, sometimes featuring anthropomorphized creatures engaging in adventures to outwit their adversaries. There were also folktales featuring more ancient characters, albeit placed in more familiar settings and using language more like that of the audience than the Old World places from where they originated. Here, we give you a sampling of previously unprinted tales in our archive.

Pat Cotter was a great storyteller as well as a local educator and just a great contact all around. Here, Pat shares one of the rarer Jack tales in our collection, as it appears to combine the folklore of two "Jacks"—that of the trickster figure Jack as well as that of the jack-o'-lantern.

How the Jack-o'-Lantern Got Its Name

Oh, this is a long tale. Do you know what Jack tales are? Okay. Jack tales are tales that Appalachian people used when they couldn't explain something to their kids, they'd tell 'em a Jack tale. And it was more of an entertaining process. And there was some truth to it, but most of it was half-truths. But, it would either put the kids to sleep or get them off their back for a while. Okay, so, the Jack tales.

This is a Jack tale that my grandfather told me how the jack-o'-lantern got its name. There was an old Irish farmer who lived pretty close to him and he was very, very mean. He didn't go to church on Sunday. He didn't go to PTA meetings. He didn't pay his paperboy. He was just all in all a bad character.

But, he did have one attribute that made him famous in East Tennessee. He grew the best apples in the state of Tennessee. On his farm there, he had apple trees and he grew the best, biggest, and sweetest apples in the state. The governor would come in and get his apples and he was just, they were great . . .

And, the devil heard about Jack's apples. It don't happen so often now, but the devil used to drop in and see people every now and then, okay, and so, the devil dropped in at Jack's house one day and said, "Jack, I hear you've got the best apples in the state." And he said, "I have. I've probably the best apples in the eastern United States." And the devil said, "Well, I'd like to have some of 'em." And Jack said, "Well, what you'll have to do is you'll have to go to the very back part of my farm on the highest hill, you'll recognize it, on the tallest tree on the very top limb. That's where you'll find the sweetest apples."

So, the devil said, "Well, think I'll go and get some of 'em." So, he left and started to the apple tree. And Jack followed him with a hatchet. And the devil clumb (that's one of those terms that we use even though I'm in education), he clumb up the tree and the devil was on the top limb. He set down and sure enough, he picked the apples and it was the sweetest, best apples he'd ever eaten. While he was up there partaking in the apples, Jack took his hatchet and he carved a cross on the bottom of the apple tree. And, I don't know if you know about devils and crosses, but the devil couldn't get by [the] cross because it was on the tree trunk, so he was stuck there for something like forty-three years. He couldn't get down. And he was up there and of course he was mad all this time.

Well, Jack eventually died of meanness and old age and his last stop was Heaven, and Saint Peter said, "You've been so mean and so bad, you can't stay here." He said, "You'll have to go to Hell." And, of course, when Jack died, the spell was released, so the devil came out of the tree and he walked back; he was walking back to Hell and he was mad and thirsty.

He'd been up there for a long time, you know, with nothing to drink.

He and Jack got to Hell about the same time and they fit (that's one of those words we use). They had such an awful fight. The devil was mad and he was ripped and Jack was ripped because he'd got kicked out of Heaven, and the devil said, "You can't stay here in Hell." And Jack said, "I've got to. I hadn't got any other place to go." And the devil said, "No, you can't!" And they fought some more. And the devil got the best of Jack. And I tell the guys that the devil gets the best of a lot of us from time to time, you know, and I kind of turn this into a religious service. No, not really.

But, the devil and Jack, the devil started to get the best of Jack and Jack took off running and he lit out running (I use some of this terminology). And, when he did, the devil picked up a hot, he hadn't had his 'nuff, and he picked up a hot coal out of Hell and he flung it at Jack and come bouncing along, you know. And Jack saw it and he said, "You know, I've been condemned to wander through eternity in darkness now, I can't go to Heaven and I can't go to Hell. I might be able to use that coal." And he started to reach down and pick it up to use for a light and he realized it was hot, so he looked over in a field and, sure enough, there was a pumpkin.

And he took his knife and he hollowed out the pumpkin and he cut a hole in it and he put the hot coal in there and Hallow-een night, now, you can still see him going up through Union County [Georgia] and some of the other places with his light. That's how my grandfather told me the jack-o'-lantern got its name.

Minyard Conner was another great contact for Foxfire over the years. He was an incredible wood craftsman and all around re-naissance man of the sort common to this area. He was also a fair storyteller and told us a story of a peculiar technique for hunting raccoons.

Nobody Likes a Lying Dog

There was a coon hunter and he was out hunting all the time and he never married. He had a good coon dog, but another feller was catching all the coons and [the first coon hunter] wasn't catching none. So, he asked the other feller why. This other feller had a little monkey along with him. That feller said his monkey helped him.

"I put him down in the swamp where the moss is on the tree and you couldn't see him."

Minyard Conner (center)

Well, this feller would tree one—his dog would tree one—he had a little .22 pistol and when his dog would tree one, he would give his monkey the pistol and tell him to go up the tree and find the coon. The monkey would go up there and hunt around, find the coon, shoot him, and come on down.

Now, this feller got so interested in it, he wanted to buy the monkey, and [the other feller] told him he'd sell him the monkey.

He took the monkey and went off hunting with him and his dogs treed—and moss was hanging down from the tree—you couldn't see no coon. He give the monkey the pistol and told him to go up the tree and the monkey went up the tree and he was gone and gone and gone. He couldn't find the coon. He come back down to the foot of the tree and shot the dog.

The next time [the coon hunter] saw that other feller, he said, "Your monkey killed my dog." And [the other feller] said, "Well, I forgot to tell you about that when we traded, but if there's one thing that monkey hates it's a lying dog."

Another Foxfire favorite, Kenny Runion, shared with us a rare secular folktale about the biblical Samson. This particular tale is quite interesting, as Samson is generally found in American folklore in the context of the African American gospel tradition.

How Samson Lost His Eyes

That Samson was a stout man. They jobbed his eyes out. Let's see how that story went:

He growed up to be a man, and he got to likin' a woman the way it reads. And on the trip down there, his daddy and mother

Kenny Runion

went with him. And he left the road and went out in the edge
of the woods, and he found a lion there dead. There was a lion
layin' there dead. He went on and he come back. He went on
and he come back. He wanted to come back, see? And a swarm
of bees went in that lion. He got all the honey he could eat, and
he took them some, and he made a riddle about that.

So, he went on down. He kept on till he married. I don't
know whether he was married then or not, but anyhow, he got
him a woman. Then he got in trouble. But they made it a while.
And I don't know what happened, but her daddy got her back
home and showed her a letter that somebody else had sent her.
Samson went up there to get her, by the way, and she was gone.
And the old man told him, he said, "I got another girl here if
you want her. She is a pretty one. I'll just let you have her."

So, he wouldn't have her, I don't think. And he went on
back and he got to studyin' what to do. He caught three hundred foxes. Three hundred foxes. Tied 'em together—tied their
tails together. Then he took pitch—that's a kind of tar, ain't it?
He set that afire and turned them loose in their territory. Burnt
everything they had up. Everything they had. Completely burnt
it up. Three hundred foxes with their tails afire—that'll fire the
woods!

There they went back down, and they was having a big
feast. They was going on seven days. And [Samson] put a riddle
in front of 'em and he told them, "Now, if y'all riddle this I'll
give y'all thirty-five change of garments, and if you don't, you
give me so much."

So, he went on down and had his wife with him. She got
after him so he told her what [the answer] was. Went on down
and sure enough, when it come up, she unriddled it right there.
He didn't do a thing in the world but picked up some kind of
a jaw or something or 'nother and went around and killed—I
don't know how many hundreds he did kill. Took the clothes
and give 'em back to 'em. It just went on that way. Just one
thing and another.

They couldn't do nothing with him. You could tell him anything in the world you wanted to and he'd break it. Just break it like it was sewing thread.

And he just kept on and on thataway till he got him another woman somewheres. And she thought she had him. And did. She got atter him to tell where his strength lay. She just kept on worrying and worrying till he told her. It lay in his hair. He had seven locks of long hair. That's where his strength lay. And just as quick as he told her, she got him down in her lap and got him to sleep. And stayed there awhile. And she sent after her folks to cut his hair just like they do in Clayton—short. He got up and he thought he was as stout as ever, but he wasn't. His strength was all gone.

Then they went into penning him up. They worked him to a syrup mill—just all kind of hard things. Jobbed his eyes out. And they put him in prison—I reckon it was prison—in chains.

Then they was having a big time down there. The King, I guess it was, told 'em, "Go up and get Samson and we'll make light of him, and we'll have fun of him."

Kenny Runion

And one of them went up there and turned [Samson] loose and brought him down there [to the King]. I guess they had to lead him. He was blind. They got him down there to the side of the house. Stood there awhile and [Samson] told the boy, he said, "Would you mind me a-stoopin' down?" And that boy said, "No. Go ahead." He stooped down, you know, and he got them sills—one over here and one over there. And when [Samson] come up, she turned a summerset bottom sides upward. There were three thousand on top of [the building]. Killed every one of them and Samson, too. And that's the way it went.

And he never asked for a thing in the world but revenge for his eyes. Said he *would* like to have revenge for his two eyes . . .

Chapter Five

ANECDOTES

Perhaps the most abundant verbal art genre in our collection is the anecdote. These kinds of stories tend to come from first-hand experience and center on either the teller or someone in his or her immediate community, most often a family member or neighbor. Like legends, anecdotes are purported to be true but also contain some element of whimsy. Some resemble a jest or jocular tale—there is often a "punch line." What makes anecdotes especially interesting is what they can tell us about memory and how events stay with us over time. These are the kinds of stories told by grandparents to grandchildren or those most often shared among close family and friends at social gatherings.

Our archive is full of wonderful anecdotes, largely due to the nature of our interview process. In the last twenty years or so, the bulk of our collected interviews led to what we call "personal stories" or biographical pieces on individuals in the community. These articles often included first-person accounts of the contact's upbringing and journey through life. More often than not, what was printed in the magazine during this time period were entire interview transcripts, albeit organized in some linear fashion. However, these personal stories frequently included "memorates," or short, stand-alone narratives about specific events from the teller's life. These memorates are what make up many of the anecdotes that follow.

As is the case with legends, we found that anecdotes typically revolve around things like place, hunting and fishing, and the supernatural. Additionally, we have found a great many stories revolving around work. Occupational lore is an abundant genre in folklore, especially as it relates to those jobs that require a special skill set (loggers, train engineers, miners, etc.). These kinds of jobs lead to the creation of folk groups that can be as close as family and thus produce their own cultural matter such as stories, superstitions, and other customs.

Hunting and Fishing Stories

These hunting and fishing stories were collected from David Callenback in 1999.

"That Ain't Playin' Fair"

Daddy said, "Do you want to go to turkey huntin' up in the morning?" I said, "Yeah, I'll go with ya." Daddy said, "Well, you're seventeen. You never killed a deer or turkey. Let me call him up, but you git down below me. He's gonna come to you first, but let him get real close and shoot him. Don't be a-movin', or he'll be gone." So, we got out thar bright and early that morning about four o'clock, and I about froze to death. I was mad. I said, "Thar ain't no turkeys this early in the morning." I was sittin' over thar, and the sun came up. I a-heard, "gobble, gobble, gobble." I said, "Daddy, right down thar . . ." Boy, I made Daddy mad. He said, "Shut your mouth. Sit down." I set down, and Daddy called him and called him, and I just set thar. I just had that gun layin' thar. I didn't know to have it ready. I just had my gun up thar lookin' through the woods. Here he come with

his head up and his tail all spread out. I said, "Goll, thar he is!"
I grabbed my gun and throwed up, and he was as far as here
to my mailbox, way too fer to shoot. I fired down on him and
cut bushes everyware, and the turkey went Brrrrrrhthththth-
ththththt. Daddy said, "Dang Almighty, boy, can't teach you
nothin.' You shootin' a hundred yards." I said, "But, Daddy, he
had a beard that long!" Daddy said, "It ain't gonna do you no
good 'cause you ain't gonna get it!" So, next time he took me,
we got up thar, and Daddy says, "Now, let him get close like
I told you, but have your gun ready." So, I sat up thar. Daddy
called and called, and I seen [a turkey]. I seen him comin,' and
just when I heard him stop, he had his head stuck up. I was too
fer. I let him come on up. I was gonna shoot him when another
one walked out right above it, and I didn't know that it was a
hen. I killed it dead. Daddy came down thar and said, "That's
a hen." Boy, he got a hickory and striked me all over. He said,
"You ain't supposed to kill hen turkeys." I said, "Daddy, you
said a turkey." I said, "Is that not a turkey?" Daddy said, "Can't
you see? A hen ain't got no beard, but a gobbler got a big, ol'
long beard. Why didn't you shoot the one right by him that
had the beard? Both of 'em close enough." I said, "Well, I'll
just kill one myself. I ain't foolin' with you no more." Dad said,
"Well, just pitch a fit. I don't care." He said, "I ain't takin' you
no more." Mama told me, "Don't worry about your daddy. He
got a bad temper."

   Mama took me out thar way up on the hill. Mama told me,
"I'll show you somethin'." She built a cage out of [wire], and
she took a hoe and dug a little ditch. She said, "Take this cord
and put a little corn in thar." I put the corn in thar. She said,
"Go back and just wait." She said, "They'll eat the corn, and
we'll bait them two or three times." I'd go back every mornin',
and the corn'd be gone. About that fourth time I baited it, I
went up thar, and thar he was in the pen, the big gobbler. He
went in that pen, but he didn't have enough sense to come out.
He'd go round and round with his head stuck up just lookin',

but he wouldn't go back out the same way he come in. I said, "Mama, Mama, come out here." Mama come up thar. Mama said, "That's the way to get a turkey." I said, "Now, how you gonna get him out?" Mama said, "Right here." She had a little, bitty, short twenty-two rifle. Mama said, "Just like this." And she put her hand over one eye like that and [took] the rifle and went STAP! [The turkey] went flop, flop, flop, flop. I said, "You killed him!" She said, "I was tellin' you to." I reckon I pulled him out, and Mama said, "We'll fool your daddy." Took him down thar, and Daddy, in his favorite rockin' chair with his pipe in his mouth, said, "Ol' David and all them a'turkey huntin' ain't killed nothin'." Mama said, "Well, he's a lot better hunter than you are, Ralph!" Said, "Look here!" Mama held him up and said, "He don't need no shotgun—killed him with a twenty-two rifle." Daddy said, "Lord have mercy, how'd you do that?" And you know, Mama ought to have told me not to tell. I said, "Hit him in a pen. He had his head stuck up and Mama shot him." She smacked me right in the mouth. She said, "You tell everything you know." He said, "Baited him?" I said, "No, Mama did." Daddy said, "Baitin's illegal. That ain't playing fair."

Bait & Sting

Me and my brothers were goin' fishin' for trout, but we couldn't find no fish bait. It was so dry, and there 'as a big hornets' nest hangin' on the limb. I said, "Right there's the bait, boys." Cliff said, "Reckon how many're in there?" Frank said, "Well, a man told me in town the other day that the way to get a hornets' nest is to cut you a stick and stop the hole up, take you a knife and cut the limb off, and stick the nest down in the water. It'll drown 'em." I said, "Well, that makes sense." And we all agreed, you know. Frank said, "Well, I'm the one that's got a knife, so let me try." He was always the bravest one. He cut him a stick. He whittled it down and said, "That about right?" I said, "That's about the size of the hole that'll fit." Well, he went up there. He got in, but [the hornets] were comin' out of the air. Boys, when he stopped that hole up, I mean, you talk about pourin' it to Frank! They just started comin' in out of everywhere, and one popped me right side of the head. I took off, and them things followed us plumb to the creek. I had to jump in the creek, and I like to never got 'em off me. I run home cryin' to Ma all swelled up like a bullfrog. Mama said, "Is the stick in the hole?" I said, "Lord, yeah." She said, "They won't leave that nest. They'll sting you if you get [within] ten foot of it." Daddy said, "Wait a minute. I'll get the nest for you tonight." So, he took a long cane pole and tied him up a big ol' *Clayton Tribune* on it and lit it and stuck it to it. He said, "Here's your bait." He went up there and got the bait. We went up there the next day, and we caught eight or ten big, brown trout. I guess that's one of the biggest browns I ever caught. It was about eighteen inches long. I caught him down yonder on Big Creek.

In 1991, Foxfire students Lee Carpenter and Leigh Ann Smith interviewed David Land. Here is a somewhat humorous tale that he shared with them about a pretty smart hunting dog.

Treed in a Creek

Well, I had these tree dogs. They'd tree any kind. They'd tree a bobcat, a coon, or anything that went up a tree. One of them, Troop—well, they was all good—but this is about the most dependable dog, I guess. He was a little older than the rest. He was a rabbit-hunting dog. Most tree dogs don't run a rabbit much. They don't like to run rabbits, but he would, in the daytime, run a little bit. He was down on the creek where I couldn't see him, and this man was hunting with me and all. You know, when a dog trails, they change their voice when they tree. He had a big IEEOW, IEEOW. He was just as calm. He'd set [at the tree and bark] all night till you come to him. And he all at once started barking and the man said, "Well, he's treed. He ain't been a-running nothing, but he's treed." I said, "But there ain't no trees down there. There's a creek." The man says, "Well, I guess he's treed in the ground." I said, "No, he's not treed in the ground, I can tell by the way he sounds." We went down there, and he's standing out in the water. He had his head up out of the water. It was nearly too deep for him to stand. He's just a-standing there, IEEOW, IEEOW, IEEOW. I went in there, and he'd got in a steel trap. Somebody had set an ol' steel trap for beavers or muskrat. I don't know what he was trapping for. Anyhow, Troop had stepped in that trap in the water, and he couldn't get out. He wasn't trying to get loose. He knew he couldn't and he was barking that tree bark so I'd come to him to get him out. That was remarkable to me. He was a smart dog.

Vaughn Billingsley was featured for a personal story in the 2004 Spring/Summer issue of The Foxfire Magazine. *As part of that interview, Vaughn shared with us this little hunting story.*

Don't Shoot Till It Moves

. . . I remember the first time that I ever went squirrel huntin'. I found some shells in the backseat of the car we had borrowed to go coon huntin'. I found me some shotgun shells, and I asked Daddy, I said, "Can I take your gun over there and go squirrel huntin'?" He sat me down and talked to me a little and taught me what to do and how to act. He told me that if I seen a squirrel not to shoot until I saw it move and knew for sure that it was a squirrel. "Don't waste a shell," he said. So, I went up across the edge of the field and into the woods. I had to walk about a mile or two up there before I could go huntin'. I walked up quite a bit, and there was a squirrel sittin' on a limb, just sittin' up there, lookin' at me with his tail bowed up over his back. It was a perfect picture. Well, I 'member standin' there, waitin' for it to move. I waited and waited, and it never did move. It just sat there and looked at me. I said to myself, "Well, I know that's a squirrel, so I just better shoot it." So I did, and out it fell. So, I went on around until I finally killed one more. Then I went home 'cause I was pretty happy over killin' those two squirrels. That was my first time.

Vaughn Billingsley

In 2003, student Samantha Tyler interviewed Walter Stancil about bear hunting in the region and recorded several hunting stories. These two are our favorites.

The Dog That Wouldn't Quit

I took Cale, my son, huntin' when he was about ten, and he's made a good bear hunter. We were goin' huntin' one time, and we got out of the truck at this place that takes a long time to walk into. Cale had two or three dogs, and I had two or three. It was a pretty steep mountain we were walkin' up. We got in there and turned the dogs loose. There was lots of bear signs from three or four bears, and they were tryin' to, to start somethin' up. This little female gets on one bear by herself, and it's, like, on a Wednesday. Well, some of our dogs got on one bear, and they treed it. Some of the dogs got on another bear, and they didn't tree it. This little female had followed the bear by herself. I didn't get her that day, but the next day I tracked her with a trackin' collar. I followed her 'cause I knew she'd treed. I'd follow her to one place, and that bear would have come down and made her run until she'd treed it again. I could tell all this by the signal on her collar. Well, I hunted her Thursday and Friday. I got up early Saturday mornin' and got a good signal on her. I got out of the truck and walked back in the country for, I guess, about three hours. I get back there, and I get that tracker out, and that signal's gone. Well, what had happened was there was this kid, and he'd heard the dog barkin' in the woods about nine o'clock on Saturday mornin' with that bear up a tree. She'd had him treed part of the time, but she hadn't had any food all that time. [The kid] had a rope in the pocket of his coat, and he saw that she had a tag on her collar, so he was gonna bring her out and bring her home. He reached in his coat to get the rope, and that bear just come down outta that tree, and off they go again. That night, I called my wife from a mountain on my cell phone, and she said she knew where my dog was. That kid had called. Well, I come outta there, and I knew where my dog was. I had lost the signal, so I was just lookin' for her. She'd dropped off on the other side of the mountain. I came on home, and I went back after her the next mornin'. She had that bear. She had followed it Wednesday night, Thursday, Friday, Saturday, and part of the day Sunday, all because she wouldn't give up. There aren't many dogs that'll do like that.

"You're Crazy. I'm Coming Down!"

One time, me and this old Indian had this bear treed. We'd been waitin' on the dogs for about thirty minutes, and we didn't hear 'em. So, we went and got in the truck and went to where we thought they were, and when we got around there, we heard where the dogs had treed. We didn't have guns. A lot of times, we don't carry guns. We got to where the dogs were, and they had the bear up in a big hemlock. That hemlock forked about thirty or forty feet up. We had the dogs tied back, and that boy that was with me thought he'd go up there and get that thing to come down. Well, we took a stick and beat it, and that thing wouldn't come down. That boy said, "You go up that other side and make a noise, and that thing'll come down." Well, I went up there, about eight feet up the other side of the fork, and that thing started hissin' and slappin' at me. Well, I eased back down a little bit because I didn't want that thing comin' after me forty-five feet up in the air, you know. It'd get pretty rough. That old Indian was down there on the ground, and he said, "Do not come down. If it comes after you, I'll kill it." Well, we didn't have any guns, so I didn't know how he would kill it, but I picked at that thing for about five or ten more minutes, and that thing kept on hissin' and slappin'. Finally, I looked at him and said, "You're crazy. I'm comin' down!" I decided from then on that if a bear gets up in a tree, I'm gonna take my dogs and go on back to the truck. It can come down on its own.

Supernatural Stories

We begin our journey into the supernatural with an account from Liz Shaw, recorded for the 1984 Winter issue of The Foxfire Magazine.

The Thorny Desert

I remember, it was a spooky gray day one day and it was real cloudy. And I think the power might have gotten knocked out 'cause it was dark as it could be in [that church], and they were singin' one of those scary ones [shape note hymns] and I got spooked. Yeah, when I was a little girl, I got scared. I wanted to go home right then. I mean, look at all those old faces and these wrinkled old faces and this white hair. Maybe they weren't that old, but I guess when you're little, old really is old. And they smelled old. I mean, they smelled like roses, you know, and mothballs and stuff. And they'd be sittin' there and it was dark and it was rainin' and thunderin' outside. And that's the day I went in and learned "Thorny Desert." That's the day. And I was sittin' there next to my uncle Vaughan. I can remember thinkin', "I'm so glad I'm sitting next to my uncle Vaughan. I'm so glad I'm sitting next to my uncle Vaughan." I was scared. It sent goose bumps up my neck. It was scary. It was like they was calling down the wrath of God. And He was going to come down. "Fiery darts of Satan." Oh, that image was in my mind. Sometimes I just think about it and I almost scare myself.

In 1990, Eula Carroll shared this haunting tale of an encounter with the ghost of her mother to Foxfire students Aubrey Eubank and Renee Richard.

"Don't Be Afraid. I'm Here."

[When we got home] it was just misting rain. Papa made me go to the barn and milk the cow. It was dark as pitch on across there [from the house to the barn], and [it] opened with a big door. That was a livery stable, they called it. They rented stalls y'know, and it was court week. Well, it was dark, and we had an old collie dog, and she was the sweetest thing. He wouldn't let me take that dog. He wouldn't let me take the lantern. I started down there. Brother always stood by me, and he got right in the first gate and had the dog and had the lantern. I didn't know he had it, though, till after. So, I went on down there, and this hack that I was telling you about that carried mama to the cemetery [was sitting there]. I went on through that big hall, dark as it could be, on through there and opened the big door. And it screeched, because it was a very big door. It opened going into the other pasture—the big pasture, and I opened that gate. [The cow] knew which way to go and she came on. We got real close to that hack. Something said, "Bam! Bam! Bam!" The cow stopped, and you know a cow or a horse either one will blow (whew, whew) like that when they're fighting or scared. She wouldn't move, and I stood there, and in a minute it started again. I should have known that if somebody wanted to get me, they wouldn't have made that noise, and I was just sitting there praying. I was so hot, I was just scared to death. I thought I was gonna die. The cow was just blowing. She was really scared, too. It sounded like somebody was trying to get out of that big ol' hack. There was a big loft all the way across the barn. I went up to the steps and looked up and somebody said, "Eula, don't be afraid." I recognized my mother's voice. Nobody believes me, but I know what I saw.

Something says, "Eula, don't be afraid, I'm here," and I looked up there and she was sitting in a straight chair. It was the most beautiful light I've ever seen in my life. It was just a halo of light. She had on a navy dress with white dots, and white lace on it. She said, "Don't be afraid. I'm here." And you know, that cow just started walking into her stall. She knew where it was, and I wasn't afraid and I started walking up the steps and [my mother's] hand was going down like she wanted to hold my hand, and of course it went away before I got to the steps.

I went on and milked the cow and fixed the feed for in the morning. I went on up there, and poor ol' Brother was sitting up there at the gate, and he had something over him, and a lantern under a big raincoat and he had the dog there with him. He was going to come a-running if I called him over there.

When I went over to him, he was crying, and I said, "Brother, don't cry," and he said, "Well, I was gonna go down there and get 'cha, 'cause I was scared." So, I went into the house and my stepmother and my daddy were in there. We hadn't had supper yet and she was in there taking some biscuits out of the stove. I said to Papa, "Papa, I saw Mama." He began to cry. He said, "Oh, Eula! That was the wrong thing for me to send you down there. Somebody could'a'been there in that barn."

"Well, I saw Mama and she told me not to be afraid." He said that he believed every word I said, 'cause I looked so happy when I came in. Brother was cryin' and he said that he wanted to see Mama, too. I never was afraid to go in that barn again, but he didn't send me anymore when it was dark. I was sixteen when that happened.

At another moment in his 1991 interview, David Land shared this spooky story that involved his father and a possessed toolbox.

The Signaling Toolbox

[My father] never did believe in signs and things happening, but this thing happened when he was building. I told you he was a builder. He'd work, too. He was building this house over in Pickens County. He got the house pretty well done and was working on the back side. My daddy had a toolbox. They's working on the back side, and they heard somebody knock on the front side. It was like somebody knocking like they wanted to come in. They said, "Who's that around there knocking? Surely they can hear us around here working." [They said], "Why won't you come around here? We're not in the house." [My father] told a boy to go around and see where they was.

He went around there and come back and said, "There ain't nobody around there. Sounds like it's in Mr. Land's toolbox." They all went around there then. They got around there and stayed there just a little bit. And then PECK, PECK, PECK, in the toolbox. He said, "Well, it does sound like it's in that toolbox." [The house] wasn't underpinned. You could see under the house, so there couldn't nothing be under the house, you know. And they raised the lid up [on the toolbox] and waited a little bit and PECK, PECK, PECK. They says, "It's down under the tray down in the bottom." Well, they took all the trays out, and there was nothing in there. But ever once in a while something would just PECK, PECK, PECK. And they never did know what it was. Now, if he had been a man that was bad to tell tales and yarns and things . . . but [my father] never did tell anything. What he told was just the facts. After the people moved in there, they had one child got burnt up, I believe one gouged his eye out with a fork trying to untie a shoe. He slipped and gouged his eye out. And there was a lot of bad things happened. He said he always believed that was a warning, some kind of a warning, that something bad was going to happen. What he heard, I don't know.

Family and Community Stories

Granny Toothman was a favorite among our Foxfire students. In this 1985 interview, she shared with us a couple humorous tales about the domestic world of her childhood.

A Cat in the Oven & Two Birds with One Stone

[My family had a wood cookstove.] It had a big oven with two doors that swung both ways. I'll tell you a little story about that oven. It was a cold, cold day, and Mother had left both oven doors open so the heat could come out, and we had a big ol' cat there, and the cat crawled up in the oven and went to sleep. Mother got ready to get dinner. Why, she shut both doors and built a fire! [Laughter.] And we heard this cat a-screaming, and we were running around the house but we couldn't find it. We got out around the house and we came back in and we could still hear that cat a-screaming. All of a sudden, Mother thought, "It must be in the stove." She opened the stove door and here came my cat. Its paws were scorched and its hair was singed just a little bit, but the cat really wasn't hurt. But it sure never went back in that stove!

So anyway—we had chicken or turkey. Up until I was twelve years old, I had to kill those chickens with an ax and "whang" on the chopping block! Then I plucked them and all that. After I was twelve years old, I shot them. By then I had me a .22 rifle. It was one of the first bolt action rifles that was ever put out. A single shot. I ordered it from Sears and Roebuck. It cost $4.98. I remember that very well because I had got five dollars for hoeing corn that summer and I paid for that rifle myself. First evening I got rifle, I got my shells and went over the hill and killed a squirrel. Dad thought that was great.

But that first Christmas I had the rifle, Mother sent me out to kill a chicken. She had some special blue hens that were extra

Granny Toothman

good layers, and then she had these dominickers that were a whole lot bigger and better to eat, and they didn't lay like the blue ones did. She said for me to get her a big hen and "Don't kill a blue one!" So, I went out and shot that dominicker right in the head, and there was a blue one in line with the shot and it went right through its neck, and I'd killed a blue one and a dominicker both at the same time.

I was really nervous about going in and telling her about shooting her blue hen. Dad was in and I knew I had protection, so I said, "Oh, Mother, I shot one of your blue hens."

She said, "I thought I told you not to shoot a blue hen."

I said, "Well, I couldn't help it. It was right in line with the dominicker. I got the dominicker, but I've got a blue hen, too."

And she said, "Well, I reckon if you killed two birds with one stone, it's all right."

While Jud Nelson was making the wagon we documented for Foxfire 9, *a friend stayed in his blacksmith shop, and they began to visit. The following story is one his friend shared.*

A Turnip Tale

This is damn fact and there ain't no doubt about it.

I was running an ice plant. It was during the war. I had some good friends that run a service station across the street. They sold a few groceries over there—canned goods, you know—that people need on the weekend.

Well, during the war, I sold my car. I didn't need it. I wasn't going nowhere anyhow. I could drive the ice truck to go a-fishing or go over to the bootleggers or something like that, you know. And anyhow, my wife and kids would walk up to that store and get what we needed. It was handy, and they didn't have to cross the street. They'd go up there and get what we needed and I'd go up there and pay 'em whenever I took a notion—every two weeks, month, whenever I took a notion to pay my bill. And if I needed a case of something, he'd get it for me wholesale and sell it to me at cost. And I'd bought a case of turnip greens. Big cans, you know. I just carried them over to the house and set 'em in the pantry, and when it come wintertime, they'd be there.

Well, when you get up in the morning with a grouch on, you can find something to bellyache about. That ain't no trouble. Sometime during that morning, I went up there and paid old Ed my bill. So, it was ten or twelve dollars more than the usual—well, I might have been ten or twelve dollars late, you know.

When I got back over to the house to eat dinner, I said, "What in hell is it we have been eating around here that costs so much? The damn bill's shot plumb out of sight!" And I opened the pantry door and said, "Look. There's a whole damn case of turnip greens, and when have we had any?"

I knew damn well [by] the time I said it I'd done played hell. But I'd done said it, and you can't put it back. It's done out. And the next day at dinner I had a tall glass of tea and a big bowl of cornbread and a big bowl of turnip greens. That night at supper, I had what was left of that can of turnip greens and what was left of that bread.

Well, at breakfast I always had the usual couple of eggs, you know. But at dinner, [it was] the same damn thing. And there was twenty-four of them cans . . . It got to where [my wife] was wantin' me to raise hell, but I wouldn't'a done it if it'd killed me deader than hell. If I'd turned *into* a turnip, I wouldn't have.

One evening I was getting pretty tired of them damn things. [My wife] went to the picture show, and I got in there and counted them cans so I knew how much farther I had to go. That last dish that was served of turnip greens, I lapped 'em up like a hound dog. I wadn't going to let her beat me.

For a while there, I guess I was the slickest-running young-ster in Gordon County. But it was a while before I wanted any more turnip greens! And I never did buy another case.

Your mouth can sure get you in trouble if you don't shut it. When it gets out, it gets out, and you can't take it back. Don't you forget it.

Della Cody

In 1992, Della Cody shared with us two chilling, dark tales about death and the cruel nature of some men, including the story of how her grandfather was killed.

"There He Is"

I was about twelve year old, I guess, and uh, this family lived right down the river below us. Well, my aunt owned a farm and this man didn't do anything but make liquor. You know, about the only way for anyone in there to make a living was for them to make liquor. Well, that man wanted to know if my aunt would let him come across our land to get in a big cove where he was making a big still. They called it the Indian Cove. She told him that if he would keep her fences up and don't let her cattle out of pasture, he could go.

He said, "Oh yeah, I'll keep your fences laid up."

I was just a little old girl, but I remember that. He came through there with a wagonload of meal just stacked as high as it would go in a wagon, pulling the wagon up through there with them bulls. His son was driving them with a whip. He had a plaited whip made out of leather. He would give it a shinny or two over his head and crack it over them bulls' heads, and I've never seen such pulling as they did across that road. They stalled one time. The road wasn't traveled none, and going up that steep bank there was gullies washed out. They somehow or another got the wagon wheels off in that gully, and them poor bulls couldn't pull it out, it was loaded with so much meal. Well, he whipped and he whipped on them bulls. They just pulled for all mighty! Well, his daddy was over at the still. He had done give his son up a-coming. When he left, he found his son still there on that bank.

Well, one Thursday, when that man came [home], he was drunk. And he started knocking the dishes off the table, and his wife said, "Don't you do that. These children need their milk."

He said, "I'm gonna kill every one of you and pile ya up in a pile and leave ya here." Then they just got into it. The two oldest ones tried to get their daddy off down to the neighbors' house 'cause he was threatening to kill them all. Well, somehow or another in the big racket, he shot at his wife sitting at the table. His wife and daughter gave the pistol a knock, and it hit the baby laying in the wife's lap and killed it. She got him off the halfway down there, and he said, "I ain't going nowhere.

I'm going back up to the house. I'm gonna kill ya all and pile ya up in a pile and leave ya."

She said she couldn't do anything with him.

His son said, "We'll see about that." He got his gun, and when his dad started in at the yard gate they went to shooting at him. Folks said they shot one of his arms nearly off. They said that he kept begging them not to kill him, but they kept shooting him. His son went out there after they shot him, and he had the pistol and gave him three licks right in the top of the head. Laid his daddy's head wide open. He was a bald-headed feller. I remember that 'cause we went down there and seen him and the baby after they were laid out. Back then they laid people out at home. We went in and the children stayed there, and they didn't leave. When people come in to see him, you know, after they laid him out, his son would just pull the sheet back and he would say, "There he is." He didn't care no more than if he was a rabbit laying there.

Dog's Best Friend

My grandpa got killed over a dog. This man come, and the dog was with Grandpa. He said, "Does the dog bite?"

Grandpa said, "The dog ain't gonna bite nobody unless they bother me." Well, this man didn't believe him.

He said, "You mean, that dog will fight for you? Well, let's just put on a show. I'm gonna fight you and see what that dog will do." So, the man acted like he was gonna fight Grandpa. The dog jumped on him. Then he was gonna kill the dog, and that is what they fell out about.

Grandpa said, "People don't kill my dog!" So, they got into a fight, and they fought and fought, since this man was gonna kill Grandpa's dog and Grandpa was gonna get him. Well, the man started running and he cut into the house, and then Grandpa cut into the house. As Grandpa was coming around, the man hit him in the back of the head with a rock and it killed him.

Local storyteller and author Janie Taylor penned an article about an alligator that escaped from the Tiger Zoo for the 2006 Spring/Summer issue of The Foxfire Magazine.

An Alligator in Tiger

In the 1930s, before World War II, there was a zoo at Tiger. Travelers visited this zoo as they drove Old US 23, which was the main highway between Atlanta, Georgia, and Asheville, North Carolina. Tiger was the halfway point between the two cities and thus a convenient stopping place to rest and tour the zoo.

This facility was located on the property of Bertha and Jable Cannon where the Rabun County Senior Center now stands. Until recently, there were visible remains of the zoo, including broken sidewalks and bits of the concrete foundations of the animal cages. The population of the zoo included two black bears (one on a chain; the other in a large cage). There was a collection of caged creatures native to these mountains, including foxes, raccoons, wildcats, and squirrels. There were also monkeys, snakes, and exotic birds, but the main attraction at the zoo was an alligator! This nine-foot-long reptile was truly KING OF THE ZOO—with his own personal pool, shade trees, and a special diet. A doctor of veterinary medicine and graduate of Auburn University was in charge of the daily operation of the zoo at Tiger. The zoo was truly a tourist attraction.

On a warm, sunny summer day my dog, Toddler, and I were at Grandma's house over at the base of Tiger Mountain. Toddler was [a] black-and-white wire terrier who was my constant companion and best buddy. As usual, Grandma sent Toddler and me to get the daily mail from the mailbox over on Syrup City Road just outside of Tiger. So, we two left the cabin and walked down the hill, playing in the sand, watching the flying birds, and checking on the anthills. Then we stopped by the willow tree in the swamp and began throwing rock pebbles into the water and watching the ripples. Then up the hill we went and over the gap to the mailbox. As instructed, I counted the pieces of mail—one newspaper and two letters—and stuck them into my back pocket.

Back over the gap we went, and Toddler and I trotted down the hill. When we came through the willow tree in the swamp, Toddler began barking frantically, shoving against my feet. I looked to see if a mud turtle was visible or a water moccasin, but I saw neither. Then I saw IT! A large alligator was lying under the branches of the willow tree in the swamp. As he opened up and closed his massive jaws, I could see the rows of teeth and his beady black eyes. Toddler had known that danger lurked and had protected me from this ferocious creature. Needless to say, we ran the long route by the pasture and barn to the safety of Grandma's house.

As I went into the kitchen, I saw Grandma at the wood-stove frying chicken as she prepared the noon meal for the work hands. To her, I gave the mail—one paper and two letters. Then I said, "Grandma, there is an alligator under the willow tree in the swamp." Before Grandma could answer, my aunt Ruth exclaimed, "She doesn't know an alligator from an earthworm, and Janie P. needs her mouth washed out with soap—lye soap, for telling untruths."

Since Grandma was too busy for such, she told me to go sit in a rocking chair on the front porch and think about my sinful ways! So, with Toddler by my side, I rocked. Now, Toddler knew that we had found an alligator, and I knew that to be so, but who was going to believe us? Certainly not my aunt Ruth. Then I remembered that the work hands, riding in a mule-drawn wagon, would come to the house for dinner. I knew that they would cross over the gap, drive down the hill, and when the mule team sensed the presence of the alligator under the willow tree in the swamp—well, somebody would believe me then!

Toddler and I waited and watched. Soon we heard the

creaking and rattling of the farm wagon as it crossed over the gap and came down the hill. Sure enough, when the mules saw that large reptile, they became frightened and out of control. My uncle Joe jumped off the wagon, saw the slimy alligator, and realized the frantic behavior of the mules.

To the cabin, Uncle Joe ran shouting, "The alligator has escaped from the Tiger Zoo and is under the willow tree in the swamp." With these words, my grandma hugged me and started crying, "Janie P., you could have lost an arm or leg, and Toddler could have been eaten alive!"

The menfolks went over to the Tiger Zoo, notified the veterinarian, who immediately brought a '34 Ford pickup to load the alligator on. The reason the alligator had not attacked Toddler and me was the fact that the alligator was suffering from a near heatstroke after wandering away from the zoo. The snout of the alligator was tied, and with his tail thrashing, he was loaded and returned to his pool, shade tree, and proper diet at the Tiger Zoo.

Later that day, as we were all on the front porch of the house, my aunt Ruth said to me, "I'm so thankful you were not injured, and Toddler is indeed a hero! Too, I know that you know the difference between an earthworm and an alligator, but promise me, Janie P., that you will never, ever tell a falsehood!" So, I did promise, but I still tell my tales of Tiger!

Today, some seventy years later, the green willow tree and the swamp still exist. The alligator and the zoo at Tiger have vanished, with only vivid memories left for a few of us who can recall that eventful day at the zoo at Tiger.

Occupational Stories

Robert Harris was truly a rare interview. The self-proclaimed "Last Circuit-Riding Preacher in the Nation" (which probably wasn't far from the truth) was interviewed by Foxfire students in

1985 and shared some of his tales as a ministering throwback in a modern age.

An Unlikely Collection

As a circuit-riding preacher, I attract people from all walks of life and from all ages of life. As you can see here, I have the kids flocked to me. Then you have your grandmas and grandpas and everyone in between. Many people come out of curiosity. They ask me if I'm Doc Holliday or Cowboy Copus or the Lone Ranger. Of course, I don't mind that because it's a point of contact and it gives me an opportunity to talk and I get into various kinds of conversations.

Now, last year I was in Maggie Valley, North Carolina, for the North Carolina Harley-Davidson Motorcycle Association's rally. We had something like seven thousand motorcycles and one horse. You can imagine the interest that created. In the minds of most people, motorcyclists are considered to be a rough group, but that's because they don't know the cyclists. You have a clientele of all the different levels of society. You have people that are very high class on motorcycles, and then you have a lot of ruffians. Not everybody that rides a motorcycle can be tabbed as a rough person. I've met some of the kindest people anywhere on these motorcycles. In the heart of Maggie Valley that year, they had a beer joint, and there were about three hundred of these cyclists at the beer joint. I wanted to go into the crowd, but I was a little hesitant about whether to penetrate or whether to work around the fringe. I decided, "I'm going to penetrate the crowd."

The horse decided right then to throw up his tail and he relieved himself right in front of everybody. Of course, I carry in my saddlebags equipment to take care of that if it happens in a place where I'm expected to clean it up. So, I got off my horse to clean the mess up [and] there was a lady standing there. She was about half-drunk. I said, "Would you hold this horse while I clean up this mess?"

And she said, as a half-drunk person would say, in a sort of slurred voice, "Why, sure, Preacher. I know exactly what to do with that horse."

And I got my plastic bag out to pick up the droppings from the horse and when I stooped down to scoop it up, you never heard such a round of applause in your life! You would have thought you were out at a football game and they had scored. They whistled and they clapped their hands, and this was applause for my cleaning up the mess. It was coming from this kind of people. I looked back to see how my horse was getting along, and one of them had his head up in the air and was pouring a can of Schlitz beer down him. I said, "No, don't make my horse drunk, Brother." I said, "I've gotta ride that rascal out of here and if he's drunk, I'll have a hard time." Now, the animal would go for the beer because of the hops that's in it. That's part of the ingredients of beer.

Well, when I stood up, one guy said, "What kind of a hat is that that you have?"

I said, "My hat is a John B. Stetson."

He said, "Let me have it."

Now, if you were in a motorcycle gang and they said, "Let me have your hat," what do you do? You hand 'em your hat. Well, I thought, "Good-bye, hat. I won't see that anymore." And I talked on with the people and I had my brochures. I was passing them out right and left. I said to a lady standing by, "What happened to my hat?"

She said, "Oh, they'll bring that hat back in a little while. He's gone to get the collection."

I said, "I didn't come in here on no collection deal. I came here just as a minister with no commercial thought in mind."

"We know that. If we'd thought you were in here for commercial reasons, we'd never took your hat." He came back with about twenty-five bucks in my hat. I got my hat back with twenty-five dollars to buy gas with. So human interest stories of that nature go along with this type of ministry.

Robert Harris

The Last Circuit Rider in the Nation

I do get criticism. I have to absorb a lot of things. Many people do not understand what's going on. Well, it's like the circuit-riding bit. Now, you go down a strange street in a strange town or offer an attraction—a man on a horse in a frock coat and a ten-gallon hat. You look like you just came in from Mars. They want to know, "Are you the Lone Ranger? Or Doc Holliday? Or just who are you?"

This is especially true when I go to Gatlinburg (Tennessee) on Friday or Saturday night, when it's not unusual to have twenty, twenty-five thousand people on the street. And of course, I can't take the horse in because of the traffic congestion. I do walk around on the street and talk to people who are sitting on the benches or in the rocking chairs in front of the stores and shops. You have to be real good to get one of those rocking chairs. You have to go early to get a rocking chair. They sit there and rock and watch the world go by. Well, that's ideal pickings for what I'm doing. I come walking along the street and I pass my brochure out. Some of 'em say, "What are you running for?" They think I'm campaigning as a politician.

And I say, "Well, I'm running for the Lord, and my candidate has got to win. There's no way he can lose."

And they say, "Well, we thought you were politicking."

I say, "No, I'm the last circuit-riding preacher in the nation."

Mildred Story served as a schoolteacher for much of her life and, as you may expect, had many stories from her days of teaching. Here she shares a story from one of her earlier days in the local school system.

"No, I Wouldn't Hurt You for Anything"

Would you like me to tell you the time I was most scared? That was one of the years that our local board would not allow married teachers in the system. One day at noontime, we started in to lunch and I was at the back of the line, and I heard Mrs. Annie Perry in the lunchroom. And she says, "Mrs. Story, come here right quickly!" So, I went running in there. Jesse [one of the students] had decided he didn't like that lunch, so he had just poured it on the floor. She had undertaken to make him pick it up, and he wasn't going to do it. So, by the time I got there, Jesse had his knife out. He was taller than I was and bigger then I was. Now, Jesse was known to be a pretty good fighter and I was really scared, but there was not a man on the hill and I was supposed to be the oldest and the bravest one. Therefore, I said, "Lord, just give me strength."

I edged just a little closer and a little closer to Jesse. I knew that if I could get my hand on Jesse . . . He was a lovable sort of person, but when his dander was up, he was really angry. I edged a little closer and said, "Now, let's listen—listen now, Jesse." And by that time, I had my hand on him. I said, "You wouldn't do that to me."

He says, "Don't you come a *bit* fudder! I'll cut your gizzard out!" I backed back a little bit. Then I went a little bit closer and a little bit closer and when I touched his hand, I looked at him and smiled. Jesse smiled back.

I said, "You wouldn't do that to Mrs. Story, would you?"

"No, I wouldn't hurt you for anything."

Albeit marginalized as an illegal activity, moonshining was, none-theless, an occupation for many in this area. Here, Conway Watkins shares a tale that involves him and another well-known Foxfire contact, Buck Carver.

"I'd Rather Be Caught up Here Making Liquor Than Caught for Stealing"

My daddy never would make liquor, but I tried it myself. Buck Carver and me got caught one time up there on the Highlands Mountain. It was above the old rock quarry up there. We had [our liquor] in thirty-six fifty-gallon barrels. We were running a pretty good-sized place. That ol' federal man said, "Didn't you know you couldn't come up here in North Carolina and make liquor!"

I said, "Didn't figure it would last forever." [Laughter]

He said, "What did you come for?"

I said, "To start at the beginning, it's a long story. I've got a wife and six children to feed." I didn't have no job, and I said, "I'd rather be caught up here making liquor than caught for stealing."

He said, "Well, I'll have to agree with you. I would, too. I've got to ask you boys some questions. You can answer them to me or answer them to the judge."

I said, "Any reasonable question. I'd just as soon answer it to you. Don't make no difference to me."

About the first thing he asked was "Who else is in with you boys?"

I said, "Just me and Buck." They had both of us caught. [The other fellow working with us] was gone after a load of sugar, so there wasn't no use in naming him.

About the next thing he said was "Where did all this sugar come from?"

"It's been a long time ago, but when I went to school, history taught that the majority of it came from Cuba." [Laughter.] So, he asked two or three more questions like that, and I answered him about the same way. Directly, he dropped back to the one asking me who was tied in with us boys, and I said, "Now, you asked me that question a while ago." And then I said, "I'm gonna tell you

Conway Watkins

the truth this time." His eyes got about that big, and he thought I was gonna name somebody, you know. I said, "I wish there was somebody who could take the whole thing off from us."

There was six of the North Carolina law [with the federal man]. There was a police from Highlands and a deputy sheriff from Franklin—well, there was three or four deputies who'd been deputized to come with them, I reckon. They wasn't looking for me and Buck. They was looking for another fella and just happened to run on me and Buck. There was this fella living there at the foot of the mountain that we was selling two cases of liquor to a week for eighteen dollars a case, six gallons to a case. (That was what we was getting.) We was selling him two cases, and he was taking it to Highlands and pinting it out to people. And they thought he had a little ol' place of his own and was a-making it down there. They was a-hunting for him when they found us.

That ol' federal man was talking to us there [at the still]. Me and Buck kept a clean place. We made good whiskey and we kept it clean around there, everything cleaned up. That ol' federal man said, "Boys, I hate to cut a place like this down." He said, "This is clean! I've seen kitchens not as clean as this is!"

I said, "Well, as far as I'm concerned, sir, you can just leave it." I thought it was just as well to have a little fun out of it. I was already done caught.

They went ahead cutting down the place. We was right there when they cut it down. [The North Carolina law] had Buck and me handcuffed together, setting on a log. Lamon [Queen, the Rabun County, Georgia, sheriff] and his deputy, Faye, came on up there, and Lamon said, "Take them damn handcuffs off them boys. You ain't caught no outlaws, just 'cause you caught 'em up here making a little liquor."

So, they taken the handcuffs off of us. Buck had done told 'em that he'd help tear the bowels [of the still] out if they'd take off these "bracelets," he called 'em. They didn't take 'em off till Lamon got right up there, though.

Well, we had a right smart of groceries there, and I *knew* that we wouldn't get the groceries back because I knew the law would take them. So, I just went ahead and spread dinner for the whole crowd. I made two four-pound lard buckets full of good, strong coffee and spread dinner. By the time they got the place cut down, I said, "Boys, come on, and let's eat dinner." All the rest of 'em come right around and went to eating—the law did, you know—and just sat down and visited and talked. There ain't no use in getting scared 'cause you get caught. Old Buck, he'd washed his hands and come around there and leant up agin' a hickory bush and was just standing there. And I said to Buck, "Buck, come on and eat your dinner."

He looked around over the crowd at everybody like that, you know, and he said, "These fellas just about took my 'appytite.'"

There was seven of the law. They had us surrounded good! And then Lamon and Faye come down on the Georgia side, and they made nine.

[We didn't have to go to jail.] The federal man had our driver's licenses and everything, you know, and he told us, he said,

Buck Carver

"You all go on home, come over to Bryson City, [North Carolina,] tomorrow and make bond." Since it was in North Carolina where we got caught, we had to go to the judge in Bryson City. Well, we had to get someone in North Carolina to make our bond, so I asked him, "If we're going to wait till tomorrow, how about waiting till the day after tomorrow? We've got to bring somebody with us to sign our bond."

He said, "Well, that's all right. Come in Saturday morning, if you want to."

I said, "No, Wednesday's plenty of time." (They caught us on Monday.) Lamon brought us back into Clayton, but they didn't put us in jail.

We had got out before the other fella [that was with us on making the liquor] come back. We headed him off. He paid half my fine, but they never knew about him. We went in Wednesday and made bond. We never was locked up. I got a six-hundred-dollar fine and three years' probation. I'd never been arrested before. Oh, yeah, Buck had been caught before, but that was my first time. Well, the *only* time I ever was caught. That was sometime in the [1950s], I guess. I don't remember just how old I was. My wife and I had six children then.

Hoyt Tench worked the railroad for most of his life. His stories are both thrilling and, because of the kind of storyteller he is, humorous. Though these tales involve some fairly serious accidents, Hoyt's "seen it all" experience helps to soften his delivery and endears him to his audience.

"At" the Tracks, Not "On" the Tracks

Another time I was going out of Toccoa on a steam engine. I left about four o'clock going down by Elberton. I saw a white something out, it was foggy, and it was a lady in a nurse uniform. She was running around on the tracks. I blew the horn to get her off the tracks, not realizing what she was trying to do. She got off, and we missed her. Then there was a brand-new Plymouth sitting right there, and we hit the thing. We just ruined it. So, we had to have an investigation the next day. At the depot I told her, "I had the headlight on, blowed the horn, blowed the whistle, and didn't see it." She said, "He's right. I heard him coming, and I was trying to flag him down, but he could not stop." It wasn't her fault or anything, so the railroad went and bought her a new Plymouth, at the Plymouth place in Toccoa. She said that she did not believe that there were people in the world that would do that. It was completely her fault. She said that her mother told her to be sure and stop on the railroad tracks, but her mother meant for her to stop *before* she got on the railroad tracks. Anyway, she did, and the car went dead, and she couldn't get it cranked again. We weren't running that fast, but we hit the car running twenty-five miles per hour with a big old engine. There are just so many things that can happen.

Hoyt Tench

"You Again"

One day we were going into Greenville. We went downhill and up over a hill and down another hill to go into the yard in Greenville, so you have to use a lot of dynamic braking on those big old diesel engines. If you didn't, it would jump out. I had pulpwood, shavings and all that. I would tighten up, run, and get within a yard, and one of them was an old bad switch. I turned over nine cars, and three or four of them just turned over with the pulpwood and all the shavings on the underpass. It filled it full. We couldn't use the underpass for a good while. The superintendent came up and looked at me like "You've done it again." Everybody has done these things sometimes, and I couldn't help it. These things just popped up, regardless of how bad or how good you were, or who you were. These things just happened.

There used to be a fellow named Matthews, a track man. One day it was snowing, awfully cold. They had put in this centralized train control business. If you are familiar with what they do with a one-man, like in Greenville—they'd run all the way from Atlanta and throw all the switches for you and put you where you were supposed to be. You didn't ask any questions; you just got by over his motor car and just tore it all to pieces. It wasn't too long after that, I was running down the Athens branch, and I went around the curve into central Georgia down there. We had been running in the evenings and at night, but we changed it and started running in the mornings. They had not told [the track man], and I went bouncing around there with the engine and hit his motor car and tore it all to pieces again. It caught on fire, and Lord, it was hung under the engine part. I knew that the engine would explode after a while. I got the brakes off and reversed it and backed off it. He came and looked up with tears in his eyes and said, "You again." That made the second one we had torn up.

For many around Southern Appalachia, the church plays an important role in all aspects of daily life. Here, Vera Sawyer relates a humorous tale about a congregation coming to Jesus with a bang!

Finding Religion in Possom Hollow

In Possum Hollow, we grew up much like the young people here in Rabun County, with church and with a religious focal point. Sometimes went to church every night. We also had big tent revivals that came around. Someone would pitch tent out in an open field, and evangelists would come and preach to us for about a week. Then they'd move on to other rural areas.

One particular night, there was a little man preaching. He was a tiny man, so, to impress all of us, he got on up on the altar to preach. He was jumping up and down really hard and the altar cracked in the middle and he fell. A couple of guys took the pieces of the altar away, but the little man just kept jumping up and down, preaching about the end of time.

Suddenly there was this tremendous explosion. It was deafening, and then the entire sky turned bloodred. Everybody jumped up and started screaming, and all of the bad people who stayed drunk in the community all ran and fell down where the altar had been and started praying.

This little man started shouting, "It's the end of time! It's the end of time!" He was really impressed with himself because he thought he was preaching right to the end of the world.

What had happened was an explosion at one of the chemical plants that surrounded us. West Virginia, at that time, was known as "the chemical valley of the world" because of all the big chemical plants were there. Surrounding Possum Hollow was Nitro, where nitroglycerin is manufactured, Carbon and Carbide, where carbon and carbide were manufactured, and also the Goodyear Rubber plant. That particular night, there was an explosion at the rubber plant, and the fire burned for days.

I know that some of the people that got "saved" that night went back to the beer joint and started doing the same things they were doing in the first place, but everyone got religion really quick when they heard that explosion.

For the 1993 Spring/Summer issue of The Foxfire Magazine, *students interviewed several folks in the community to share their favorite stories of local physician J. C. "Doc" Dover. The collected stories are a great tribute to a local legend.*
        Stories from Jerry Carter:

The Crooked Arm

One time he amputated a man's arm, and he buried it in the backyard of his office. A few weeks later the man came to him and said that he was having terrible pain in and on his arm, the one that had been amputated. He allowed that Doc had buried it crooked. He begged Doc to please dig it up and straighten it out. Doc did just what the man said and dug it up. The man never had any trouble again.

House Calls

Even after the day of good automobiles, roads in the mountains were so bad that the doctor had to put his car aside after the first freeze and depend on his horse for transportation over the mountains until spring came. Medical facilities were often crude in those days, too. More than once he had to perform an operation on a kitchen table, and a greasy one at that. Sometimes he had to wash his instruments in a kettle of water boiled on the kitchen stove.

Doc said, "Once I was called to see a man who had been shot through the elbow. The arm had already gone gangrenous when a neighbor man walked ten miles in to town to tell me. 'That man wasn't worth killing,' he said, 'but he's a human being, and I [thought] the doctor ought to know. I've delivered my message. Whether you go is up to you.' I told him that if he had walked ten miles to tell me, I'd surely go. When I reached the house, I had to clean a pot to boil water in, and I had to wash off the kitchen table myself. I gave the patient ether and then got somebody to hold the mask while [I] amputated the arm and made him a pretty good stump. He thought he would die, but he didn't."

Another time, Dr. Dover had an emergency call after an accident that occurred during the building of the Tallulah Falls Dam:

"Tom Hunnicutt," he said, "a man who lived in the community, got his foot under the wheel of a flatcar hauling sand. That was before the day of so many automobiles, and the foreman sent a locomotive up to Clayton to get me. I found Tom lying on a table. All the tissue on his foot had been scraped off, leaving only the bones.

Doc Dover making a house call
to Frank Gibson and his granddaughter, Peggy

"I told Tom that he lost his foot, and he said, 'You think so?' 'I know so,' I told him, and I knew it would have to be amputated. [Tom] decided he wanted another doctor down at Tallulah Falls to see him and pass judgment. They sent for the doctor and we waited and waited, but he didn't come.

"After several hours I said, 'Tom, it's serious to lose a foot, but you've already lost yours except for finishing up the job. I'm not wanting to hurry you, but it's getting way over in the afternoon. If you use me, I want you to make up your mind pretty soon.' Tom looked at me a moment, and then he looked up at the ceiling and said in a loud voice, 'Oh, Lord, I want you to lay all your other business aside and come to Tom Hunnicutt.' Then he turned to me. 'Now I'm ready, doctor.' He didn't even flinch during the amputation."

Mabel Garner shares a recollection about Dr. Dover's driving habits.

Crash Cart

I worked at Camp Pinnacle down on Warwoman during the summer while my mother [was] in real poor health. Me and my sister would go up there at night lots of times to see about her. My husband stayed with her and worked, too. One night we went up there and my mama was feeling real bad and she begged me to stay. My husband said he'd take me back to camp in plenty of time to help cook breakfast. I asked my sister if she was afraid to go back to camp by herself. She said she wasn't afraid, so I stayed. I guess it was about ten o'clock at night when she left. She was going up through town [on Main Street], and she was going to turn in the middle of town and take Warwoman Road to go to camp. Dr. Dover come out that street between where the Sunshine Home and Daniels-Mize Mortuary is now. He came bailing out of that street just as hard as he could come. He didn't slow up for nothing and smashed in the passenger side where I would've been if I'd been with her. She thought he'd slow up since it was on Main Street, but he didn't slow up. He just kept highballing it. He stopped and told her to take it to different mechanics and get estimates on what it would take to fix it and he'd pay for it. She took it to several and got the most reasonable one to fix it. The one that fixed it for her told her that he didn't know how many cars they had fixed for Dr. Dover! When she got her car fixed, she took the bill to him, and he just handed the money over and said, "Here's your money. I told you I'd pay to have it fixed." He didn't pay attention to red lights nor nothing else. Of course, there wasn't a red light there at that street then. He wouldn't have cared if there had been one. He just went right on. Somebody said something about running the red light there in the middle of town, and he said he was there before them red lights was, which he was. I remember when they was put there good as if it was yesterday.

One last story from Lucy Kimbell about Dr. Dover and his not-so-hygienic habit:

"Well, You've Got to Spit"

I used to work at Rabun County Memorial Hospital as a nurse. I remember [the doctor] coming in one day. He had a patient that was getting ready to deliver her baby. She was ready to deliver, and he was still in his office. I called him, and I said, "Dr. Dover, you'd better come right on over because it's not going to be long before she has her baby." He did. He came right over. He was bad to chew tobacco. He came in the door, and I could tell he had been chewing. I didn't know whether he still had some or not. He didn't talk a lot. He was kind of quiet. He went over and scrubbed up and got ready, and I said, "Are you ready to put your mask on?" He nodded his head, so I went ahead and put his mask on him. Before the baby came, I noticed him squirming. All I could see was his eyes because of his mask, but I could see the tobacco coming through the mask. I said, "Dr. Dover, do you still have that tobacco?" He gave me a huge nod. I said, "Well, you've got to spit." The tobacco was all over the mask. There was a bucket sitting in front of the patient to catch any waste. All of a sudden when I got the mask off, he spit and when he did, the tobacco went all over the patient, all over the drapes and everywhere. We had to re-drape the patient. He said, "Well, I just made it!" It was on her next pain that she had the baby. That was really funny, but it didn't bother him a bit, though.

Carroll Lee worked in radio for many years, but his days in Toccoa, as told to Foxfire student Lori Lee, may have been his wildest!

Radio for Assistance

After a period, he left and went to Toccoa, Georgia. After he had been there a short while, the station had an opening, and Sammy wanted me to come. He talked to the manager, and they asked me to come over to Toccoa, which I did in 1945. The station's call letters were WRLC, which stood for the "Robert LeTourneau Company."

Having mentioned this gentleman's name, I must take a moment or two for a very unusual story, probably the most memorable happening in my entire radio experience. . . . Mr. LeTourneau, or should I say, the Reverend LeTourneau, was a highly religious man. If my memory serves me well, he was an ordained minister, as well as being the head of this worldwide manufacturing company with a plant in Toccoa, Georgia, and plants equally as large in Longview, Texas, Great Britain, and Australia. He traveled from one plant to another by his private plane, which was a small, limited-passenger, one-pilot plane. Just a short time before this excursion, he had grounded the small plane in favor of a converted A-26 military bomber, which weighed tons. The LeTourneau Company had leveled the tops of hills to fashion an airstrip near the plant, and the end of the runway was less than a quarter of a mile from the radio tower. To further complicate the upcoming series of events, Currahee

Mountain stood nine hundred feet above the local terrain, only a meager four airline miles away. I was on duty and alone at the station, when all of a sudden, I heard the roar of a heavy plane circling the area. I rushed outside, peered up, and could see nothing but heavy clouds. I listened for a crash, but heard instead the phone ringing. It was the Greenville, South Carolina, airport calling with the message that Mr. LeTourneau had left the airport without clearance and was heading for Toccoa; he had had just about [enough] time to get there. The message continued, "If there's anything you can do to help get him on the ground, we ask your assistance."

Carroll Lee

Let me stress the fact that in radio broadcasting there are rules and regulations by the Federal Communications Commission prohibiting direct communication on the air, which put me in a dilemma of how to handle the situation. About twenty feet stood between me and the doorway. I dashed out to determine the cloud ceiling and gamely opened up the microphone to deliver this quote, "For the benefit of any aircraft flying in this area, the cloud ceiling is approximately three hundred feet and has been most of the morning; we will continue to monitor the clouds and report the first break in the cloud cover that we observe." I walked back outside, and would you believe [I saw] a break in the clouds. I rushed to the microphone with another "ad lib": "For the benefit of any aircraft in our area, I can report a break in the clouds directly over our radio tower." I no sooner delivered the last word, "tower," than that lumbering A-26 came through that opening.

When he came through the clouds to see where he was, the plane was below the embankment at the end of the runway and at an angle to the runway. The pilot instantly saw his predicament, revved the motors, nosed the plane upward and rolled that plane to an almost perfect landing. Within minutes I answered the phone to hear this tall Texas pilot relate his thanks and gratitude for our assistance in "talking him down"—he had only five minutes of fuel left.

As the son of Sheriff Luther Rickman (Foxfire's very first interview contact), Frank Rickman had a very interesting childhood. Here he shares a favorite story from life in and around the local jail.

"I Think I'm Santa Claus"

Daddy was out serving some kind of papers or doing something. Me and my mother were sitting in the kitchen getting my lessons. I didn't have my mind on the lessons. I heard this sand pouring out on the roof. When I heard that, I told Mama, "They're getting out up there. I can hear that sand pouring out on the roof." Mama said, "You know what to do. Run to town and get help."

I went out there in front of the jail. I got down on my hands and knees behind a wall and crawled out of there. [This way], they couldn't see me. Then I got up in front of Mr. Bill Long's place and ran [by what is now Foodland and on up the street].

The only one of Daddy's deputies I could find was Mr. Elbert Long. I brought him down there [to the jail], and then we went up there. He was the only one who had a gun, but my mother wasn't scared. We all went up there [to the second floor] and opened the door to go back in the bullpen. It had a hallway all around it. The cage sat in the middle. Mr. Long went around the left side of the bullpen while Mama and I went around the right side. When one of them came running around the side, Mama grabbed him. Where he was going through that plastered wall and bricks and stuff, he had that white plaster all over him. Mama was all excited. She grabbed and went to shaking him. She said, "Who do you think you are?"

He said, "I think I'm Santa Claus." Mama held right on to him, though. She brought him back around there and made them all go back through that hole that they cut through the bars.

Frank Rickman

When she got them in there, she told Mr. Long, "Now, you stay here and watch that hole until I get somebody else." I think she sent a taxi to go up on the head of Wolffork to get Mr. John McCurdy. [He was] a great big old man with a white mustache, like I got. She gave him a double-barrel shotgun and sat him down in the chair right outside that hole. [She] told him to stay there and not let them come through there until daddy come back.

Well, in two or three hours, Daddy came back. [He] goes up [to the cell] and makes everyone strip off butt-naked. The reason he made them strip off was to see which ones had been trying to get away. The hole was so small that where they had went through it so fast, they had skinned their sides up and down. They looked sort of like rainbow trout.

Then I remember when court came [for those prisoners]. Daddy got up there and told the judge, "This man may have a bad reputation, but [I wish you would go easy on him]. He was nice to my wife. He could have hurt her or done something to her, but he respected her. I hope you'll respect him for being nice to her."

Historical Anecdotes

Over the past half century or so there has been a growing trend in how historians approach the historical record. Oral histories, or histories collected from people through interviews, has proven to be one of the most valuable resources available to our understanding of the past. Perhaps most famously with soldier and civilian accounts of World War II, we've come to appreciate the intimacy and detailed minutiae of the oral historical record on some of history's most profound moments.

Oral histories are another form of anecdotal narrative. And, whereas personal anecdotes can give us insight into an individual's life and times and provide us a specific perspective from within one community or another, as it relates to a major historical event, the historical anecdote can tell us much about a person's or community's response to some of the past's most profound moments. For the generation of adults who made up most of Foxfire's earliest interviewed contacts, one such event was the flu epidemic of 1918. It just so happens that this horrible tragedy, one that took so many lives in our native postage stamp of Southern Appalachia, was a worldwide epidemic that led to the death of some 50–100 million people around the globe. For the Summer 1973 issue of *The Foxfire Magazine*, students interviewed more than a dozen individuals about their experiences at this time in history. The stories and experiences vary in their details but share a number of common threads, chief among them the ways in which the community came together in love and support of one another to see each other through a truly devastating event. That little piece alone demonstrates the importance of this particular genre of oral tradition, for it not only gives us a glimpse into the experiences around a particular event but also shows the character of a community:

Lawton Brooks: It killed people just like hogs dyin' from the cholera. They was diggin' a bunch in the graveyard all the time. I was down there one evening while they was diggin' for an old boy, and an old man come rushin' down on a mule, told 'em to dig the grave a little bigger, 'cause his brother died, too. Buried 'em together, right in the same grave. I don't know how many double graves they is down at Hayesville. Bunch of 'em died out of every family.

I was a rabbit huntin' when I took it. I thought this boy with me shot me when I took it. It scared him. I told him, I said, "You shot me!" He said, "No." I said, "There's somethin' wrong with my knees." I never had 'em hurt s'bad in all my life. It seemed like somebody just took 'em and beat 'em in two, right across there. He run down to the house and got my daddy and went to get the doctor; then my nose started to bleedin'. I had a temperature of 105 degrees [Fahrenheit] and he said, "He got that flu." And the doctor didn't have nothin' to give ya—just somethin' to ease y'. Nothin' more than an aspirin tablet. We did all of us happen to live over it, but m'daddy lost his voice—couldn't speak over a whisper for eighteen months. And he worked every day when he got to feelin' well, but he couldn't speak over a whisper. And later his voice came back to him just like it left him.

I'd say maybe two out of a hundred wouldn't have it. The rest of 'em, by gosh, had it. All of us got it at the same dern time. We was so weak, we couldn't even hand each other a glass of water.

If it wasn't fer a boy stayin' with us a-workin', [we wouldn't have made it]. And that fool never did take it. And he stayed there and cooked what he knowed to cook. 'Course we couldn't eat, we was so dern sick nobody wanted to eat. All they'd think about, if they was gonna git well or just die. You didn't care 'cause you hurt so bad. You didn't care if you did die or not. He never did take it, but we couldn't hand each other a drink of water—we was all of us a-layin' around there in the house. He got out there—I don't know how many people he waited on that lived roun' there close to us. He'd go and see 'bout 'em ever' day. And git 'em in a little wood to build 'em fires and things. He helped 'em all he could, that's the way they done, they helped each other. Them that was able. But the big majority of them layin' there about dead, what wasn't done dead. But that's the awfulest thing ever come through there.

It was durin' the wintertime. If it'd been in the summer—the crops—good God, they wouldn't a-been nothin'. If you took it today, you die with it tomorrow. It wasn't a thing that lingered long on ye. By God, it hit ye, it hit ye. If anything's wrong with ya at all, it would kill ye—ye just had to be good and stout to go through with it.

The stores just closed up. They wasn't anybody to run anything. They's the most people died you ever heard tell of—most I ever heared of. Just that winter—it went on through. That's the last time [it's been around]. Oh, these bad colds commence comin' now and they call *it* the flu, you know. Hell, they ain't never been but *one* flu ever hit this country. And that was that in 1918. It went on for several months like that, and it just quit out. But that's the only flu I ever heard tell of. Now days they claim, "Oh, they got the flu." They never was but one flu, and that was that one. And it was the *flu*. You just either flew away or got better, one or the other, let me tell you that right now. I'll *swear* I thought that old boy shot me. That hit me in the leg, it felt like somethin' went right straight through both my knees. I thought he shot me through the dern leg. I hollered at him, and he said he didn't, and he come runnin' out there, and I told him I couldn't move. He says, "Can't ye work yer legs?" I said, "No sir, I can't work my legs." I couldn't move my legs, and they was a-killin' me, boy. I was just a-hollerin'. If I *had* been shot, I guess it wouldn't hurt a bit worse. The doctor came over to the house a little later—he just lived right over the hill, and he said, "He's got that flu." After I took it, ol' Grady, that's the boy was with me [hunting], hung around a little while, and derned if he didn't take it, and he was there at our house, and he couldn't get home. And he stayed there. We was all piled up in 'ere. And the next mornin' then my daddy up and got up with it. Didn't git up with it, he was in the bed with it. Wasn't no gittin' up about it. It hit you, you wasn't a-gonna git up, and if you was up, it knocked you down. That was the worst thing I ever knowed of to hit the county. Now, boy, they was a-buryin' people out here. Anytime you passed, you'd see a bunch in the graveyards a-diggin' all the time. They just stayed in that graveyard. A hole here, and one there, and one over on the other side—just about dug one big graveyard. Diggin' somebody else's grave, not knowin' when theirs was gonna have to be dug.

Harriet Echols: I got married on the second of December in 1917 and my first baby was born the eighth of October 1918. Then in January of 1919 was when it hit in our community; that was in Wilkes County, Georgia, at the little town of Tignall, between Elberton and Washington. We had three doctors there in the little town, and you know those doctors went day and night for weeks and weeks. They couldn't get to all of the people, and they wasn't enough people up and able enough to get up and help the people that the doctors couldn't get to. They'd send medicine, but they couldn't get out to see 'em all. And the doctor was on the go when my baby was born. He hadn't been in bed for twenty-four hours and it was a home delivery; he came out to the house because we was twelve miles from the hospital, and back then they took care of the patient at home. He said he had been at the Prison Camp all that day and with other patients and if he wasn't needed, he would just have to go to bed and rest, so he laid fer a while and got a nap. And before he up and left, they was sick people there for him to see.

We had these two young men, Mr. Dunaway and Mr. Lassiter, that had opened a funeral home in the little town, and they had a real good business goin', and both of them got sick. And [the doctor] told us when he was down there to deliver my baby, that neither one would live but he was doin' everything he could and both the other doctors was helpin', too. Mr. Lassiter died but Mr. Dunaway finally got well. It took him several months before he was able. So, that discontinued the business, and all the funeral business went to Washington and Elberton.

And the Negroes, it was awful. There wasn't enough people to bury the dead. They managed to do it somehow, I don't know. Some days with the colored people that lived around there, they had three and four funerals a day.

Back then, ye see, they didn't know what to do when it first started, they didn't know what it was. The doctors couldn't cope with it and they was just so many that was sick and they didn't have medication for 'em, but just the mercies of the good

Lord we managed to live. And we had it all three of us—me, my husband, and the baby. And they was times you couldn't tell hardly if we was alive. How we lived, I don't know. One morning during January 1918, when my husband got up—he hadn't eaten anything for days—he said, "Well, how do you feel this mornin'?" Well, I had the cow to milk, the horse to feed, and a bunch of chickens (we was out on the farm), and he worked extra days with his father at the sawmill; and I said, "Well, I'm still here." He said, "Ya feel like gettin' up and fixin' me a cup of coffee?" and I said, "Yeah, I'll get ya a cup of coffee." I don't know how I done it, but I did.

Every bit of the wood was outside, and I burned it up. I had to keep the fire day and night. I burned up every bit of the wood I had. And my brother lived about as far as from here to Mrs. Cabes's, and I called and I called over there and he didn't answer. He was gone to see about his wife's people about four miles from where he lived. So, he was gone down there and it was way after dark when he got back. But I got out, as sick as I was, and cut wood enough to do me through the night.

And we just did our work ourselves. We didn't depend on anybody else. I got out and helped my husband saw up trees and helped him saw up wood. The neighbors couldn't come in [lots of times]. Used to a bunch of the men got together and got wood fer each family. And so, my sister-in-law answered and I told her I just didn't think I could get wood. Several of their children had it, but her and her husband didn't. He came the next mornin', it was cold—it was cold, it'd rained just like it rained last night—and everything froze over—ice everywhere. But he came in and got us some wood. Up in the day, about twelve or one o'clock, my husband said, "Have ya got any canned tomatoes?" And I said, "Yeah, I've got canned tomatoes and soup mixture." Back then we didn't know what freezers was, ya see. I got up and opened him a can of soup mixture and fixed him some soup, and he sat down and ate some soup and got up and went out—gone all evening seein' about the sick folks—and he come back and I was still in the bed and he said, "How come you didn't tell me you was sick?" I said, "I was sicker than you was, but you went on to bed and I had to stay up and look after the baby." But the next day the baby was better and my brother brought us medicine from the doctor. We didn't even see the doctor. He couldn't get to where we lived. And they was so many people, he just helped all he could.

Harriet Echols

People was just so hot it seemed when you'd touch 'em they just burn your hands, and some of 'em it got so hot they didn't know anything. It lasted anywhere from a week to ten days and two weeks. The ones that was real sick didn't get over it. They didn't let 'em get out fer several weeks, at least three weeks or more. Some of 'em was down fer a month. And some cases developed into pneumonia. That's what caused so many deaths. I had a little niece that died from it. She never got over it. She lived about a year, but she never was well, and the doctors said it was caused from the flu. She'd get up and play around; she was about six years old when she died, but she never got over it. And there was a lot of cases like that. Of course, over the years, I couldn't tell ye who all it was, but that doesn't matter so much. Durin' that flu siege my brother (just younger than me) lost a baby. The flu had kind of died down, and it [the baby] had the whoopin' cough but it had also had the flu, and that made it so weak it couldn't fight the whoopin' cough. And with all of it together, it was quite a few people that died. Especially among the Negroes. They thought they wasn't able to have the doctors and tried to doctor it with old-fashioned remedies.

Richard Norton: I guess I was twelve, thirteen years old. Me and my first cousin up here was the only two that went through it [that] didn't have it. I guess we had fifteen families to look after; and I mean eight and ten in a family and them all sick. I'd go and milk their cows, and she'd [Margaret, his wife] bake 'em some bread and try to fix 'em somethin' to eat what *could* eat. They was a lot of 'em couldn't eat, they was so sick, y'know. And children—go out here and them just a-screamin'. Little children just a-cryin', and their parents and nobody couldn't do nothin' about 'em hardly.

There was a lumber company in here at that time, and they was houses ran all through these hollers just plumb on up the creek a up yonder just thick. Wherever they could build one. They was workers that logged and sawmilled. And a lot a them folks had as high as twelve children, and seemed like they'd ever'one get sick at the same time. And we just went from house to house. And all of our folks here was sick, and so we had to look after the whole thing and do what we *could* do—but we couldn't do much. Sometimes we'd make 'em some kind a tea, y'know; boneset tea and stuff like that. Somethin' hot, y'know, to drink.

Richard Norton

You don't have no idea how that was. A doctor rode horses then, and it was really cold. Icy, snowy and ever'thing. Lots a times I'd have to cut wood at places, y'know. They'd get out a wood and I'd have to cut wood. Didn't have nothin' to cut with but an ax. I chopped 'em up a pile of wood, carried it in, and maybe some of 'em'd be able to keep some on the fire. Doctor Neville down here was a doctor, and he rode a good fast horse, but they was just so many sick he couldn't take care of 'em. He had to go to Highlands and ever'where like that. That's one reason I guess he died young. He had so much to do.

[At this point, Margaret, his wife, joined in]: And then about three years later that dysentery epidemic came through that killed so many children. Ever'body that had a child three or four years old died. I guess there's a dozen died here on Betty's Creek, and I don't know how many more around here. Pauline had one that died. And Ida McLane had two to die, and Lester Davis had two to die, and Arthur Dillard had two to die. They claim back in those days that it was [caused by] eatin' new potatoes. It was about the time new potatoes come in. And they thought it was some disease that the children got from eatin' new potatoes. So, they stopped all the children from eatin' 'em. But I reckon it was just supposed to have been. I don't know.

Richard Norton

Aunt Arie Carpenter: Those of us that had it was scared to death of it. My brother and his wife and Willard lived right up above my family and me. Well, we got down with the flu, Mommy got down with the flu, and I took the flu, and everyone took the flu except my daddy, and my daddy had this old-fashioned grippe, and ya only have it once. Well, Doc Neville was a-waitin' on us and a-carin' for us. I had done every bit of the cookin' for us, and two other families, and me sick. Poppy carried the rations up to Mount [her brother].

Mommy got the flu on the third day of March. She never got over it and she died on the eighth of June.

Arie Carpenter

He give me all the medicine, Doc Neville did. I remember one kind had thirty-two doses in it. A lot a people died from that flu. Hit's bad—I like to never got over it. The reason I didn't die was 'cause God took care of me.

Oma Ledford: It was at the end of World War I, November 11, 1918. My brother was going to service. It was the last call in the county, so he went to Clayton to leave. My older brother took him. The next afternoon I saw them comin' back, and my older brother was holding up the one that was supposed to have gone, and we thought he was drunk. We had never seen him drunk before, 'cause they didn't get drunk.

Oma Ledford

My whole family except an aunt came down with it. People came in and they got wood for us, and the ladies would come in and wash the clothes in water with real strong lye soap.

They wouldn't touch people who had the flu 'cause they was afraid they'd catch the disease.

Ethel Corn: I remember when the flu first hit, I was just a little girl, and they called it influenzy. I didn't know much about it, and the doctors didn't know much about it. It was something that killed people.

Back in them days, the neighboring people went in and done for the sick and set up beds, and took care of 'em. Nowadays, if anything's wrong with 'em, ye take 'em to the hospital, but back then they wasn't no hospitals. People helped each other then. They visited neighbors that was sick or anything. The house was always full.

S. F. Ledford: We was all down with it. We lived next to Willey Burton, and of a mornin' he'd come and feed fer me. He'd

Ethel Corn

just come up to the barn—wouldn't come on into the house. Then in about two weeks he come down with it, and I had to go and feed fer him.

But that flu was bad back then, brother. Ever'one in Clayton had it. People wouldn't go in the houses. They'd bring us food and put it on the porch. They wouldn't come in the house. They claim it came from the Army, y'know. From the war.

I was of a town the day I took it. Oh boy, I never felt as bad in all my life. I had a headache. I thought my head was a-goin' to bust. And somebody—I've forgot who it was—said, "You sick, ain'tcha?"

I said, "Yeah, my head's just a-bustin'."

And he said, "You want me to take you home?"

"No," I said, "I can get home." And I went over to the house—it wasn't but about two mile. Boy, I go there and mister man, that's the last I knowed. Never did have the doctor. I was so weak I couldn't walk. I got up one night and May had the heater up—it was in the wintertime—and I fell right backwards and she grabbed me. Y'know, I almost hit that stove. I guess I'd a-burned up if I had hit it. It was red hot. I was chilled to death.

Uncle Alex: I had it. I was so bad off I didn't know. I was out about thirty days with it. They died all around. There was two country doctors and nurses, and they never give us anything only we had to eat plenty of oatmeal and water. I thought they should have give us somethin', but they never. Just plenty of oatmeal and water. That's all we got.

People would go to town after the things we needed. They'd come and put it on the porch. Of course, they'd have to wear a mask.

I know how bad that flu was because they was forty dead bodies in Greenville, South Carolina, that they had to put in cold storage 'cause they couldn't get caskets fer 'em. That's what the doctor told me. That's right.

My wife had it and was unconscious with it. Didn't eat anything. They wouldn't give her any medicine. Had a swab or somethin' they'd swab in her throat with it. They was two army doctors that come in and brought a nurse with 'em. I had all the doors closed the night when they come, and they said, "How do you expect to get well with all this dead air?"

I said, "My wife's cold."

They said, "Put plenty of cover on her."

I said, "We've got it." And it was a-rainin'—they, Lord. Now, that's the truth if ever I've said it. If she was alive, she'd tell you so herself.

I stayed in the bed. My wife was as bad off. She carried me water till one night she brought my water to me and she like to not've got back to bed. I knew then. I got up and stayed up and set around the house. But, Lord, you talk about a man bein' weak—I was weak.

That come from the war. It could have come in a letter. It was so bad they died all around. They was a family right across the river from me. They *all* died. I worked on a railroad track, and when I went back, they was ever'one dead. They had to bring them out of the camp on a pushcart. Lord, it was a time.

Bessie Kelly: People would wear masks over their faces, and cut wood for people and put the wood on their porches. The neighbors would go look after the sick people's cattle.

The flu makes your head feel as big as a wash pot and made you sick at your stomach. People would talk crazy talk.

Lex Sanders: Don't talk about the flu. It like to have killed me. Oh, it like to have killed me. I laid in the bed, Lord, I don't know how long. It affected me all over. It affected me in the stomach and the head. I had the swim head with it, and I was

Lex Sanders

so sick I couldn't live. For about twenty-four hours I was in a coma. I thought I was in France. And I turned and turned and I just couldn't sleep. I just turned and twisted. But my neighbors, they just come in and took care of it. They'd come night and mornin' and milk and feed the stock and do all the washin' and cookin' and strainin' the milk and ever'thing. I stayed indoors for six weeks. The second day of March is the day I took it. The twentieth day is the day it killed my brother-in-law. Killed him. He died.

Tom Mcdowell: My own brother and his wife had it bad. It was the worst thing that happened around. It was bad. Sam Cabe, his whole family and him was down in the bed with that flu epidemic, and all the folks around. And the saddest part about it, they was nobody able to go see him and nobody able to go to his aid. And Sam died. Just one a them things. When you was sick, and he was sick, and you're sick—well, we just couldn't go. Lots a people died. Oh, they did die. It was a blessin' to him even for someone to give him a drink a water. He wasn't even able to get *that*.

Ada Kelly: It was just before Grandma Norton died, when they had that awful flu epidemic. It killed people and people were down with it. Folks wouldn't go in the sick people's homes for fear of catching it, too. Folks would go outside the house and put the wood and the groceries and things like that on the sick folks' porches. And then they'd go back and look after themselves because some of the folks that helped the sick folks were sick, too. You know, we've always had good neighbors in Rabun County and Macon County; I mean they sure do take care of the sick folks.

The flu wouldn't affect the animals, but the sick families couldn't get out to feed the animals. So, the neighbors would come in and feed the cows and horses and things like that.

Lillie Cannon: I was the first one in our family to take it. I was running a temperature of 104 degrees [Fahrenheit]—was out of my head. Anyway, Dad came up the steps two at a time and waked me up—said I was groaning and muttering incoherently. So, he picked me up and carried me downstairs. Mother had the guest-room bed ready for me. Dad hurried off to call the doctor and came back about thirty minutes later; said to put an ice cap to my head, open all the windows, put hot water bags to my feet, and start on the buttermilk and soda treatment. I stayed in bed two weeks, and none came in the room except Mother and Dad. And cousin Bob Wallace. He'd sing, dance, blow his harmonica, and I had rather he had stayed out, for he shook the floor dancing, and his singing wasn't too professional. But it was the first time I enjoyed being sick in bed, even though I wasn't allowed to read or have a light in my room or even have the shade up. All I could do was recite poems I had memorized through the years.

Later, when anyone in the community took flu, they'd come for me to nurse them because I had had it and survived, so people seemed to think I knew more about it than the doctors. I just used the ice cap, hot water bottles, raised all the windows, spread blankets on chairs around the bed to keep drafts off the patient, and I laughed with them when they told some funny joke. I let them do the talking because I knew how it was to try to listen with one's mind wandering or going blank.

Happy Dowdle: I had it. It kinda hit our settlement up yonder. If one in the family took it, seemed like ever'body got it. Boy, she was rough then. But the neighbors would go right in and take over—milk their cows and feed 'em and tend to the stock and do the cookin' just like it is at home. This is the best county fer this I ever saw. This county has always been noted fer that. But now it's gettin' away from it to what it used to be. Folks right over there don't care if you die tonight. I've got good neighbors here, now. I could whistle fer 'em and they'd come. But they don't visit one another and see how they're gettin' along or nothin' much; everyone's so busy. Ever'body's a-tryin' to do somethin' to make a dollar now. Yep. Ever'body used to come, but now! It's different now than what it used to be.

―――

I really appreciate the patterns in these stories—as a folklorist, it's something I look for in collections of related stories like these. Recurring themes, such as how weak folks felt, the harshness of the winter, and how the communities pulled together to help those who were sick demonstrate the value of anecdotes. They make this historical event more real, put a human face on it. This is, in part, why we have seen such an increasing interest in oral history, which can be largely made up of folk anecdotes. There are things we can learn about the

Happy Dowdle

1918 flu epidemic from the historical record, but it's the perspectives of the folks who lived it that give our understanding of this event its pathos. This has been demonstrated again and again in documentaries on historical events, such as those by Ken Burns and others that place great value on the personal narratives of the people who lived through historical events.

Chapter Six

SONGS

In the Spring 1969 edition of *The Foxfire Magazine*, the students took on a four-part article about folk music that included interviews with instrument builders, performers, and song collectors. Additionally, the students used this opportunity to explore the function of folk songs in those communities where folk music was still prevalent in an organic context. These early articles represent the students' first forays into the exploration of folk music, perhaps a precursor to the robust Foxfire music program that developed under Foxfire teacher George Reynolds in the 1980s.

It should be noted that these articles on folk music were collected amid the American folk revival movement, during which time folk music in all forms—from old-time string music to Delta blues—enjoyed a surge in popularity and led to many popular folk music acts, such as the Kingston Trio; Bob Dylan; Peter, Paul and Mary; and others. This was a unique time in American popular music in which the line between popular forms and folk forms was blurred to the point where popular revived versions of folk songs were almost indistinguishable from their "authentic" folk and traditional counterparts.

Depending on your perspective, this was both good and bad for traditional purveyors of folk music. On one hand, the sudden spike in interest raised the visibility and legend of great folk musicians, living and dead, such as Robert Johnson, Jean Ritchie, the Carter Family, and Bo Diddley. On the other hand, the movement led to the exploitation of some folk forms by budding popular artists in genres such as rock 'n' roll and rhythm and blues.

Perhaps inspired by this changing tide in American popular music, Foxfire students pursued the collection and documentation of related topics, including producing several articles on instrument construction over the next ten years or so. We've published much of that information, most notably in *Foxfire* books three, four, and six, and in *The Foxfire 45th Anniversary Book*. However, over the course of some forty years of producing books, it is surprising that we never published the following pieces.

In the first article, performers and song collectors Harry and Joyce Roberson share with Foxfire students a short repertoire of four traditional folk ballads, including three of what folklorists term "native American" ballads, or ballads that originated in the New World, and one descended from a traditional English ballad. For the article, the students researched song origins and made note of prominent previous collections of those titles.

The second article is a great example of how folk songs can serve as a vehicle for protest. While examples of folk songs addressing political or social injustices date back as far as the fourteenth century's "The Cutty Wren," which has been attributed to the English peasants' revolt of 1381 (though this origin is up for debate), protest songs in America really came into favor during the Great Depression and the growing American labor movement, best popularized by Woody Guthrie and Pete Seeger. Interestingly, songs from this tradition made it into American schools and were sung by American schoolchildren well into the 1980s—"This Land Is Your Land" and "Where Have All the Flowers Gone," for instance.

In a piece from that same 1969 issue of *The Foxfire Magazine*, students interviewed members of the Appalachian Volunteers, an independent student group from Berea College in Kentucky (later funded by the US Office of Economic Opportunity, or OEO) who worked with poor communities in Appalachia, mostly in the coal-mining communities of Kentucky. In those interviews, the students became aware of two protest songs being used by those challenging the influence and corruption of coal companies operating in the region. The songs underscore the hardships of coal miners, their families, and the negative impact of the coal industry on the land. It's an important glimpse into this particular time as well as a still-relevant example of how rural communities can be exploited for natural resources.

It would seem that particular issue from 1969 was just full of gems, which is why we've included a third excerpt from the magazine, though this one was not part of the four-part article on folk music. The article in question is an in-depth exploration of a common chant associated with churning butter. Folklorist Chuck Perdue, at the time a graduate student in the University of Pennsylvania's folklore program, contributed the article to *The Foxfire Magazine*. Chuck grew up on a farm outside of Atlanta and no doubt encountered the churn chant at some point in his life. In the years that followed, Foxfire students came across the chant in interviews with some local residents, most notably Margaret Norton. Chuck's work illustrates just one of the ways the magazine program impacted folks outside of our immediate community.

Finally, we end with two songs published in the Winter 1971 issue of *The Foxfire Magazine*. These songs come from a stand-alone piece that simply identifies the songwriters, with a brief note on their contexts. Relevant to the previous piece on protest songs, this article includes a new composition from

Jim Miller, the person who penned the two songs about the social injustices surrounding the coal industry in Kentucky. This third piece is also about the coal industry and the challenges faced by those affected by it. The second song is by Varney Watson, brother to Foxfire student Andrea Burrell, and speaks to the divide between the wealthy and the poor and alludes to the inequities related to Vietnam and the draft.

Songs from Harry and Joyce Roberson

The first song included here, "Kidder Cole," was written by Judge Felix Alley, a superior court judge of North Carolina, at the age of sixteen. Alley was born near Whiteside Mountain in 1873. His mother was Sarah Norton, the first white child born in Whiteside Cove. The following quotation concerning "Kidder Cole" was obtained by [student] David [Wilson] from a book, which was authored by Judge Alley.

The three other songs [student] Mike [Cook] and David got for us follow the Alley ballad.

In order to satisfy hundreds of people writing me about my banjo ballad, "Kidder Cole," I will tell the story. The ballad speaks for itself and adheres closely to the facts. The ballad has been sung for many years. It is sung and played wherever mountain melodies are used.

The ballad and its origin have often appeared in various newspapers and magazines. The ballad itself has been included in several editions of Folk Songs.

Let it be here understood that all this has been without my knowledge. Like all songs that have been handed down by word of mouth, many words have been changed.

Let me say that Charley Wright, whose name appears in the ballad, is the same man who performed the heroic and miraculous feat of rescuing Baty from the brink of a two-thousand-foot precipice on Whiteside Mountain.

Kidder Cole

My name is Eugene Felix Alley.
I got a girl in Cashiers Valley.
She's the joy of my soul.
How I love that Kidder Cole.

I don't know, but it was all by chance,
Way last fall I went to a dance.
Boys and girls all fell in line,
But Charley Wright had beat my time.

I may never have a fight,
But I can't stand that Charley Wright,
Just because, confound his soul,
He danced that night with Kidder Cole.

I went to the valley about half tight,
But Kidder wouldn't dance all that night.
Went to the valley about half lit,
But Kidder wouldn't dance a doggone bit.
But Kidder said now don't begin.
I'm going back to the valley
And I'll dance with Kidder every set.

Kidder Cole is prettiest girl I know
There is in this wide world.
She's the joy of my soul.
How I love that Kidder Cole.

It's all hands up, we'll play big ring,
The fiddle will squall and banjo will sing.
I never saw a prettier thing,
than Kidder Cole—come change and swing.

This song was recorded for Columbia University in 1935 by Dr. William Cabell Greet and George W. Hibbitt, professors at Columbia. It was sung for them by Bascom Lamar Lunsford.

The Little Rosewood Casket

There's a little rosewood casket
Sitting on a marble stand.
There's a package of love letters
Written by my true love's hand.

Go and bring them to me, brother.
Gently read them o'er and o'er
Till I fall asleep in Jesus,
Fall asleep to wake no more.

I saw a man last Sunday
Riding by a lady's side,
And I thought I heard him tell her
She could never be his bride.

I saw him coming up the pathway.
Brother, meet him at the door.
Tell him that I will forgive him
If he'll court that girl no more.

When I'm dead and in my coffin
And my friends all gathered round.
And my narrow grave is ready
In some lonely churchyard ground,

There's a little rosewood casket
Sitting on a marble stand.

There's a package of love letters
Written by my true love's hand.

Both the author and the history of this song remain unknown. The Brown Collection of North Carolina Folklore lists twenty-four separate versions of the song. See volume 2 of that collection, page 631, for additional information. Mrs. Corson notes that she can remember hearing her mother sing this.

Weeping Willow Tree

My heart is sad and I am lonely,
Yearning for the one I love,
For I know I will never see him
Till we meet in heaven above.

Chorus

Tomorrow was our wedding day,
But God only knows where he may be.
He's gone to see his other sweetheart,
And he cares no more for me.

Chorus

He told me that he dearly loved me,
And he often proved it true,
Until an angel softly whispered,
He has been untrue to you.

Chorus:
Go bury me beneath the willow,
Beneath the weeping willow tree,

And when he knows where I am sleeping,
Then perhaps he'll weep for me.

Again, little is known about this song or its author. Only that it has been around a long time in the mountains. The Brown Collection lists eleven different versions (see volume 3, page 314).

Butcher Boy

In London City where I did dwell,
A butcher boy I loved so well.
He courted me my life away,
And now with me he will not stay.

There is a strange house in this town.
He goes right in and sits right down.
He takes another on his knee.
He tells her things he told to me.

I have to grieve. I will tell you why.
Because she has more gold than I.
Her gold will melt and silver fly.
Then she will be as poor as I.

She went upstairs to go to bed
And nothing to her mother said.
Her mother came and found a note,
Then found her hanging from a rope.

Mother may we somewhere meet.
Place a marble stone at my head and feet,
And on my breast a snow white dove
To show the world I died for love.

This song was descended from an old English ballad, and versions of it are numerous. Many of them change the name of the town in the first line (Boston Town, Johnson City, New York City, and Jefferson City have been noted). One of its unusual aspects is the shift of the narrator in the fourth stanza. It is listed in the Brown Collection in volume 2, page 272. The Library of Congress has it on tape sung by Aunt Molly Jackson, Bascom Lamar Lunsford, and many others.

Coal Songs

[The introduction and songs are pulled straight from the Spring 1969 edition of *The Foxfire Magazine*, found on pages 76–81.]

The Appalachian Volunteers (AVs), at first Berea College students working independently, and later funded by the OEO (Office of Economic Opportunity) and partially staffed by outsiders, moved into the Appalachians to do what they could for the poor. Young and idealistic for the most part, they set about repairing and rebuilding run-down schools; helping the poor purify wells, build privies, organize purchasing co-ops, repair bridges, develop childcare centers, train in handicrafts, organize recreation groups, and so on. All well and good.

All well and good, that is, until they probed too deeply into the *causes* of the poverty they were fighting. It didn't take long to find one big one: coal. In the early part of [the twentieth] century, the rights to the coal lying underneath the ground were purchase[d] for almost nothing from people who had no idea (for good reason) of the potential value of these rights. Thus, via the "broad from deed," owners of the coal under the ground have rights superior to those who own the land above. Bulldozers and stripping machines move onto private land at will, strip off the land above to reveal the seams, dig out the coal, and then move off, leaving a terrifying, nonproductive "moonscape" behind. The people left receive little compensation—the coal was "paid for" fifty years ago.

In the summer of 1967, Pike County's Jink Ray stood in front of a bulldozer as it was pulling onto his land. He was backed up by Joe Mulloy (an AV) and workers for the Southern Conference Educational Fund (SCEF). The bulldozer left. Its departure was followed by a wave of court cases the eventual result of which was a victory for Jink Ray, on whose side had stood none other than Kentucky's governor Breathitt. Mulloy later said,

> The Jink Ray victory had tremendous implications for the poor and working class in Appalachia. This was perhaps the first time since the heyday of the United Mine Workers that the operators had been challenged and defeated by the people. Ray's victory could serve as an inspiration to people all over the mountains to demand and take back what is theirs, the coal. The coal operators knew this all too well.

And they were not long in reacting. On the night of August 11, 1967, Alan and Margaret McSurely of SCEF and Mulloy were arrested and jailed by Commonwealth Attorney Thomas Ratliff and fifteen armed deputies. Robert Holcomb, the president of the Pikeville Chamber of Commerce, told reporters, "We know that these people are communists. There are no ifs, ands, or buts about it . . . they intend to take over the county." The charge placed against them was sedition. Its foundation was pieces of literature found in the McSurely home. William Kunstler, a civil rights lawyer from New York, later said, "If having Russian literature in your possession is sedition, then the University of Kentucky is also guilty" (*New York Times*,

August 19, 1967, p. C12). The three were later cleared, but Governor Breathlitt, under heavy pressure from the coal industry in his state, recommended to the OEO director Shiver that funds for the AVs be cut off, and they were. "They had stepped on too many political [read coal] toes in the county seats" (*Louisville Courier Journal*, August 7, 1968).

Three days before this issue of *Foxfire* went to press, we talked with Andy Mott of the Center for Community Change, a citizens' poverty organization based in Washington. Mott had just returned from a visit to Kentucky where he found the AVs still on the job despite efforts to remove them (the new governor, Louis B. Nunn, had made a campaign promise to run SCEF and organizations like it out of the state; the Kentucky UnAmerican Activities Committee had been set up and funded with $5000 a month—"a sum greater than that received by all other committees in the state legislature combined" [*Nation*, December 30, 1968, p. 724]; and OEO funds had not been restored). But the 1920 sedition law had been declared unconstitutional, and other donations had kept AV staff in operation.

Mott felt that the AVs had definitely made mistakes. The hippie dress of some of the members; the lack of understanding of others of the distinctive mountain personality; and the lack of tight, overall organization had undoubtedly worked against them. But standing up to the coal industry was not one of their mistakes, and Mott felt that they were potentially a force for tremendous good in the mountains. Whether they will be able to remain or not is still in some question.

This brief background should serve to explain the songs that follow. They were written by Jim Miller, a young assistant professor of German at Western Kentucky University. Both have been used in organizational meetings of the Group to Save the Land and People in Eastern Kentucky. [. . .] Folk song enthusiasts will probably hear hints of Woody Guthrie's

"Do Ri Mi" in the music of the second song, "Coal and Communism."

The More Things Change the More They Stay the Same

1. Mr. Johnson made his famous talk on March thirty-first,
Pulled the bombers back from Hanoi and Haiphong.
And he said he wouldn't run again and talks began in Paris,
They were talkin' but the fighting it went on.

2. Yes, the guns were still a-firin' and bombs fell every day,
It was hard to tell the body counts from polls,
And the candidate the people liked the party wouldn't nominate,
And the more things changed the more they stayed the same.

3. A good man died in Dallas in November, sixty-three,
You remember April third and June the fifth
When good men died in the cross-hairs of the spring of
*   sixty-eight*
And the more things changed the more they stayed the same.

4. I saw Resurrection City rise, I lived there for a long time,
'Cause I thought it might help change some minds and hearts,
But the city is torn down now, all the people have gone home,
And some mother stole my wallet and guitar.

5. There was nothin' left to do but go back home to Mississippi
Where the planters draw down thousands not to plant,
And the black men out of work draw thirty dollars and
*   it rains,*
And the more things change the more they stay the same.

6. Up in east Kentucky where bulldozers strip for coal
And big boulders come a tumblin' through folks' yards,

Mountains washed down on their houses, streams ran red
    and died,
Till folks organized and stood the dozers off—

7. The legislators listened and they passed some regulations,
Still the profit's a gold river flowing north,
And the streams are runnin' poison still and mountains
    wash away
And the more things change the more they stay the same.

8. Yes, it's LIFE LINE out of Dallas and it's RAMPARTS
    MAGAZINE,
True Believers to the Right and to the Left,
O the times they are a-changin', things are blowin' in the wind,
But the more things change the more they stay the same.

Coal and Communism

1. Well, the Appalachian Volunteers,
They've been in Kentucky about four years
Teaching community action and trying to organize the poor,
Coming in from all over the nation,
Working in the mountains on their summer vacation,
but it looks like the Volunteers won't be coming back anymore.
The AVs hurt the strip-mine people so bad,
The operators started seeing red!
But it's coal, boys, not Communism,
Coal behind the charges that they make,
And their strategy's not hard to understand,
So let's show them up now for Kentucky's sake.

2. Yes, after the AVs helped Jink Ray
Put the strip mine operators out of his way,
The sheriff paid Joe Mulloy a call and charged him with sedition.

Phones were ringing in Washington,
"Now lookit what these kids have done,
Stirring up our poor folks, sowing trouble and dissension!"
Some folks in Pike County sure are irked,
Community action's fine until it works!

3. They've been seeing red for years,
The Appalachian Volunteers
Aren't the first folks in Kentucky who ever tried to right
     some wrongs.
Back in the thirties Aunt Molly Jackson
Went around stirring up union action
In the east Kentucky coalfields singing her union songs.
The operators claimed she was a red,
When she heard the charges, this is what she said:

4. "I think of them starvin' babies cryin',
Their stomachs swellin', mortifyin',
I fed 'em warm bean soup and rocked by the light of a
     coal-oil lamp.
I was fifty-two years old and past
Before I ever heard of a Communist,
I got my ideas livin' all my life in the coal-mine camps."
Aunt Molly was a ballad-singing union woman
Back yonder when the hired gun-thugs were roamin'.

Chorus:
But it's coal, boys, not communism,
Coal behind the charges that they make;
And their strategy's not hard to understand,
So let's show them up now for Kentucky's sake.

They are charging AVs with sedition,
Charging them with immorality,

In hopes that we may look the other way
While they lust for coal and rape the land.

Come, Butter, Come

Come, butter, come
Come, butter, come
Peter's standing at the gate
Waiting for a butter cake,
Come, butter, come

This chant, or a variation thereof, has ushered in countless tons of butter since Thomas Ady referred to it in his book, *A Candle in the Dark*, published in 1656 in England (Brand, 1849). The woman who recited to Ady said that it was taught to her mother "by a learned churchman in Queen Marie's day [presumably Queen Mary, 1553–1558] . . . whenas chruchmen [sic] had more cunning and could teach the people many a trick that our ministers now a days know not."

There is an interesting charm taken from the records of the trial of Annie Tailyeour, on July 15, 1624, in Scotland. To make the butter come quicker [or so the charm says,] it is only necessary to take three hairs from [a] cow's tail, three from her udder, and three from "elsewhere" (place unspecified). Then walk three times "widderwards" around the cow, strike her the left side, cast the hairs in [a] churn, and say three times, "cum, butter, cum" (Dalyell, 1835).

Charming the butter into coming faster was, no doubt, [already an] ancient [practice] when Queen Mary reigned; and it continues to this day in areas where milk is churned by hand, though today chants or sung rhymes are probably used more often to make the time pass pleasantly than to rid the churn of an evil spell.

[Stith] Thompsons's *Motif-Index of Folk-Literature* lists Number D1573: Charms to make butter come, indicating the widespread occurrence of butter charms.

In regard to the antiquity of the chant given at the beginning of this article, [folklorists Iona and Peter] Opie (1952) say:

> The strange line "Peter stands at the gate" is found in other charms, as in one for toothache beginning, "When Peter sat at Jerusalem's gate," and may be traced back to the old story of St. Peter, when our Lord relieved him of his troubles "Ad portam Galylee iacebat Petrus. Venit dominus et interrogavit eum . . ." It may be compared with a Spanish charm "Appollonia was at the gate of heaven," and can perhaps be traced back ultimately to the prayer of Seth, the son of Adam, at the gates of Paradise in the apocryphal *Gospel of Nicodemus.*

The Opies also quote several interesting variants of the churn chant. From Northamptonshire County, England, for example, about 1850:

Churn, butter, churn
In a cow's horn,
I never see'd such butter
Sin' I was born

Churn, butter, churn
Come, butter, come
A little good butter
Is better than none.

And from Lincolnshire County, England:

Churn butter, dash
Cow's gone to the marsh,

Peter stands at the toll gate,
Begging butter for his cake,
Come, butter, come.

The reasons for using butter chants are fairly obvious. As Estyn Evans says (1961):

Butter making must have been a chancy and critical business when each family had only one or two cows, ill-fed for a large part of the year, and there were fairies, witches, and blinkers to contend with. The protective charms and prognostications connected with churning are legion.

The conditions mentioned by Evans, which existed in Ireland, were little changed when the immigrants came to America, and, in some cases, life was even chancier in the New World, requiring numerous precautions in order to get through such chores as butter churning.

In Arkansas, some housewives drop a silver coin into the churn to drive out witches who keep the butter from coming (Randolph, 1964). Silver has always been efficacious in fighting witches, and I recently heard of a woman near Atlanta who would take a silver knife, draw a circle with a cross in it on the floor, and set the churn over that before beginning. One of the children in the family for whom the woman worked was red-headed, and red hair is sometimes associated with witches. This took place only about twelve years ago (Kay Cothran, personal communication, March 1968)!

The Brown Collection (1964) lists twenty-two beliefs and practices from North Carolina that are associated with butter churning. It also lists fourteen churning chants. The chants are essentially the same as that at the beginning of this article, with variations mainly centered on name changes in the third line. The names used are Peter (four times), Baby, Little Bow, John-

nie, Mattie, Sallie, Tommy, Willie, Somebody, Missus, and
Granny. Chant Number 7567 on page 445 varies from the form:

Come butter come,
Come butter come,
Cow's in the pasture,
Churn a little faster,
Come butter come.

This uniformity in the churning chants probably results
from the influence of print. The standard form given previously
has been printed numerous times: In Mother Goose collections
(Baring-Gould, 1967); in *Songs of Childhood*, a music education
book used in American schools; and in the Brownie Scout
Handbook, page 161. A part of the chant has even been incor-
porated into a poem by Wheaton P. Webb (*New York Folklore
Quarterly*, 1955).

The following collection of churn chants from Georgia has
been obtained as a result of a casual inquiry I made of my father about five months ago. I wrote him asking if he remembered the chant we had used in Georgia when I was a child.
He did not, but he passed along the request to Celestine Sib-
ley, a columnist for the *Atlanta Constitution*, and I began to receive chants from readers of the column. I sent questionnaires
to twenty-six people who sent in chants, requesting additional
information on their chant and on churning. Eleven were returned. The chants follow, accompanied by such information
as seems pertinent.

Come butter come,
Peter's at the gate,
Waiting for some butter,
To go on his plate.

From Sybil Mauldin, Dalton, Georgia

Come butter come,
Come butter come,
Peter's standing at the gate,
Waiting for a butter cake,
Come butter come.

From Mrs. Kate Cowart, Stone Mountain, Georgia

Come, butter, come,
Come, butter, come,
Peter standing at the gate
Waiting for a butter cake,
Come, butter, come.

From Mrs. Mildred C. Melton, Griffin, Georgia. Chant came into the family in 1860 in Concord, GA; name often changed to that of friend or relative; last used in 1918; sometimes dasher was rolled around horizontally as it was being moved up and down in the churn.

Come butter come,
Come butter come,
Johnny's at the garden gate,
Waiting for his butter cake,
Come butter come,
Come butter come.

From Mrs. Clifford C. Blalock, Cleveland, Georgia. This is the version found in *Songs of Childhood*, Music Education Series.

Come! Come! Come, butter come!
You's ol' mistis, standing at the gate,

Waitin' with her butter plate,
Come! Come! Come, butter come.

From Mrs. Henry Mashburn, Valdosta, Georgia. Chant came into family prior to 1860 near Milledgeville, Georgia. Cook's son (African American) did the churning.

Come, come, come butter come,
Little boy at the garden gate,
Waiting for the butter to make a cake,
Come, come, come butter come.

From Mrs. R. B. Brown, Bowdon, Georgia

Come, butter, come,
Johnny's at the garden gate,
Waitin' for his butter cake,
Come, butter, come,
Come, butter, come.

From Mrs. J. O. Bradshaw, Gainesville, Georgia. Chant came into family prior to 1900. African American cook or white children in family churned; each child usually had his special day to churn; different names used in chant; last used in 1930.

Come butter, come
Come butter, come
Johnny's at the garden gate,
Waiting for his butter cake,
Come butter, come,
Come butter, come.

From Mrs. Joy B. Gwinette, Dublin, Georgia

Come butter come
Peter's at the gate,
Waiting for butter,
To make a sweet cake.

From Mrs. R. S. Dozier, Thompson, Georgia. Chant used in Columbus, Georgia. Last used about 1950. Sometimes used a side motion to help gather the butter.

Come butter come,
Quick to my home,
I'll give you to eat,
Everything sweet,
Apple and cake,
I'll save for your sake,
Sugar and plums,
You shall have some.

From Linda J. Lord, Athens, Georgia. Chant came into family about 1875 in Ashland, Georgia. Last used 1930.

Editor's Note: The full article contains thirty-five variations on the churning chant. We elected to publish only the first ten but believe this is sufficient to illustrate the extent of variation.

Two New Folk Songs

Last year Andrea Burrell sang us a song that her brother, Varney Watson, had written. We liked it so well that we thought we'd share it with you, and also, in the process, get it protected by copyright. Mary Beth Brundage, our music teacher, was kind enough to write it out with the proper musical notations (Varney doesn't know music—he just sings and writes), and here it is.

In addition, there's a new song by Jim Miller of Bowling Green, Kentucky. Jim's songs have been printed before in *Foxfire* (vol. 3, no. 1, pages 78–81), and they have been very well received.

Cripple Creek Revisited
by Jim Miller

Waded up Cripple Creek Sunday last,
Cut my feet on broken glass.
I'm from Cripple Creek, mosta my clan's
Living up in Flint, Michigan.

Chorus:
Had me a gal in Shady Grove,
She left with the feller from OEO.

Sister married, Mom works in town,
Brother's off fighting in Vietnam.
Dad, his minin' days are done,
Got the coal dust in his lungs.

Roof leaks, we're out'a tar,
Go out some nights and sleep in the car.
Six old cars settin' in the sun,
Nary one of them suckers'll run.

Feller in here from the poverty war,
Just sets and picks his old guitar.

Said the preacher to the feller from OEO,
"To hell with their bodies, I'm saving their souls!"

Down to Cripple Creek the big rocks roll,
Dozers strippin' them hills for coal.
Cripple Creek runs down red and black,
Little fish floatin' on their backs.

Lived on Cripple Creek all my life,
Don't even own a good pocket knife.
I'm leavin' Cripple Creek, yes I am,
Got my papers from Uncle Sam!

I Ain't No Hypocrite
by Varney Watson

Yonder comes a Rich man and there's money in his pocket you
*   can bet,*
and poor people all around us workin' hard and getting deeper
*   into debt.*
A non-profit org'nization, and the Rich men preach salvation
*   while we sweat,*
Well, they say I won't get to heaven —
But at least God knows I ain't no hypocrite.

In my life of tribulation, I have seen one revelation,
That the poor man seldom ever speaks his peace.
He's workin' hard when never asked,
Giving when the plate is passed,
Never knowing where his ten percent will reach

But money ain't no Road to heaven.
It takes faith in God and honest toil and sweat.

Well, they say I won't get to heav'n,
But at least God knows I ain't no hypocrite.

When there's fighting to be done and the poor man knows he'll
*   send his son—*
Never questioning whe'er fighting's going wrong or right—
To help his country he don't mind, but to this thought he still is
Blind: that it's a rich man's war but the poor have to fight.

No you can't buy back the life for on his son there was no price.
You can't mortgage back the livin' from the dead,
Though he may cry into the night, wondrin' if what he's done
*   was Right*
At least God knows he ain't no hypocrite

If you're wond'ring at this time what is the purpose of these
*   Rhymes*
If a story then what moral does it tell?
Well, to tell the truth I can't be sure.
I wrote it down while drinking beer and while pondering the
*   mysteries of hell.*
Down there a drink must cost a lot
And since money's what the poor ain't got, to go I guess you must
*   have to be rich.*
So to end this song I'll say one thing,
I guess it's what I really mean:
Just do your best to be no hypocrite.
Just do your best to be no hypocrite.

Chapter Seven

PRANKS & JESTS

Humor is an important component of any community's folk-lore. In the days when oral tradition served as a primary source of entertainment, jocular tales were a great means of raising the spirits of those participating in a storytelling context. Additionally, the performance of pranks and other lighthearted activities helped to break the monotony of what was often a hardscrabble life.

Over the years, we've conducted interviews with some real characters—great storytellers with a talent for delivering wonderfully humorous tales. So, we would be remiss not to publish a few more. We should note, however, that these aren't "jokes." While jokes are part of oral tradition, they are more structured than what is presented here. Jocular tales do have some structure and often include a sort of punch line as you'd expect to find in a more standard joke, but these tales are largely anecdotal, taken from the teller's own life and experiences. Over the years, based on audience response, the teller will often refine the story and its performance to achieve the best result (a good laugh), yet the story's origins still remain tied to real-life events.

Next, we move to firsthand accounts of pranks, a genre that is more performance than oral tradition and that contains its own essential "components." There needs to be, first, a prankster (the one carrying out the prank), a target (or "dupe"), and an audience to witness the events, though, sometimes, the audience is simply the prankster him- or herself. Pranking is a form of competitive or high-stakes play. With pranks, there is always the risk of someone suffering emotional or physical duress, but it often occurs within a context in which pranking is a high probability, such as on April Fools' Day. In a particularly good article in the 1975 Summer/Fall volume of *The Foxfire Magazine*, a group of students collected several stories about general pranks and about those attached to the tradition of serenading.

Serenading in Southern Appalachia is most closely related to the "mumming" traditions commonly found in rural areas of England, Ireland, and Scotland. Mumming, or "mummering," is a more stylized folk "play," complete with costumes and masks, while serenading is a less-formal brand of high jinks targeted toward pranking and disrupting the peace of its intended victims. Based on what our contacts have told us about serenading in this region, this Christmas Eve tradition usually involved younger members of the community—teenagers and the like—roaming the countryside, going house to house, making noise with guns, cowbells, pots and pans and rousing families awake, who would often, in turn, invite the merrymakers into their homes for food and drink. It was a begging ritual, akin to trick-or-treating on Halloween or to the Mardi Gras traditions of rural Southwest Louisiana. While we don't see this sort of thing today, those of us living in Southern Appalachia can still hear gunfire and fireworks set off on Christmas Eve as a last holdover from this tradition. Thankfully, we have a good record of the serenading tradition to round out this chapter.

Billy Joe Stiles tells us about the ghost in Clayton. Or was it really a ghost?

The Tale of the Haunted House

Just outside of Clayton there's this old house that's been abandoned for several years, covered up with kudzu. This house is supposed to have ghosts in it or [be] haunted or something like that. You can hear chains rattling at certain times of the night.

One morning a man got up, found out he didn't have any flour for breakfast, so his dear wife sent him to town to get a 50-pound sack of flour. So, it was kinda drizzling rain and one of those mornings he didn't much want to be out. So, he put on his big slicker coat, walked to town and got 50 pounds and put an old piece of cloth or something around it, a rag of some kind to keep it dry. And as he started back home, he had to walk by this haunted house. It was one of those mornings. There was just a little bit of light shining at that time. His old lantern had gone out, so he was stumbling up the road trying to get home. His wife was patiently waiting at home to make biscuits. He looked across the road and he saw a fellow coming down, [it] was his neighbor, John. Well, being a good neighbor he hollered out, "Hey, John." Well, John was very scared and very superstitious. He heard that this house was haunted. Here John peeped across the fog and saw a big black thing with no head. And John broke to run and as he run his neighbor kept hollering, "Hey, come back here, John; help me, John." The more the ghost (supposed to be the ghost) hollered, the faster John ran.

As time went by, this fellow didn't say a word. One morning he was out in town talking to John about the tale of the haunted house, about seven o'clock one morning when he started to work. Now, this is the way, a lot of ways, tales get started. All that ghost was John's neighbor trying to be kind to him. He never did convince John that house was not haunted and wasn't full of black ghosts. . . .

Vaughn Billingsley shares his first experiences with an automobile and an airplane.

Modern Marvels

I remembered the first car I ever see'd. It scared me to death. Me and my cousin Gene was out. We lived in an old log house down on the edge of the road. We was the only house back in there. We heard somethin'; we turned around and looked, and there was an old A-Model comin' down the field there, down the old road, and it was goin' "durp, durp, durp," comin' down through there. It scared us to death. We jumped up and run in the house and crawled under the bed. I can remember gettin' just as far as I could get up against the wall and we were just a-screamin', scared to death.

The first airplane we ever seen, we thought it was the Lord a-comin'. We seen the little white thing up in the air. Well, I was the one who seen it. I was out in the yard, and I seen that. I went to hollerin' for everybody to come and look. They all come out and looked and looked. Mama come out on the porch; she looked up and said, "Well, the Bible said that in the last days that He would send signs and wonders from the heavens before He comes." I thought that was the truth.

As the wife of a sheriff, living in the jail, Junita Queen had her share of interesting experiences, but she and her husband also had quite the sense of humor, as illustrated in this jocular tale about pranking her daughters.

Ghost in the Cell

The girls had a good time. One time there wasn't anybody in jail, hadn't been for three or four days; they wanted to sleep upstairs in the jail cells. We told them they could unless Lamon brought somebody in. Then, of course, they'd have to come down. There were rooms all wound around up in there—two beds in some, one in some, and some with four different places to sleep. They went up and then had to come back down for sheets and a blanket. They were having the grandest time. They had some girlfriends with them. While they were downstairs, Lamon slipped upstairs and got up in a cell where they couldn't see him, one where they knew someone had died before, and just waited until they got back up there and got busy making their beds up and talking. Then he drug a chain across the top of that cell. Now, you talk about girls running and screaming and trying to grab the others to get in front of them! Oh, they never did want to go back up there that night because they were so scared.

Numerous Marcus recounts a particularly raucous encounter between a bull and a hornets' nest.

The Steer and the Hornets

The hardest work you'll ever do is trying to stay on a confound steer and it a-bucking. Their old back is round or something. You ain't got nothing to hold on to much. [When we were breaking a young steer], we'd roll or waller around on 'im just to let 'im know what it was [like]. You can't put too much weight on 'em all at once 'cause it will make 'em sway-back or injure their back or hips. When they got big enough to hold a body, they could be pretty well broke to ride, but some of them never would get broke good. They'd buck you off. I laughed at a cousin I had one time. He was wanting to ride one and I said, "You better watch that one. He'll buck you."

"Bah," he said, "they never has been a steer that would buck me off."

I said, "You'll find out when you get on that one." He went ahead and got on him and got started down a little old path.

That blamed thing cut loose to bucking. It tried to get him off. It went bucking off out there in the woods and got in a hornets' nest. That steer sure did do some buckin' then. [That feller] got off of there and he took to the thicket! I said, "I thought they wasn't one that could buck you off."

He said, "I ain't gonna set up there in a hornets' nest with him." I laughed at him good. He didn't have no business up on that steer. You can stay on a mule easy again as you can a steer.

Numerous Marcus

Ollie Queen Glore shares a jest about communication and the divide between outsiders and locals.

Population Figures

I remember well when the city of Clayton had plank sidewalks and muddy streets. [That didn't stop people from coming up to the mountains in the summertime and staying at the hotels around Clayton.] We called those folks "summer tourists" or "lowlanders." There was one who asked a young girl in Clayton the population of Mountain City. She said, "Oh, they grow taters and beans and corn."

He said, "I don't mean, what do they grow? How many people are there living up in Mountain City?"

She said, "I don't know, but I could run up there and count 'em for you."

Pranks

As a folklore genre, pranks fall somewhere between performance and verbal art. First, the action itself is a kind of performative art; secondly, there is always a narrative that follows—told by either the prankster or the target of the prank. It's that narrative piece that is crucial to a prank's life cycle. It functions as both a jocular tale and also as a means of influencing action, perhaps inspiring someone in the audience to perform their own version of the prank on an unsuspecting victim. Perhaps you will find inspiration in the following accounts.

Marinda Brown: I remember back when I was in boarding school about 1919. Somebody got some rope. There was a hallway with doors all the way up and down each side of the hall. They tied this rope tightly to all the doors [crisscrossing the hall]. We never found out who did it. The girls couldn't get the doors open. It would just pull the next one tighter. My room was at the end of the hall [and they didn't tie up my door], so I saw what was going on. We tried and tried to find out who did it, but never could.

Mrs. Thad (Happy) Dowdle: Fifty or sixty years ago, they done a lot of pranks for Christmas. Sheriff Moore had a one-horse wagon, and some boys took it apart and put it up in the schoolhouse upstairs. Then they put it together and hitched a horse to it, and there it was, nickering for him to come get him! The sheriff didn't know how in the world he was gonna get that horse an' wagon outta there.

Buck Carver: I was short-sheeted when I was in the CCC camp. We would put the sheet on the bed and turn it up from the bottom about halfway. When someone started to get in the bed, he couldn't get but halfway down. He had to get up and fix the bed.

    [. . .]

They used to get buckets of water and wait till people got in bed. Then they'd fix that bucket of water so that when you opened the door, it would tip right over and drown you. I've heard John Grist tell about the time they did that to Uncle Bill Martin; it made him mad for quite a while.

    [. . .]

In them horse-and-buggy days, they would take off the wheel taps. You didn't get far till your wheels just rolled off. They usually did it when one feller had stole another feller's girl.

    [. . .]

I pulled a prank on Fred Chastain one time. He was staying with us helping us get telephone poles. Me and Fred went somewhere and I bought a pint of liquor. We drunk about half of it that night and hid the rest in a branch behind the barn. In the morning it was my job to build a fire and then go feed the mules. I told Fred that I'd hid [the liquor] behind the barn and in the morning, he could go with me and help me feed the mules; then we'd finish off that liquor. I called him the next morning and he just groaned a couple of times and never got up. It made me about half-mad, because I wanted him to help me feed the mules. I went on out [and] fed them. I went on around behind the barn and drunk about half that liquor. I set there a few minutes and thought about how he didn't deserve any of it. So, I just drunk it all. I filled it about one-quarter of the way up with water and put it back in the branch. I was out a-catching the mules when he come out. He went down to the branch and got the liquor. He turned it up and took a little taste of it. I thought he'd pour it out. By josh, he turned it up and drunk it all. I never said a thing to him. He and I walked up a trail to the top of the mountain. Daddy took the mules and the wagons around the road. We were standing there waiting on Daddy. Directly Fred said, "That shore was the weakest liquor I ever drunk in my life."

I said, "They wasn't no liquor to it. It was nothing but water!"

[. . .]

Me and Fred Chastain played a trick on Julius McCall one time. Fred stayed with us for about five years and helped us with the timber business. One evening Fred decided he wanted to go home for something, and so I went home with him. It was dark outside—so dark you couldn't see the road. The only way you could see it was to feel it with your feet. We fell all over that road, all in the gutters and everywhere. We got to Julius's house and decided to see if we could find a way to get him to let us spend the night. So, I changed my voice. I could mock or imitate just about anybody I wanted to back then. I hollered, "Hello! The house."

Julius came to the door and I said, "Me an' my partner are lost out here and it's so dark we wanted to know if we could spend the night."

It was dark, so Julius couldn't see who it was. He said, "Boys, I don't know who you are. What is your name?"

I said, "We're some of the Carpenter boys that live over in North Carolina."

He said, "Well, shucks, yes. Come on in." I changed my voice and said, "No, thanks, Julius. It's dark and I guess we'd better go on home." When I changed my voice, he knowed who it was, but it shore got him.

Mrs. Tom Mcdowell: One time my uncle had raised a whole lot of corn. He had gathered it, and put it [in] the crib. My daddy and one of [my] cousins saw that crib full of corn. Pa said, "How funny it would be if somebody got in there and scratched a big hole in that corn and scattered some of it out on the ground. Luce would think somebody had stolen his corn." So, they scratched a hole in the corn and went on home.

Pa and my mother went on to bed. Pa said, "Jule, you answer Luce when he comes, for he will certainly be here after a gun."

Uncle Luce came and Ma said, "What's the matter, Luce?"

He said, "Somebody's got in my crib and stole about half of my corn, and I'll know who it is in the morning. I want to borrow the gun!"

So, he borrowed the gun and went back home. He got a feller to stay with him overnight and they stayed all night in the barn and nobody came. He never found out what happened to his corn.

Tom Mcdowell: Percy and Bill was brothers. They milked the cows. There was a partition between the stalls. Bill milked one cow, and Percy milked the other. Percy got through milking his cow first, and Bill was setting in a chair a-milking his cow. Percy took a pin and put it in the end of a cornstalk. The partition was up off the ground, and there that cow's heels was on the other side. Percy just took that pin and stuck that cow's heel. She just hauled around and kicked Bill and his bucket of milk over. Bill didn't know what on earth was the matter with that cow.

[. . .]

My sister's girl married a boy named Bill Norton. He could mimic anything he heard make a sound. Once he just goes up from his house to a big rock called the Devil's Den. He went and got up on that rock and yelled out like a panther a time or two. It stirred the dogs and the men up in that area. So, they got their guns and went up there. He heard the men coming and he moved. He yelled out like a panther again and the dogs got all excited, and started barking. The men were trying to get the dogs running, and of course they wouldn't chase Bill. Bill took off, got out of their sight and went home. Whenever they came in, Bill was shaving. It was a little dangerous, but Bill fooled all of them.

[. . .]

There was an old man lived over on Tesnatee Creek. A bunch of boys, around Christmas Eve, were just a-going around playing tricks on fellers. They took a wheel off his wagon and carried it off. They managed to climb a tree with it and they tied that wheel right in the top of that tree. Sometime the next day, Con discovered his wagon wheel in the top of that tree.

[. . .]

I've heard my daddy tell this one. A feller named Sam Segall had some dogs. He was afraid after dark by hisself and he wasn't much better when he was with his dogs. He stayed as close to them dogs as he could. Daddy told my mother that he was gonna break Sam from hunting around up here. He got a sheet and wrapped up in it and pinned it and laid down on the bank on top of the road. When Sam come along, Daddy just rolled off into the road. "Oh, hellfire!" Sam said, "What's that now? God almighty!"

Down the road he went. He and the dogs were making ninety!

[. . .]

Some feller played off drunk. He had some associates that were on up the road. They got ready to go, and this feller laid down across the road and played drunk. The other two come along and they didn't want to leave him there. He couldn't walk, so they picked him up and carried him and got him home. They set him down outside. The door was shut and it was dark. So, he just gets up and says, "Come on in, fellers."

One of them said, "Oh, by God, let's whop him!"

Harriet Echols: Those boys went back over here on the mountain with Mr. Lake Stiles. They took his horse and carried it way across the mountain and put it in another man's stable. They took his cow and brought it over here and put it in Mr. Stiles's barn. They said that the next morning this man went to feed his horse and there was a cow instead. The cow said, "Mooo," and he didn't know what to do. After a while he recognized the cow. He knew someone had played a prank on him. Well, Mr. Stiles went to milk and found the horse.

[. . .]

Back at Tignell, Georgia, Emmel Evans was a young boy about fifteen or sixteen. He worked with old Mr. Blackman. The grandparents, parents, son and his family lived all together in a great big, huge house. He had this Evans boy to work with him. Em would go to town every night. That was in the cracker barrel days and when they had pot-bellied stoves.

Every night, Em would go up there for recreation. He'd stay out so late, he'd wake up the old folks when he came in. Mr. Blackman got tired of it. He and one of the other neighbors decided that they were going to make a dumboodle and scare Em at the ol' Methodist church.

After Em left to go to town, they got this tin can, put it on a string, got some rocks, and tied them on the string. As the string was pulled, it made a weird sound. Em would always get a bag of stick candy. Mr. Blackman and this neighbor went and crawled under the steps of the church. When they say him coming, they waited until he got even with the steps and then they pulled the string. By the time he got home, he never had stick of candy left! It was all up and down the street. Mrs. Blackman knew what was going on, so she opened the door and helped him in. She opened the back door and started yelling for Mr. Blackman, as if he was out in the barn. He came running in and said, "Now, what in the world is wrong?"

She said, "Something has scared Em. He's just about dead."

He said that it stopped the boy from going to town. He was married before he'd ever go to town again by himself.

[. . .]

My father used to tell some tall tales. My father's name was Andrew Whitner, and he was raised at Murphy, North Carolina.

A bunch of boys went over to the schoolhouse. They were having the Christmas play at school. Back then we didn't have all the little bought toys for Christmas. They popped popcorn, made popcorn balls, and gathered up apples, bought stick candy and such as that. And they made molasses candy.

So, they went to the play. There were just boys around thirteen or fourteen years old. They had started back home. Back then they had to light a lantern and have torches. So, this ol' gentleman and his wife lived on down below where my father was raised. All the boys got together—there was ten or twelve of 'em—and they went along.

Back then people wove cloth and made their winter underwear. The men wore the red flannel underwear then. The boys waited until this ol' lady and gentleman got in bed. Then they went to the branch and got a big bucket of freezing cold water. You could pour the water out and it would freeze before it hit the ground. They waited till they got in the bed and one of 'em went to the door and hollered. The ol' man said, "Who's there?" They told who it was, made up a name, and said the people who lived up above them had a sick baby and wanted his wife to come right quick. He come out on the porch and turned around to go back in and they dashed a bucket of water on him. They said that ol' man like to froze to death before he could get into the house by the fire.

Will Seagle: The railroad had paid me one day and I was comin' home through Otto that night. [Some] robbers jumped from behind a stump, and said, "Hands up!"

I said, "I guess not."

They said, "Hands up or die!"

I said, "All right now, I see." It wasn't too dark. But I run in the creek and got me a rock. I just did miss one of 'em as he went behind a tree. And so, he run back out. Thought they could get me t'run, y'know. They had them old knives—you've see'd 'em, that you open and they won't shut till y'mash the spring. I'd bought one of them that day, I happened to have it in my pocket. I grabbed it out, for I thought they was going t'take my little dab of money. I didn't get much, but I'uz going to keep it. And when one of 'em come back t'me, I made a dive f'him that way, and I stuck it in his shirt collar. And I cut that shirt and his britches, his waist and grained the hide plumb down till I cut his britches braces. He said, "I'm cut!" He ran back and that ended it up.

Will Seagle

After that happened, Priest Bradley give me a pistol. He said, "You can carry it and hide it over there and not carry it on to work."

I come back that night, and somebody'd blacked a tree stump and put a coat on it. Oh, it'uz the awfulest-lookin' thing. I said, "Now, boys, I hate t'shoot anybody, but I'll shoot you, just as sure as the dickens. Now I'm goin' to do her."

I hollered two'r'three times at 'em, "What's up?" I walked up a little closer and I said, "Speak to me!"

They wouldn't speak—[the stump] couldn't speak! [Will laughs heartily.]

I took that gun out, and it went "Bang, bang!" [The stump] never moved, and I walked up to it and kicked it and hit that dressed-up stump. [The pranksters] were way up on the mountains, behind trees. You never heard such laughing.

Filmer Kilby: I used to have some friends from Mountain City, Tennessee, who worked in a sawmill. Well, the sawyer had a special cap because the saw threw dust all over him. It was a wide-brimmed felt hat like you see in the Westerns. When he quit sawing, he would take his hat off and lay it bottom side up on a stump. I was up there one time with my brother-in-law, and he said, "That sawyer feller. He wears a cap up here and always lays it down in the same place. Ever' afternoon when we get ready to go, he'll get in the truck and we get started and he'll holler, 'Wait, fellers, I forgot my hat.' He runs back and gets it. Now we're all anxious to get out in the afternoon, and we don't want to wait."

When it came time to go, sure enough, when we cranked up and went a ways, he hollered, "Wait a minute, I gotta get my hat!"

He bailed off the truck and ran over there and grabbed that old hat brim. It wouldn't come—there was five big roof nails nailed through the top of the hat to the stump. He jerked about three times, and the whole brim just tore away from the crown! He came running back to the truck and said, "I'll getcha tomorrow," jumped on the truck and that's all he said.

[. . .]

I know these Parker boys on Blue Ridge—was raised up with one of them. He bought a team of mules, and one time when I went up there, he had ordered a German police dog. People then taught a dog to catch hogs. If hogs got out, the dogs would go catch 'em, bring 'em in. One Sunday, I went up there, and he and I begged his brother to ride this real spirited mule, and we kept on until he got on the mule. When he got on the mule, he was going up the middle of the road, and my friend hissed the [German police] dog to 'em. It was a natural-born heeler, did what he was told. Now that mule took off toward the Blue Ridge Gap, and I don't know where my friend's brother ever got off. . . .

    [. . .]

One time we lived in a old house and used wood for heat. I thought I heard a noise during the night, but I didn't pay any attention. I got up and started to build a fire in the morning. I usually get up early—six o'clock, I guess. I built the fire, went back in the living room waiting for the stove to get hot. Coffee water was what I was waiting on. All of a sudden, smoke came in the house. I didn't know what it was. I thought I'd turned the damper down. I took the eye [on the stove] out and checked that little ol' stove. Smoke was just a-fogging. I opened up the kitchen door. Smoke just poured out. I couldn't hardly get my breath. By then the house was just filled full of smoke. When I walked out on the porch, I looked out and saw a new car sitting out at my brother-in-law's. I thought then. I knew they had done something, but what could they have done?

I thought a minute, then went back and thought, "Well, nobody came in during the night. They didn't do nothing."

I went back in and checked my fire. Then I knew something was wrong. I come back out; went around the yard. The upper side of the house had been bulldozed out. It wasn't very high. I saw this little ladder there. They had climbed up there and took two burlap sacks and stopped up that stove pipe. I like to NEVER have gotten them out. I looked out there and they were out on the porch. They had come in at two in the morning and had set their clocks to alarm at 5:00 a.m., three hours of sleep to get up and watch me come out of that place.

I waited until about nine or ten o'clock to go out there. I went out there, said hello, shook hands with 'em. All of 'em dared not say a word. I waited around thirty minutes until one of them said, "I believe he's got the smoke washed off him."

Serenading

Mrs. Nora Garland: On Christmas Eve night, we'd all go a-serenading. We went from house to house. We'd put on different old clothes, you know, and carry things to beat on and cowbells to ring—all things to make noise. We went up to one place and the man told his wife, "Lula, just carry the bed out and give 'em some room." It was a great big room, and they cleared it out for dancing and playing games. And some of 'em did dance. I didn't, though. It was against my religion, but my brother would play the harmonica. They'd turn the big room over to us, and we'd all play games like "go in and out the windows" and "spin the bottle" and I can't remember what all. We'd be there till midnight.

We'd play tricks on people, too, and my brother helped do that. One place where we went to dance and play games, they had two big horses with white faces. Those boys took shoe polish and painted them black! They painted those horses' faces! Those folks never said a word about it.

I remember one time in particular when we had serenaders to come to our house and serenade us. We could just barely hear 'em a-talking. There was a great big pine thicket above the house and we could hear 'em a-coming around the hill. Daddy reached up over the mantel and got his gun and went outside and shot straight up. He was so thrilled over that, he'd say, "Well, gentlemen and ladies, I've got the tricks on you all! You've got the treat on me!" When he shot the gun, they were supposed to trick the family, you know. 'Course they didn't and Daddy would always have plenty to treat them with.

Nora Garland

Lawton Brooks: All the noise we made for Christmas—serenading people on Christmas Eve—we done with a shotgun. We'd get shotgun shells fifty cents a box and we'd got there and shoot up in the air—serenading people. Them shotgun barrels would get so hot, we'd have to set 'em down and wait a while, and then start again.

Just getting out and going around, sneaking up to someone's was our entertainment at Christmastime. That's what WE called serenading. They didn't know nothing about, and we'd just come up shooting, ringing bells, and making the derndest noise you ever heard. If they was in bed, they'd just as well to get up. They shore to God couldn't sleep! They'd just have to get up and ask us in. They'd always invite us in and feed us—they were looking for a bunch, anyway. They'd have something for us to eat and sometimes give us a present or something.

There'd be about twenty-five or thirty of us. The girls would join us, too, and we'd all go. Everybody would make some kind of noise, one way or the other. We were just serenading the people that lived around in the settlement. They wasn't thick settled, though, like they are here. There might be somebody lived here and it might be half a mile out there to the next house, maybe a mile, but we'd go and just keep a-going till we gave 'em all a good round. We had to walk and sometimes we'd go for five or six miles. Take us half the night to get back after we got through serenading people. 'Course we'd never get in till was along in the morning. We'd be going all night nearly.

We'd do tricks to people, too. That was part of serenading. People in them days would have a cow and a horse, at least, in the stalls in the barn. While they were asleep that night, we'd take the horse out of one stall, and put it in the cow's stall, and move the cow into the horse's stall. They'd go in there to milk the next morning (we liked to be there to watch) and there'd stand the ol' horse in the cow stall. Boy! They could get mad! They'd throw their milk bucket down on the ground. They'd be mad enough to kill somebody, but they didn't know who done it. Us kids got a lot a-kick out of that. We'd do all kinds of tricks like that. We'd move people's stuff, hide some of their stuff. Hide their axes or something else, whatever we could find loose, laying out, we'd hide it. Wouldn't put it where he couldn't never find it, but he'd maybe have to hunt for two or three days for it.

[. . .]

Folks didn't care, though. Everybody else done it. Just like trick or treat here now on Halloween. It was just on that same basis—everybody done it. They'd just gather up—boys and girls would—and they'd just take off.

Annie Dowdle Thurmond: We'd get together and go serenading the people [in the community] on Christmas Eve or maybe Christmas night. I didn't get to till I was twelve or thirteen (that was about 1927, because I was born in 1915). Some of the men and boys would have guns and just shoot for the noise. We'd have bells and take pans and beat on them with a stick—

anything to make a racket with. We'd go around somebody's house and holler. If they were sociable, they'd let us in. They might serve us some juice or [other refreshments]. It seemed a funny way to celebrate Christmas, but then we didn't have as many things as [young people] do now for entertainment. We just had to make up our own.

Mrs. Burma Patterson: But on Christmas Eve and Christmas night, we were celebrating—all of us together. My three brothers would be right along with my sisters and me. I had two older brothers and a smaller one. (We had big families back then.) Everybody knowed each other and we just had the most fun. I do think we had more fun than kids do now. We didn't have "wheels," but we had our legs. We walked, serenading. We didn't ride in a car. We all wanted to be together.

There wasn't nothing but just a road wide enough for one wagon or car to pass.

Burma Patterson

We'd take the cowbells off the cows, and the boys would take real shotguns to shoot all around the house. We walked in a neighborhood and was real quiet. We'd wait till we'd get just right to the house, then go to shooting and running round the house—ringing bells, shooting, and screaming to the top of our voices. They'd have every light off except for a little lamp. We wouldn't be running around there long till we'd see 'em strike a match and light a kerosene lamp, open the door, and say, "Y'all come in." They would have cake cut in little pieces for us, or an apple, an orange, or a piece of candy, and some of them would have something for us to drink. If we wasn't hungry, we'd take it with us.

If we didn't yell and whoop, why we'd to singing Christmas songs—"Jingle Bells" and "Santa Claus Is Coming to Town." We'd go serenading whether it was warm, sleeting, raining, or snowing. We didn't let nothing stop us from doing that. That was our yearly thing. We enjoyed it. I think they ought to now, but so many lights so close together, you'd know if anybody was coming. You couldn't slip up on them, unless you lived out in the country. That was fun!

When we got through serenading, the boys would go out in the woods and get firewood and we'd build a big bonfire and tell tales and play "pleased or displeased" till midnight. Our parents were at home in the bed when we got in. Maybe my dad would be asleep, but my mama would be awake, and she'd see that we were all there. My daddy would go with us lots of times and leave us young folks to have a big time.

Leonard Hollifield: We did not go caroling as I remember it back then. We done serenading, as we called it. We would use firecrackers and guns. When we would get to a house, we would start shooting the guns, and if they came out and invited us in, we would quit and go inside and have a treat. It was the same thing as caroling today or trick or treating, but that was the way we would do it. It was serenading.

It was the only time we did it, too. We didn't do it any other time. We would go on Christmas Eve and that was about it. There would be a bunch of grown-ups with us, *always* to supervise, you know, so there wouldn't be anyone hurt. The chaperones kept us from getting in trouble. They had another rule at the time: if you heard someone coming in the distance, why you'd get out and fire your gun if you didn't want to entertain them, and that was how they would pass you, if you fired on them before they could fire on you. Daddy always heard them coming, and he'd shoot the double-barrel "POW! POW!" and then they would pass us by.

If he could kind of figure out who was doing the serenading and if it wasn't a boisterous bunch, the ones that were going to be rowdy and such as that, why he'd let them come on in and give them an apple or an orange or something like that.

Leonard Hollifield

Chapter Eight

FOLK BELIEF

The term "folk belief" is probably not as well-known as its pejorative counterpart, "superstition," but to use a pejorative is rarely (if ever) a good idea. The problem with the term "superstition" is that it belittles what are, for some, closely held beliefs about the world and how things work. Folk beliefs are most often connected to our cultural or religious communities, but we also observe folk beliefs in the context of our occupations and pastimes. Just watch a baseball game, for instance, and you can see all manner of folk belief at work—from players who run through specific ritualistic movements before every at bat to the fans who turn their caps inside out for a ninth-inning rally. We may tell ourselves that we're not "superstitious," but if we take a moment to think about our own rituals, we see that very few of us are "above" having folk beliefs.

As a cousin to "ritual" or "ceremony," folk belief can be of great importance. While we may be more familiar with seemingly mundane examples, such as those we espouse when we are children ("step on a crack, break your mother's back," for instance), there are many folk beliefs that exist within cultural communities that carry much deeper value and meaning. To help us better understand the role of these beliefs and how they work, folklorists have separated folk belief into two categories, empirical and magical.

Empirical folk beliefs are those built around experiences or observations, such as those held by seafaring cultures about the things they observe in the weather—"red skies at night"—and how they affect the waters—"sailor's delight." To use an example from our work here at Foxfire, the practice of planting by the signs of the zodiac is a great illustration of an empirical folk belief. Those who follow this practice do so because of experience and observed results from following (or not following) this practice. Those outside the culture may view this as "backward" or "simpleminded," but for those who practice this belief, it is something that experience and observation tells them has value in their lives.

Magical folk beliefs involve elements of the supernatural and the mysterious, though, like empirical folk beliefs, they are often believed because of experience or observed outcomes. Over the years, Foxfire has published several articles about this kind of folk belief, specifically how it pertains to healing. Practices such as talking the fire out of a burn or whispering away warts fall into the category of magical folk belief. For the purveyors of such practices and the communities for whom these folks serve as healers, faith in these beliefs is strong.

The following is a collection of folk beliefs collected by students over the years. For the purpose of better illustrating the differences between magical and empirical folk beliefs, we've identified them for you.

Magical Folk Beliefs

A blister on your tongue means that you told a lie.

If you go in the house through one door, you must go out through the same door.

Never retrace your steps.

If you cut out a window somewhere in the house and replace it with a door, someone in your family will die soon after.

If a spider writes your name in his web, you will die.

If a person won't take a bath, it means that one of his folks died by drowning, and he is afraid of water.

If it comes a hard rain after somebody's been buried, they said he was going to heaven.

You can't bury anybody until they have been dead for three days. If you bury them in under three days, they might come back.

If you go to bed singing, you will get up crying.

Never sweep after dark.

Never sweep twice in the same place.

Never step over the broom.

You'll never get married if someone sweeps under your feet.

It is bad luck to sweep trash out the door.

If you sweep your trash out the door on New Year's Day, you will sweep your luck away.

If a man is the first one to come into your house on New Year's, your chickens will be roosters; but if a woman is the first, your chickens will be pullets.

Whatever you do on New Year's Eve is what you will be doing for the rest of the year.

On New Year's Day eat turnip greens and black-eyed peas. Every turnip green you eat is every dollar you will make the next year, and every black-eyed pea you eat is every penny you will make the next year.

If you leave your Christmas lights up past New Year's, you will have bad luck.

To keep witches away, put a broom under your doorstep.

Put a pullybone over the door, and the first boy that walks in will be your husband.

If you break a mirror, you will get seven years' bad luck.

If you break a mirror, throw salt over your shoulder and you will counteract bad luck.

It is bad luck for a baby to look into a mirror before he is one year old.

It is bad luck to start something and let someone else finish it.

It is bad luck to sneeze at the table on Sunday morning.

It is bad luck to leave a rocking chair rocking after you get up.

You will have bad luck if you turn a chair around on one leg. It will bring a hole into the house.

It is bad luck to crawl through a window.

It's bad luck to move a house cat when a family moves from one house to another.

If a bird pecks on the window near you, you will have bad luck.

If you open a knife, you have to close it because if someone else closes it, both of you will have bad luck.

If you start to go somewhere, do not go back to where you started from or you will have bad luck.

Don't walk with one shoe on—bad luck.

Don't put shoes on a table—bad luck.

Throw spilled salt over your left shoulder or you will have bad luck.

When you drive by a graveyard, hold your breath or you will have bad luck.

Do not watch anyone go out of your sight. It is bad luck.

A man will have bad luck if he speaks to his mother-in-law.

Don't open an umbrella in the house or you will have bad luck.

Never bring a hoe into the house.

If you drop a dishrag, someone is going to come visit you that is dirtier than you are.

Itching Foot—you are on strange ground.

Itching Hand—you are shaking hands with a stranger.

Itching Ear—someone is talking about you.

Itching Nose—someone is coming to see you.

If your right eye itches, someone will make you mad.

If your left eye itches, you will be pleased.

If the inside of your hand itches, it is a sign that you are going to handle money.

A fly in the house in winter means good luck.

If you hang a black snake in the branch of a tree, it will rain in three days.

Don't leave a cat in a baby's room because it will suck the breath out of it.

Do not let a black cat cross your path. If it does, put a mark, a cross, on your window.

Dog howls at night—Death is coming.

If a crow is sitting on your house, then someone is going to die.

If a fox calls near a log, someone will be ill.

Turn a snake's belly to the sun and it will rain soon.

Catch the first fence lizard in the spring, scratch his legs downward, and you will see no snakes all summer.

Turkey feathers worn on the head or made into pillows cause baldness.

Male children should sleep under a panther skin to give them the panther's strength, cunning, and agility.

One can ward off sickness by eating buzzard meat. The buzzard has immunity from sickness due to his foul smell, which keeps the disease spirits at a distance.

Eating all the food placed before you brings good weather.

Friday begun is never done.

A baby will be like the first person who carries it across water.

If a baby looks in a mirror before it is a year old, it will be hard for it to cut its teeth.

If you say something has never happened or you don't want it to happen, knock on wood and it will counteract the effect.

If someone vacuums under your feet, you won't get married.

Hold your feet up going over railroad tracks or you won't get married.

Hold your breath going over a bridge, or you won't get married.

Don't set a purse on the floor—you will lose money faster.

Bubbles in coffee mean money.

Play in the fire and you'll wet the bed.

If you dream of having your teeth filled, you may recover lost valuables.

If you dream about your teeth falling out, someone is "stabbing you in the bag."

Tell a dream before breakfast and it will come true.

If you dream about feces, you'll receive money.

If you dream about dirty water, a friend is being deceitful.

If you dream of a dog's approaching, a witch is watching you.

If you dream of a fish, you will lose your appetite.

Do not point at a rainbow, or your finger will swell at the lower joint.

If you go away and leave your lodge, put a hemlock branch across the doorstep so no ghosts will come.

If you ask for the debt someone owes you on Sunday, they don't have to pay it.

Carry a rabbit's foot for good luck.

If you step on a crack, you will break your mother's back.

The crow has a sweet song that humans never hear.

Do not walk under a ladder or you will get seven years' bad luck.

If you hear an owl hoot in the day, someone will die.

If you hear bells ringing in your ears, someone will die within three days.

If you leave your house and have to turn back, make a cross in the dirt with your toe and spit on it.

It is unlucky if you swing a chair from side to side.

It is unlucky to set out a cedar tree because when it grows tall enough to cast a shadow, a member of the family will die.

It's unlucky to step on someone else's shadow.

Empirical Folk Belief

If the cows are lying down, bad weather is going to come.

If you hang a dead chicken in a tree, a hawk won't come around.

When deer move on a night when the moon is not full, you see a fox in the day, and frost on a cloudy morning, you will have bad weather.

Exactly three months after the first katydids begin calling, the first killing frost will come. There may be earlier, light frosts, but no killing ones.

On the first of Dog Days, all the mockingbirds stop singing until the end. Watch the mockingbirds from the second to the tenth of July.

When cows follow you around, there will be bad weather the next day.

When you see a hog carrying a bed of sticks and straw, it will be a cold winter.

If you hear an owl hoot, it will rain that day.

Always stir the batter of a cake in the same direction or it will fall.

When the hornet builds its nest near the ground, it is going to be a bad winter. The same is true if the smoke from the chimney settles to the ground, if the corn has a heavy shuck, if the hair on the mule is thick, and if the hair on the dog is thick.

An early Easter means an early spring, and a late Easter means a late spring.

For every foggy morning in August, there will be a snowy day during the winter.

If the first snow stays on the ground three days, another snow will come to top it.

Before planting, soak the seeds in the same water which you have soaked lightning-riven wood.

When the red root (*Ceanothus*) puts out leaves, the young fawns are in the mountains.

Plant taters on dark nights.

Plant corn when you see the first catbird.

Put corncobs under tomatoes to make them prosper.

Kill a hog on the wrong phase of the moon and meat will spoil.

A good hair tonic is sap from the wild grapevine gathered during the spring.

Trees laden with leaves are a sign of cold weather. A heavy crop of holly and dogwood berries means the same.

If it rains the first Sunday in a new month, it will rain two more Sundays in that month. If the first Sunday is pretty, two other Sundays will be pretty also.

If it rains on Easter Sunday, it will rain every Sunday for seven weeks.

Destroy germs from a sick person's bedding on the Sun's Day, or Sunday.

A red sunset means clearing weather; a yellow sunset, rain.

Dig a grave before a full moon, you get not enough dirt; dig after, you get too much.

If there is a ring around the moon and there is a star in the ring, bad weather is coming. If the ring contains no star, there is no bad weather in the near future.

[On] February 2, if a groundhog comes out and sees its shadow, there will be six more weeks of winter.

If you trim your hair in the new moon, it will get thick.

Never cut a dress on Sunday; it will never turn out right.

If the leaves on a maple tree are turned upside down, then it is going to rain.

If a spider weaves its web in the morning, it is not going to rain that day.

THE TELLERS

Looking through the archive for distinct storytellers, we were excited to discover that some of our best yarn spinners had yet to be presented in a Foxfire book. Some striking omissions were folks like Stanley Hicks, Lloyd Arneach, and Davy Arch. The first comes from a great storytelling family that includes his cousin Ray Hicks, best known for his collection of Jack tales. Stanley has been primarily featured in Foxfire publications as an instrument maker and banjo picker, but it turns out he's got some great tales of his own. Lloyd Arneach and Davy Arch come from the Cherokee community and were not interviewed by Foxfire until 2013, in spite of being renowned storytellers. They are representative of a larger cultural identity that has only been recently explored by our students but one that is incredibly significant to the history and culture of this region.

The next two tellers, Don Patterson and Kimsey Hampton, are representative of a brand of interview and article that dominated the pages of *Foxfire* from around the mid-1970s through today: the "personal story," or memoir. These biographical features focused on individuals and their experiences, but what was overlooked in the process were the great stories that often came out through the interview process. Don Patterson's recollections of witch tales from the Burton Community are a great example of how students discovered great stories just by sitting down and allowing their contacts to speak on whatever he or she wanted.

In the case of Kimsey Hampton's interview for his personal story, we were able to get a great collection of humorous anecdotes about his time growing up in Rabun County, Georgia. Kimsey, as it turned out, worked almost exclusively in story when weaving together the details of his colorful upbringing in these mountains. Whereas most of the folks we interviewed for personal stories gave us a linear timeline of their lives, Kimsey threaded together a collection of entertaining jests that illustrate his life. Even more special is that we know the interviewer, Tommy Lamb, was Kimsey's grandson and, as such, had the kind of intimate relationship with Kimsey that put him at ease and allowed for a truly great storytelling session.

The final two storytellers are very recent interviewees that demonstrate both the continuity of folk tradition and the rise of new material informed by folk culture. The first of these is with Ronda Reno, a fifth-generation herbalist and faith healer from the Warwoman Community in Rabun County. She was interviewed in the summer of 2018 for an article on the topic of folk medicine and its growing popularity in the modern age. Ronda was an incredible person to sit down with, and our students admired her so much that they recorded a second interview to collect more information and to just spend some more time with this self-identified "granny witch." In the context of sharing her knowledge on native herbs and folk remedies, Ronda also told a few stories and provided us with a folk-historical perspective on the early days of European settlement in the New World, including information on the identification and persecution of "witches" through the lens of her own family's history. She also went on to provide us with a new variant on the popular local legend of the War Woman, for which her community is named.

Also from the Warwoman Community, Kip Ramey is a folk

artist who has amassed quite a following for his mixed-media paintings and sculptures. Kip has worked in the area as an artist for years but also has deep roots in this region and has heard his share of great stories. As a fan of great storytelling, Kip knows how to enrapture an audience. While it's not his primary mode of artistic expression, he can spin a good tale, especially about the supernatural. This region is full of all kinds of great legends about mythical or exotic beasts, from tales of panthers or other wild cats that are commonplace throughout these mountains to more fantastical stories such as those about the Mothman in West Virginia. Kip's contribution to this tradition is an example of the growing legend of Bigfoot, which is generally associated with the Pacific Northwest but is now appearing in areas throughout Southern Appalachia. Told as an experience narrative, or anecdote, Kip's tale demonstrates how the storytelling tradition lives on in this part of the country.

Stanley Hicks

Stanley Hicks was one of those interview contacts who entertained everyone he talked to. Foxfire students made a number of visits to Stanley's home in Watauga County, North Carolina. Primarily featured as a banjo maker and picker, Stanley was also a great storyteller and verbal artist in his own right. His cousin Ray Hicks was known as the "Storyteller of Beech Mountain," and has often overshadowed Stanley as a teller of tales, but Stanley was no slouch. It is partly for that reason that we wanted to feature Stanley's stories in this volume.

In 1980, Stanley, along with a handful of other traditional artists, was featured on Foxfire Records' very first production, *It Still Lives*—a project that came out of interviews students conducted for *Foxfire 3*'s section on the banjo and dulcimer. The main focus of the record was traditional string music played on those instruments, but Stanley's incredible riddles and stories inspired the students and Foxfire music teacher George Reynolds to include a bit of his verbal artistry. Included with the record, the students also published a booklet of extensive liner notes, transcriptions, and annotations. This section includes the excerpts from that booklet, including Stanley's own introduction of himself and his life in Watauga County, a short collection of riddles, and two stories: a first-person anecdote about an experience with a rattlesnake and a wonderful telling of the folktale "Jack and the Giants."

Stanley Hicks

Life on Spice Creek

My great-grandpa, his name was David Hicks. He came from England. When he come to this country he settled first in Wilkes County and then he come to Watauga County and settled up at Valle Crucis. He gave twenty-five cents an acre for about two hundred acres of land. A year or two after he was there, he traded it for a black-and-tan dog and hog rifle and a sheep hide, and the black-and-tan dog is what he got out of it. He couldn't raise his family on a farm, and he'd take the hog rifle and his dog and kill game, you know, bears, deer, and turkeys, stuff to feed his family.

He come on down the river just a little ways from here. Bought another place and cleaned it up there. Then he later went up to the Beech Mountain, and that's where my grandpa Sam Hicks settled.

He said that when he started farming and raising his young-uns, he said he couldn't make enough to feed 'em, and lots of times he'd run out of corn and stuff, and he'd work for old man Eli Mast for a hat full of corn. Then Eli would take his toll out of it, and he said he'd get home with enough just to feed his younguns one mess. One mess of meal and he would have to go back the next day. He said that he told his wife, Grandma Becky, he told her if he got through that year he'd never buy another grain of corn. He always raised enough stuff to do him.

I was born in 1911 and raised on Spice Creek in Watauga County. My daddy was Roby Hicks, and he was seventy-five years old when he died. My mother is still living—she's ninety years old and she's still living. They was nine of us younguns that got grown and two that was born dead.

It was pretty hard times when we growed up—had to work old yokes of cattle and stuff like that, you know. We'd break 'em and then Dad, he'd sell 'em. We'd take and go to the Beech and cut bark and stuff, you know, to get stuff to our tax with 'cause they wasn't no jobs. The first job to come to our country was Ritter Lumber Company, I think. Come into Boone's Fork.

When they built the roads then you worked what they called free labor. Went and built the roads, you know—dug and built and fixed 'em without any money. They didn't pay anything at all. You'd have to work about a day a week or four days a month. Dad would go and work, but when he'd get something to do somewheres else, I'd go and carry water in his place. You know. Somebody had to carry water to the crowd a'workin'.

You couldn't get over the roads much only on an old sled or something like that. First car I seen was an old T-Model; then they got the A-Model. They could go part of the way some of them could, but you couldn't hardly go, you know, in the roads that they had. If you seen a man with a team of horses, he was a rich man then—that was a rich man. A man that had a team of horses and a wagon was rich. Now then you'd have a hundred to two hundred thousand dollars to call him rich.

Back at them days, you know, a wagon is what they hauled their goods in. My uncles hauled in goods in one—they'd run a little store, you know. Coffee, it was about seven cents a pound; cloth about seven cents a yard. Stuff was very cheap then to what it is now. Back then, you see, people raised what they eat and eat what they raised. They didn't have nothing to buy it with.

I growed up on a farm and we growed our stuff that we eat. We growed hogs and chickens and guineas and stuff like that. We killed our own hogs and beefs and cured the meat, you know. Then we had our chickens. They laid their eggs, and we ate them or sold 'em for twelve cents a dozen. We'd take mattocks and stuff and clean up new ground. Raised our cane to get 'lasses and corn to get meal. We raised wheat to get flour. We'd thrash out buckwheat and all that stuff, you know. Take what we called a thrill and thrash it out.

In the summer, people would make spicewood tea and sassafras tea and stuff like that. And lots of times we parched chestnuts to make coffee out of. Parched wheat and ground it and parched corn and made coffee out of it.

People were a lot healthier then than they are now—much more healthier. We cooked over the fireplace—had these old skillets. They baked the bread in on the fireplace and had these things, you know, you hang your pot on to cook your beans. Put in a big piece of hog meat, and boys [it was] real good, mmmmm, mercy! Now then, you put a big pot of beans on the fireplace and cook 'em so quick, you cook all the vitamins out of 'em. Ain't no vitimins in 'em now. That's the reason so many [people are] sick. They don't ever cook stuff like we used to. They run and get 'em a little hamburger and grab it and eat it and that's about it.

Then people don't walk like they used to. They ride there and back and get out of the car and go in the house. They don't walk like we used to did. I walked three miles back to school when I went. Why, we cut our own wood, built our own fires, and walked to school back and forwards in the snow. We didn't have no buses to go in. We'd have to walk there and back. I'd have to walk [back] and [forth] when I'd work too, you know. After I was married, I'd have to walk about five or six miles each way.

When I was married . . . the way we started out, her daddy and mother give her a hog shoulder and a quilt or two and Mother give me a featherbed. We didn't have no pans or kettles or nothing. I think Mother gave me one pan and maybe a fork or two, and Dad gave me a bushel of corn. That's what we had when we started out.

We cooked on the fireplace and on an old wood cookstove. We've still got our wood cookstove. But I don't use my fireplace no more. The first woodstove I had was an old steel barrel. Cut and fixed it. Then I took metal roofing and bent it round a pole to make the piping out of.

Me and my wife cleaned up the ground—cut the trees off of it and rolled the logs off of it and then dug our holes in there and planted our corn in it. We'd raise these old field beans, what we called babyface beans. We'd raise them and sell 'em by cold weather.

The first job I worked was WPA, worked seventy-five cents a day. Then got a job at Whitings, when they come into this country, on the railroad. Worked in hit two years for a dollar a day. If you could get a half a dollar a day, you worked for it, or twenty-five cents. You just work for whatever you get. When I was growin' up, overalls like I'm wearing now cost thirty-nine cents a pair, and now they're fifteen dollars. 'Course, I can get the fifteen dollars now easier than I could get the thirty-nine cents then.

They called it hard times but we made out awful good. I'd swear it was better than it is now. Everybody wasn't running and breaking their necks then. They'd set down in the road and talk to you half a day. Now then they just, "Hi," and they're gone. And they get a car and it—it's a big go in hit. It ain't like it once was when I growed up.

You know, back in them days, we made a lot of stuff. My grandpa made the first pair of shoes I ever wore. He was a shoemaker—made dulcimers, banjos, shoes, anything. First pair of shoes I ever wores, my grandpa made 'em. Mother made our clothes, knitted our stockings and knitted our gloves and all that. Daddy sharpened mill rocks and made mills and made banjos and dulcimers. My daddy was Roby Hicks, and that's where I learned to play the banjo and make all this stuff.

Stanley Hicks

I made my first banjo when I was fifteen years old, and I've made them off and on ever since. I'm sixty-seven now. You could figure, I say, about fifty-two years. We used to use cat hides for banjo heads. Now I use groundhog hides in mine. I still use cat hide, though. The cat gets to messing around, and I get ill with it and put its hide on the banjo. If it's a good old cat, I don't do that, but t'ain't many good cats. You don't find many good ones—they're always into something. I had about fifteen here, and they got to catching birds and killing them and catching young rabbits and killing them and stuff like that, and I got tired of it, and I got rid of them but two. I think there's two around here somewhere if someone ain't got their hide on a banjo . . .

Riddles

Stanley: So here's a riddle I'm going to tell you, going to tell you this riddle—and all, and you'ns can guess on it. Now I'm going to give you, I'm going to tell you'ns two. If you'ns will ask me, then I'll tell you what they are.

They's some of them—I'll not tell you none that sounds bad. They ain't bad, but I'll not tell none of them. I know quite a few.

Here's one:

Old Granny Wire jumped in the fire,
Fire was so hot she jumped in the pot,
The pot was so cracked she jumped . . . jumped in the sky,
The sky so blue she jumped in the shoe,
The shoe was so deep she jumped in the creek,
The creek were so shaller she jumped in the taller,
Taller was so soft she jumped in the loft,
Loft was so rotten she jumped in the cotton,
Cotton was so white she asked to stay all night.

Now here's another one I'm gonna tell. You'ns be studying on it:

Through a rock
Through a reel
Through an old
Spinning wheel
Through a sheep shank bone
Such a riddle's never known.

And this "through a rock, through a reel, through an old spinning wheel, through a sheep shank bone, such a riddle's never known"—it's lightning. Lightning strikes and it goes through a sheep shank. Such a riddle's never known.

And Old Granny Wire, see, when she done all of this and when she jumped in this cotton, it was so white and soft, she asked 'em to stay all night. So she stayed all night with 'em.

Yeah, and right here's one now you'ns can study and hit, uh, it's about dogs, you know. It's:

Trim, Tray, Try,
Which is the bitch's name?

Trim, Tray, Try, Which is the bitch's name. Can you'ns get this 'un?

Mike: Which one of the ones . . . ?

Stanley: Trim, now listen, Trim, Tray, Try. Which is a bitch's name? Which one is the bitch's name? See, it's Trim, Tray, Try, *Which* is a bitch's name.

George: "Which"?

Stanley: "Which" is her name, you see.

Cotton: Trim, Tray, Try!

Stanley: Trim, Tray, Try, but "Which" is the bitch's name. I've done told you her name. "Which" is the bitch's name. "Which" is her name. So you've done and got it there then.

There's a lot of these, you know. And here's one more I'm gonna tell you'ns. And used to, I knowed it well. I'm gonna tell you'ns this one now:

It goes all over the field in daytime, all over the field in daytime, and sits at the table at night.

What's that?

Mike: Sits on the table or at it?

Stanley: It goes all over the field, travels all over the field in the daytime, and then sits on the table at night. Keep a studying. When you say you don't know, I'll tell you'ns. When you get where you don't know what it is.

He travels, now this thing travels all over the field in the daytime, goes all over the field in the daytime, and then sits on the table at night. And it might sit in other places, but back when I growed up, it sat on the table all night. Might be in other places now.

Cotton: George said milk.

Stanley: Huh?

Cotton: George said milk.

Stanley: Milk's what it is. Cow travels all over the field in the daytime. And the milk sets on the table at night. And here's one more—one more and it's very hard. Now he'll probably know it, he's up on his riddles and stuff.

What goes to the water with its head down and never drinks?

Goes to the water with its head down and never drinks? That's very hard one in a way, and in a way it's just very easy. But it goes to the water every day now. It goes and it never drink, never drinks.

Cotton: Oh, is it a spring?

Stanley: No. It goes to the water every day, it goes every day to this water—creek or ever'where it goes—to the water every day, and it never drinks, never drinks and its head's down. Hit's a horseshoe nail. Ha, ha, ha. This horse goes . . . this horseshoe nail head is down and hit never drinks . . .

Stinger Snake

Cotton: Have you killed any big rattlesnakes or something like that?

Stanley: Rattlesnakes . . . Well, I'll tell you now, I'm a goin' to tell you this, and it's a fact, son. Ain't no joke about this. Yeah, I've killed rattlesnakes—come pretty nigh gettin' . . . bit by one. But I killed a snake, I'd wished I put in alcohol and kept it. Now you'ns might not believe it but it's the truth. I'm goin' to tell you the facts.

I stayed in Beech Creek. Years ago I stayed over there. I been here since '52 and, uh, went on down, it's been, I couldn't tell you now. I'd say it's been thirty-five years ago—thirty years, anyway, and they, uh, cradled oats and stuff, you know, back then they cradled oats and stuff. And they was a patch of oats where they'd cradled at and, uh, they was an old [place], where they'd stacked 'em at and they tore this stack down. And the stubble, you know, was about this high and the grass was a comin' up in it.

And I went up there to get some of these old pieces of rails and stuff, you know, to clean it up off the ground, for a feller. And was aiming to take some of 'em to the house for wood.

I don't know whether you ever heard tell of or not, but this was a stinger snake. And it had a stinger in its tail about this long [one inch], with a joint in it that was as hard as a bone.

It come up and I got to fighting it and I fit it, and fit it, and fit it, and fit it. And its head was slick and it had hair, like you saw birds, it had hair on it about like these wooly worms not hardly that long. And I fit that snake for thirty minutes and I was give out. Sweat was rollin' off of me. And every time I'd strike, it would disappear, you know, it's just gone. I'd say I fit, anyway, a half hour. Finally I just happened to, happened a good lick and hit it right in back of the neck and knocked it and killed it. And it had a stinger in the end of its tail. Hoop snakes is what they called 'em, you know, roll. You know, they call 'em Hoop snakes. And that's the only one I ever saw and I've heard Grandpa and them talk about 'em. They roll this a way and when they get to you this stinger goes in you. And hit stand straight up on that, it'd stand straight up. I took it down to the road and hung it up in a bush. Tied a string around its neck and hung it up in a bush and it stayed there for two months. You know, till it just . . . And people came from everywhere's to look at it. And it had hair—it was just a fine. Pretty coarse, but it wasn't long, about this long. About, ah, I'd say about eighth of an inch. And the stinger in its tail had a, it had a joint in it, had a joint in that and its head was slick. And I've never see'd one since and nobody else ain't. And if I'd a took that snake and a put into the, you know, put it in alcohol or something, I could have been rich.

Stanley Hicks

Jack and the Giants

Here's one now about Jack and the Giants: Jack he was out a huntin' for a job. And the old King had land, it was down there in these Giant's land and . . . every time he'd send anybody up there to clean the new ground up, these Giants would kill 'em. Cut their heads—kill 'em, you know.

Well, Jack he come along the road and he made him a paddle

about so big and bored him a hole through it back here and tied it to his gallus. And he's goin' along this road and he come to a mudhole and [there was] a big bunch of butterflies in it. Great big, you know how they'll gather in on the mud. So Jack he just took his paddle off and he walked up and he whammed away in that and just—he killed no tellin' how many of 'em. So he just took and cut on his paddle—"Killed a thousand and wounded a thousand more," on his paddle and tied it back to his gallus and went on.

Came to this old King's house. Knocked on the door and the old King come out and said, "What do you want?"

He said, "I'm looking for a job."

"Huh," [the King] said, "you're too little and weaselly to handle a job that I want." He said, "I need a good hand but," he said, "I just can't handle you." He said, "You're too little and weaselly."

And he looked at Jack's paddle, you know that paddle he had. And it said, "Killed a thousand and wounded a thousand more—killed a thousand head and wounded a thousand head more."

"Huh, bedads," [the King] said, "that might, you might just be the man I want." He said, "Just come on in."

Jack went on in, and he had him an old leather bag sewed around him, you know, so he could get somewhere where he was eatin' at and if he got hungry, he could just put food down in this, you know, while he was eatin' he'd just pour it in there, pour milk and stuff in it and when he got out and got hungry he'd have it to eat. So he was in there eatin' away, just a pouring it to him eatin'. Every time old King and his wife turned their heads, Jack would pour a little milk in there and stick a big piece of cornbread in there.

"Well," [the King] said, "I'll tell you what I want you to do now, Jack." He said, "There's three of 'em [giants]: one's got two heads, and two of 'ems got three heads apiece, and the old man's got four heads."

And he said, "I want 'em killed." He said, "Every time I send my men up there to clear up new ground, [the giants] kill 'em."

"Huh," [Jack] said. "Bedads, I don't know whether I want that job or not. Well," he said, "how much do you pay?"

[The King] said, "I'll give you a hundred dollars a head. Every head you bring me back I'll give you a hundred dollars."

"Huh, bedads that's pretty good money."

Well, he stayed all night. And morning old King said, "Now there lays a ax right there and a chip block."

Jack went up and he looked at 'em . . . little old hatchet laying there. Jack picked up the hatchet.

Old King says, "You can't clean up new ground, you can't clean up no new ground with that."

Jack says, "Bedads, I can."

So he went on up . . . got to this tree where the giants had killed all these people. So Jack clumb a tree. He got way up in and he started hacking away, hacking away, hacking the brush down. And he heard something coming up through the woods. He looked down and there come a giant with two heads—just a crashing and breaking the brush a coming on up . . . comes up and looked up at Jack.

Said, ". . . what's your name?"

Said, "Jack."

"What you doing up in there?"

He said, "Cleaning up new ground."

"Huh," he said, "I never heard tell of nobody cleaning up new ground like that." He said, "Always cut the tree down then cut its brush off!"

"Huh, bedads," [Jack] said, "that's where they're wrong at." He said, "I climb the tree and trim all the branches off and then I get down and pile 'em all up and get 'em out my way then cut my tree down, and that's the way I clean up!"

"Well," said [the Giant], "I never heard tell of that." Said, "Come down Jack, come on down, come on down."

Jack was scared to get on the ground. Jack, he got down

to about the second branch down . . . talkin' to the old Giant. Well, he didn't know what to do.

[Jack] said, "I'll tell you what I can do." Said, "I can do something you can't."

"What's that," [the Giant] said, "what's that?"

He said, "I can squeeze milk out of a flint rock and you can't do it." Said, "Pitch me up here one."

And Jack had a needle, you know. So he pitched Jack up a flint rock. And Jack took that needle and jabbed through this ol' leather bag and squeezed it, and the milk just drop, drop, drop on the ground. Dropped down to the ground.

"Pitch it down here."

He pitched it down . . . old Giant and the Giant just ground it up. Just ground it up in crumbles. "No, no, no milk at all, huh."

Jack said, "That's funny." Said, "I told you I could do something you couldn't do."

"Huh," [the Giant] said, "that's the first thing any man's ever done that I couldn't do."

[Jack] said, "I'll so something else you can't do."

"What's that?"

He said, "I can cut my stomach open and sew my stomach back up." And he said, "It won't bother me a bit and you can't do it."

"Let's see ya do it."

Jack, he took a knife and ripped this old leather bag, and milk and bread just begin to squirt out, you know, he grabbed it, you know, took his needle and he whooped around, he sewed 'er back up, you know.

"Pitch me down your knife."

Jack just pitched him down the knife and the old Giant just layed his stomach from one side to the other open. Then he got to trying to get it back in, get his guts back in, got 'em down in these leaves and in the dirt and stuff. He'd wad 'em around and get all this trash in 'em, you know, an all. Wad 'em up in there and trash and all into his, into his innards there and him a trying to get 'em back in. Directly he got sick, you know, just plumb sick and just layed back and passed out. And Jack he just went down the tree and took his hatchet and chopped his head off. He put it in a tow sack and took it back to the old King.

"Ah," he said, "I, ah, see you can do pretty good, Jack." He said, "You got one. Nobody else never was able to get one."

Give Jack two hundred dollars. They sat around there and talked that night. And the next morning, Jack, he was sorta dreading to go back.

[The King] said, "Jack." He said, "There's three more." He said . . .

"Uh," [Jack] said, "I don't know." Said, "I don't care much about killin' Giants no way."

He said, "Go back up there." And he said, "There's two with three heads apiece." Said, "They're dangerous."

Jack, he went back up the next morning, and he didn't know what in the world to do. He was aiming to slip around and go home. He heard everything a comin', just felt like the whole, the whole everything was a breakin' down, you know. And he looked down the holler and there come two giants, three heads apiece, just a pushin' the trees down as they come. Jack, he looked at 'em a little bit and down the tree he went, you know, and [there was] a big old hollow log and he run in this hollow log. Grabbed his shirttail full of little old rocks, just tied his shirttail full up with rocks and went in the hole. Got in there and up come these two giants. Said, said, "Law, law, law." He said, "I don't see how in the world no one killed our brother." He said, "His head's chopped off and it's gone." Said, "I don't see how in the world he done that." Said, "I'd just like to meet up with the man that done that."

Well, they talked around awhile and said, "Now Mother ain't got no wood to sit up tonight." Said, "We'll have to sit up with our brother tonight."

So they picked up their brother and they put him on this log and, big log—twenty feet long—one got on one end and one the other and got it on their back and then started out with it. And Jack, he crawled to one end of the log and he cut one in the back of the head with a rock.

"Quit that hittin' me."

"I never hit you."

"Yes, you did."

"No, I never."

"Yes, you did, and if you hit me again, I'll kill you."

He crawled to the other end of the log and he potted the other on the head.

"Quit that hittin' me."

"I never hit you."

"Yes, you did."

"No, I never."

"Yes, you did. Hit me again, I'll kill you."

[Jack] eased back and got a little sharp rock just as teeny as he could get and just popped that other slap in back of the head and they throwed the logs and went into it. And they fit, and they fit, and they fit, and they fit. They fit and fit and directly they got so weak, you know, [they was] just hold of one another. Jack, he come out [of the] log and took his hatchet and cut their heads off. And he had to get 'em [to the] top, drag them to the top of the hill and he rolled 'em down to the old King's house, he couldn't carry 'em. Just rolled 'em off down to the old King's house.

Old King gave him six hundred dollars. So that made him eight hundred dollars, you know, and Jack, he just didn't want no more money. That was all the money he wanted.

"Law, law, Jack," [the King] said. "You're the best giant killer I've ever hired." He said, "You're the best." He said, "Now you'll get rid of all them. Got one more over there; the old man." Said, "He's got four heads."

"Uh, bedads, I just don't like to kill giants."

[The King] said, "Jack, one more."

"Well, bedads, all right."

As he eat supper and all, [Jack] decided he'd just slip off an' go home. Wouldn't kill no more giants. So he come way around, you know. Goin' to slip way around. And this old giant, that had four heads, had done and been there and found all his boys layin' there with their heads cut off. Ground all tore up and all. And he spied Jack. Jack just run right up on him, you know.

An' "Hello there stranger." Said, "What's your name?"

He said, "Jack."

He said, "My three boys here killed and all." He said, "Who done that?"

"I killed them. You fool with me and I'll kill you, too."

He said, "Pray don't, Jack." He said, "Don't. I'm, I'm the last one. Don't do that."

"Well, just don't fool with me."

"Well," he said, "will you help me carry this log off?"

"No. Bedads, if you want the log carried off, you carry it."

The ol' giant laid his three boys on it and picked it up and put it on his back, and off the mountain he went.

Got down in the valley, "Now," he said, "Jack." He said, "Uh, my wife'll be awful mad and awful tore up and all." Said, "You stay right up here till I go in the house and talk to her." Then said, "I'll take you in."

Well, he went in there and Jack went up to the keyhole in the door, you know, and he listened.

Ol' Giant said, "Mother." Said, "Little ol' feller out here." Said, "He won't weigh nothin', little ol' scrubby thang." Said, "He just looks like nothin'." And said, "He said he killed the three boys, cut their heads off. Told me that if I fooled with 'im, he'd cut my head off. I just don't believe he's that strong." He said, "Let's try him out, and if he ain't no good, we'll kill 'im and eat 'im for supper."

Well, he went back out and he said, "Jack." Said, "The old lady's going to fix supper." And said, "Let's me and you uh, uh, pitch the crowbar a little."

Had a ol' big crowbar weigh about five hundred, three or four hundred pounds. And uh, Ol' Giant, he just picked it up, and he pitched 'er way over in the bottom and just stove it into the ground.

Jack, he went over and [the Giant said], "Now you'll pitch it back."

Jack went over and looked at it and he m-m-m-ed around a little bit and rolled his sleeves up and said, "Hey, Uncle. Hey, Uncle."

[The Giant] said, "Jack, what you gonna do?"

[Jack] said, "I have an uncle in France." And said, "He ain't got no steel there. He's a blacksmith. I'm gonna pitch this crowbar to 'im."

"Pray, don't, Jack," [the Giant] said. "That's all I've got," he said, "to play with." He said, "pray don't do that."

"Well, huh. Bedads, I'll not pitch it a'tall."

"Well," [the Giant] said, "just don't pitch it a'tall."

So [instead] he went in to the shed there and picked up two, uh, picked up three pails that'll hold about twenty-five gallons o' water a piece or thirty. Give Jack one and took two in each hand. Jack just barely could get his'n down to the creek, barely could get it down there, it'uz so heavy. And the old giant just, wap down 'n' he picked this'un up full and wap down he picked that'un up full. Picked 'em up, you know, about seventy gallons of water in the jugs, them big ol' things. Jack, he rolled up his sleeves, got his breeches legs rolled up. Rolled up his sleeves and he went down in the creek. And he went to feelin' around under it. Feelin' around, feelin' around.

"What you gonna do Jack, huh!"

"Bedads," [Jack] said, "I ain't gonna bother to take just a little pail of water back!" He said, "If I can't take the whole creek back, I won't take none!"

"Lord have mercy, Jack," he said. "My wife [would] get drowned in that. Be out after night and get drowned in that."

"Well, huh, that's all right then."

He said, "Jack just don't get none, just let the creek stay there."

"Bedads, I'll just take the whole creek back."

So [the Giant] went on back to the house. Said, "Now you stay out here Jack." And said, "I'll just go in the house and tell my wife all about it." And said, "Then, uh, you can come in then for supper."

Well, he went in there and he said, "Mother." He said, "I don't think Jack's worth a thing." He said, "I just don't believe he's worth a thing." Said, "Don't believe he's one killed them boys." He said, "Let's kill 'im and eat him for supper."

Well, they had an ol' big oven, you know and a big lid on it like these skillets, you know, they used to bake bread in. Then they had board up here in the chimney.

And Jack went in.

And she said, "Law, law, law me, Jack." She said, "Law me." She said that, uh, uh, "I was to treat you just exactly like my boys." So it, uh, said, "Come here, come here, come here."

Jack, he went up. She said, "Set on that, set on that board right there, Jack."

He got on it and she started to comb his hair and he'd fall over this way, fall over that way.

She said, "Ah, let me show you how to sit up straight."

She propped up on it and Jack took a running go with his shoulder and he just popped her right over in this oven, grabbed a big prize and popped the lid on it. She was in there crackin' and poppin'. Jack went under the bed. Here come the ol' giant back (with four heads).

[Sniffing] "Huh, huh, huh. Mother, Jack's a burnin', huh, huh, huh, Mother, Jack's a burnin' [sniffing] huh, huh, Mother, [sniff, sniff] Jack's a burnin' [sniff]."

Raised the lid up and it was his wife in there just a crackin' and poppin' and grease comin' out of her.

He said, "Lord have mercy, Lord have mercy." He said, "Jack's killed them all but me." And said, "I'll be the next one."

Jack come out from under the bed, "Yes, sir, you fool with me erry bit," and said, "I'll kill you right now."

Said, "Don't come, come, don't, Jack."

Well, [Jack] said, "I'll tell ya," he said, "they's a big army a coming here," said, "and they'll be here any minute to kill you." And he said, "You got erry a team of horses?"

He said, "Yea, I got a good team up there and a wagon."

So Jack, he just run up there. Got the horses and all and run back down. Put the ol' Giant in a chest, took down to the depot. Carted him up and shipped him out of the country.

The ol' king wouldn't give him nothin' for that. Said, "You didn't bring the heads back for that."

"Bedads, don't want it nohow," [said Jack].

So last time I see'd Jack and his mother and his daddy they was a livin' real good.

Davy Arch

In 2012, Foxfire students decided to do an issue of *The Foxfire Magazine* focused on the Eastern Band of the Cherokee Indians. Geographically, we are only about an hour's drive from the Eastern Cherokee reservation, located in western North Carolina. The students took a trip to the Oconaluftee Indian Village, a living history museum in Cherokee, North Carolina, that interprets eighteenth-century Cherokee life. The village is full of indigenous artists demonstrating traditional Cherokee arts, including pottery, weaving, tool and weapon making, and storytelling.

The Cherokee oral tradition is one that is rich and full of legends and myths. These storytellers carry with them the full, rich history of the Cherokee people, stretching back to their origins and through complicated, at times terrifying relationship with European explorers and colonizers. On their trip to Oconaluftee, the students met one such storyteller, Davy Arch.

As noted by Katie Lunsford, who put together the article about Arch and his repertoire of traditional Cherokee stories,

[. . .] I realized why Davy Arch is such a celebrated storyteller; he tells a story from his soul. To see him tell a story is almost as good as hearing the story itself because of his passion for his culture. Spanning from humor to horror, his traditional stories captivate all who will listen.

It is largely for that reason that we choose to include Davy Arch in this collection—his passion for his culture and its stories is contagious. Another reason, evident in this piece, is how stories weave their way into conversation. You can see the mind of the storyteller at work, which is a wonderful thing to witness.

Davy Arch with Foxfire students

Introductions

My name is Davy Arch. I'm Eastern Cherokee, and I'm the assistant manager of the Oconaluftee Indian Village in Cherokee, North Carolina. I am a storyteller, and boy, I can tell some big ones. I tell mostly real-life adventure stories. I got into storytelling because of my artwork. I'm an artist by trade, and I do a lot of traditional arts, some of what I call pre-Columbian art. I make arrowheads, instruments, weapons, tan hides, and all that kind of stuff. I'm a sculptor. I carve stone and wood. I get inspiration from stories for a lot of my carvings. A lot of times, I'll go to an event and I'll set up and demonstrate. I'll be working on a piece of sculpture and somebody will ask, "What is that? Where did you get the idea?" Then I would tell them the story behind the carving.

The Story of Flint

One of my favorite stories is about flint. You know a lot of people identify Native Americans with making arrowheads. It's one of the few things that has survived over thousands of years. I'll be sitting around making arrowheads, and I'll think of its origin story. In the beginning, flint was contained all in the body of a giant that lived here in Cherokee country. This was in a time when all the plants and animals and human beings could communicate with one another. Everyone would talk about how much easier life would be if they could have some of the flint. They said, "We could make tools and weapons. We could build fire. You know, life would be much easier if we could just have some of this flint off the giant's body." But, everyone was afraid of the giant.

One day, the animals were talking about it. The rabbit was kind of a trickster in our culture; he always liked to brag and boast. He said, "Well, I'm not afraid of that giant. I think I could get some of that flint." Everybody turned to the rabbit and asked, "Well, why don't you?" He realized he had stuck his foot in his mouth, but he came up with a plan.

In the history of our people, there have been times where it was so difficult that families didn't have enough to eat, but it has always been tradition to offer company or a stranger something to eat and drink. It's always been bad manners to refuse that. Even if you're full, you go in and take a little bit. The rabbit knew this, so he approached the giant and asked if he would

[like to] come share a meal with him. Out of respect for the tradition, the giant accepted the rabbit's invitation. This was part
of the rabbit's plan. He planned to feed this giant until he got
so full, he'd go to sleep. He had prepared a hammer and wedge
to knock a piece of the giant's body off when he went to sleep.

The giant came to the rabbit's house, and the rabbit had
laid out a big feast for him. The giant ate and ate until he was
full. He told the rabbit he was full and that it was time for him
to leave. The rabbit said, "Wait just a minute." So, the rabbit
went into his house and brought out another dish of food that
was even more delicious than what the giant had just finished
eating. Out of respect, the giant had some of that food, and
each time he got ready to leave, the rabbit would do the same
thing—go back in and get more food. He fed the giant until the
giant was gorged. The giant went over to this huge chestnut
tree and went to sleep. That's the moment that the rabbit had
been waiting for.

The rabbit went back in his house and got the hammer and
wedge, and he snuck up on the sleeping giant. He set the wedge
on the giant's chest and was going to knock a chip of flint off of
the giant's body. He drew back his hammer, and when he hit
his wedge, instead of it knocking a chip off the giant, the giant
had gorged himself to the point that he exploded and went all
over the universe. Now, in every country in the world, you can
find flint. Flintstone is on every continent there is. They claim
that the shooting stars across the sky at night are still parts of
that giant's body.

A lot of people wonder what happened to that rabbit. When
that giant blew up, it didn't kill him. A lot of people thought
that an explosion like that may have killed the rabbit, too. Well,
it didn't, but a piece flew off and cut his tail off. The rabbit
used to have a long tail. Since that day, he has had a short tail.
Another piece of flint hit that rabbit right in the upper lip. If
you'll look at a rabbit's lip, it still has a split lip. He carries that
scar to this day.

After that, everyone had flint, and it made life much easier. We used it for everything. We used it for tools. Men and women both learned how to make arrowheads and how to work flint. It's easy to make fire with. So, that's how we got flint. That's one of my favorite stories because I make arrowheads, and I can tell that as I'm demonstrating what I'm doing.

The Cherokee and Bears

Another story I used to tell a lot was about a carving I made of a half man, half bear. It looked a lot like a Greek centaur, a half man, half horse, but this has a bear's body and a man's torso. The story is about a boy who went to live back in the woods with the bears. He would come back home, but he got to where he was spending more time with the bears than with his family. The village got into a crisis and didn't have enough food. So, one day the boy left and told his parents that he was going to live with the bears forever, but that if they ever needed food, they could come get him and use him for food. That was one of

Davy Arch

the stories that I used for inspiration behind that carving, the boy turning himself into a bear.

I've got another story that was about the same where a man was changed into a bear through magic and was condemned to roam the earth as a bear for the rest of his life. We have another story where a whole clan of people was transformed into bears to provide food for the rest of the tribe. They claim that way back, we had nine clans. We had a Panther Clan and a Bear Clan, but those are two clans that don't exist within the culture anymore.

The Wampus

I've got several scary stories. There is one story I have told a lot. Everybody has ghost stories and scary stories and stuff like that, but when I was growing up, I hunted a lot with my grandfather. We'd be back in the mountains walking a trail, and sometimes we would find just little piles of bone splinters in the middle of a trail. Grandpa would say, "Well, that was that wampus cat eating something right there." I asked him one time what it was he was talking about. He said, "Well, thousands of years ago, the men had their medicine, and the women had their medicine." We still do, and this is medicine that you are not supposed to talk about in mixed genders. One time, there was a young couple married, and the young man was a doctor. In the evening, he would leave and go talk to the men about the men's medicine. Well, he was driving his wife crazy; she liked to know everything. She couldn't bear to think that he was getting information that she didn't know anything about.

One evening, she decided she was going to sneak down to the council and find out what these men were talking about. She disguised herself with a panther skin, but these old men knew she was coming. These old doctors know a lot of times before the patient does that they're coming to see them. The doctors waited on her, and when she snuck up on the men's council, they came up, caught her, and brought her into council. Because of her disrespect to the men's medicine, they condemned her to roam this earth forever as a panther. They changed her into a panther through magic because she had disguised herself with that panther hide. They told her that she would have to roam these mountains for eternity because of her disrespect. They also gave her the power to change back into a woman. They told her if she wanted to eat, she would have to change into this cat and eat while she was a cat. Sometimes, people see a woman walking back through the mountains. They believe that is the woman that shape-shifts from a panther back into a woman. If you ever hear a panther's scream, it sounds just like a woman screaming. My grandpa told me one time when we were back in the mountains and heard one, he said, "That's that ol' wampus cat shape-shifting. It must be awful painful for her to shift from one thing to another." All through the woods, even nowadays, you will find those little piles of bones.

That's one of my favorite tales. I think about that a lot when I'm back in the mountains. I've never seen a big cat back in the mountains, but one time when I was digging up some Christmas trees way back in the mountains, a cat came down and walked around my truck in the snow.

On Storytelling

I think a good storyteller is somebody who is telling real-life adventure stories, has a vested interest in that memory, and they get the enthusiasm of the time. They almost reexperience the adrenaline they had when they were living that story. I love to hear those kinds of stories from storytellers who research the information, have a good presence, and can relay a message that people can understand. I have heard storytellers who use big words and terminology that people don't understand, and to me, their story is not as effective.

I like to listen to older people. They've rehearsed their stories, and they've got it down to a science. They can really be dramatic and even act out the stories a lot of times when they're telling it. Younger storytellers sometimes add a little flavor that is really good because they're looked at as carrying on that tradition, especially if it is a story that has been passed down.

People have asked me if stories get changed around. You know, if you whisper a message and send it around the room, a lot of times it's a different message at the end of the line. A lot of people have wondered how true our stories are to the real story. In the past, it was kind of a rule of thumb that a story had to be told the same way every time so that it wouldn't be confused by the next generation. They taught lessons, so traditional stories are told the same way by a lot of different people.

I like humor and funny stories. Those seem to be the ones you remember—that and scary stories. The ghost stories and the funny stories seem to stick with you. I have several funny stories. One popular story around here is about the opossum losing the hair on his tail. That's one that a lot of people know. He was tricked by the crickets. They told him they were preparing his tail for a dance so that he could brag on it. He liked to brag and boast on it. In reality, they were cutting the hair off of his tail in a way to embarrass him and teach him a lesson. That's a pretty good traditional story.

A Cow in the Dark

I'll tell you one of the funniest stories I ever heard. Where I grew up, over by the casino, was mostly pasture. We had a livestock barn down in the field there, and we had a barbed wire fence that went all the way around the field. Instead of the bridge that is there now, there was an old swinging bridge, just a foot bridge across the creek. It was elevated pretty high out of the creek. Off the ends of the bridge, there were two wide boards—they must have been twenty feet long—that ran across into the field across the fence. A neighbor of ours was coming through there after dark. He said there wasn't a moon out, and it was dark.

He said he made his way across the bridge and started down the planks on the other side going down into the pasture. He said he stumbled and started running, trying to catch his balance. He ran out into the field and fell. When he fell, he landed on something big and warm and hairy. It moved. He said when it moved, it scared him to death. His imagination ran away with him. He jumped up and took off running. When he hit the fence on the other end of the field, you could hear the nails pop out of the fence posts all the way around the pasture. What he had done was run out, and he fell on a cow that was lying out there in the middle of the field. His name was Bill Hicks. He was one of the chief's cousins. We called him "Sweet William" because he had those Sweet William flowers growing all around his place. Just to hear him tell that was a lot of fun. When he was telling that story, I could just imagine him jumping up from landing on that cow, taking off, and hitting the fence.

Some Local Anecdotes

I've heard a lot of stories about people wandering around these mountains at night before there was electricity. There wasn't any ambient light anywhere. If you got away from town, you were back in the dark. It was just pitch-black dark. I've heard about people seeing lights and stuff like that. Grandpa said one time he was coming down off the mountain right before dark one evening. He said it was getting so dark that he couldn't really see. He had a little dog with him, and he had been fishing. The dog started barking at what Grandpa thought was a big limb lying across the road that had fallen out of a tree.

When he got up close to it, he could see the shadow or the image of something lying across the road. He began to smell a rattlesnake. His dog started barking, and he realized, when he got up close, that what he was seeing was a giant snake. He said it was as big as his leg. Its tail was lying up on the bank in the woods, and his head was laying off the bank, off the road going down the other way. It scared him to death. He didn't have a gun or anything, so he picked up a rock about as big as he could pick up and threw it at the snake. The rock didn't hit it; it went past the snake and hit the ground. When the snake felt the vibration, it moved off the road. A log truck had wrecked, and that load of logs was still laying off below the road. He said the snake went over in those logs.

He hurried and got on around it and went home. The next morning when it got daylight, he got his gun and went back up there to see if he could find it. He said that snake left a trail across that road about a foot wide, where it crawled. That was the second one that big that he saw in his lifetime.

A guy named Cub Calonahaski used to work with my grandfather. He lived on one side of the mountain, and he [Grandpa] said that every morning, Cub would come across the mountain through what we call Jumper Gap and come down to Grandpa's house. They were digging up laurel roots to sell to the companies that make tobacco pipes.

Well, one morning, Cub came busting into his cabin just white as a ghost. He had gone up his side of the mountain, and when he had got into Jumper Gap, he stepped across what he thought was a pole lying across the trail and sat down on it. It was one of those snakes. When it moved, he jumped up and took off. Grandpa said he was scared to death. They took the gun out and went back up there. The snake was still up there, but they didn't kill it. In our culture, we don't kill things just to kill them. We call the rattlesnake our brother.

There's a story about the "Wrath of the Rattlesnake." A man came home one day, and he found a dead rattlesnake beside his dead wife. His wife had killed the snake, and the snake's mate had killed her. So, the snake and the man made a pact that day never to kill one another again. When we find a snake in the woods, we just tell it to go where people don't walk. Usually, they'll go out of the trail and leave. Once in a while, if we catch one in here in the village or something, we'll give it to somebody, and they'll take it back into the mountains just to get it away from people. I rarely kill them. Some people do kill them and eat them.

Grandpa said the snake Cub had set down on was about fifteen feet long. He said its head was as big as his hand. A rattlesnake will live a hundred years if you'll leave it alone. They have indiscriminate growth. If they have food, they'll keep growing, just like a fish. So, there were some monsters in this part of the world at one time. Land development has really taken its toll.

The Story of the Inchworm

We have a lot of stories about giants and unusual creatures. How things got their characteristics is a big part of our culture. One of my favorite stories is why the inchworm is so small and why it has no legs in the middle of its body. They claim that in the beginning, the inchworm was a giant, as big as a tree. They're carnivores; they're predators. They hunt and eat bugs and other things. When the inchworm was a giant, he started preying on the Cherokee. They said he'd come to the Cherokee village and stand straight up on the edge of it. They looked just like the bark on a tree. He'd wait until the hunters would leave the village, and he'd come down and catch the women and children and eat them.

The Cherokee got tired of that, so they devised a plan to kill the inchworm. They stacked up stone piles around the fire in the middle of the village to look like people when they knew the inchworm was going to be there the next day. They waited until light the next morning, and the hunting party got together in the middle of the village so the inchworm could see what was going on. They left the village and went back into the woods and hid. Now, the inchworm, seeing that they had left the village, reached down, but when he reached down, he reached across the fire and grabbed the pile of stones he thought was a person. The stones were so heavy, he couldn't raise up. He kept trying to raise up, but while he was trying to lift that pile of stones, the fire burnt his legs off in the middle of his body. His body started to shrink. When he let go of that pile of stones to get back in the woods, away from that fire, he continued to shrink down to an inch long. He had burnt the legs off the middle of his body, and they never did grow back. That's how the inchworm got his characteristics. There are stories like that about everything.

Uktena and the Crystal

There was a giant serpent called Uktena that guarded a magic crystal. They said it had horns. On an old rattlesnake, the place over its eyes will turn into what looks like horns. They'll raise up and get a spike above their eye. I don't know if this was an old rattlesnake that looked like it had horns or if was actually a serpent with horns. In Central America and down in northern parts of South America, they have the same image, a winged, horned serpent. Uktena was supposed to have guarded a magic crystal. Well, a Shawnee medicine man came down here looking for that crystal. They claimed that he found the crystal and killed Uktena down in North Georgia on King's Mountain.

Up on top of that mountain, there is a stone wall all around the mountain, but on the back, it is a sheer rock cliff. Well, the Shawnee lured that snake up to the wall that he had built. He had oil about every eight or ten feet in a big pit, and he set that oil on fire once the snake got inside the wall. [The snake] couldn't go down the back side because of the cliff. It couldn't get out. The snake eventually tried to get out, and the Shawnee warrior doused him with oil and lit him on fire. The snake rolled down the mountain and killed itself. He went and got the crystal. It was a clear crystal with a bloodred streak in it.

When they excavated Tellico Plains in Tennessee before the TVA [Tennessee Valley Authority] flooded that valley, we were able to go in and do archeological digs on all the old grave sites. They found that old crystal over there.

In the old stories, when the doctors were using that, they had to feed it fresh blood. That's what the crystal required. There's a prayer, or what we call a formula, to put the crystal to sleep when you're not using it. To put it to sleep, you wrap it in complete deerskin and bury it. When you want to wake it up, you go get it, take it through another ceremony, and feed it fresh blood. When they excavated Tanasi Village over there, they found the crystal. It had been wrapped in a deer skin and buried. When they got it back out and started handling it, it cut someone and got blood all over it. So, it got the fresh blood it needed to wake up. I think it is at McClung Museum over in Knoxville. A lot of the artifacts that they excavated are over there. Things like that, that have just been looked at as myths from the past, once in a while, they are confirmed through archeology and science. A lot of what we talk about and the stories we tell are backed up through scientific evidence and archeology.

The power of a crystal a lot of times is to reckon with the past or to tell the future. A lot of times, it's used to see what's going to happen in the future. Sometimes, it can shed light on how we can use the past as a lesson to make the future better. I think that has been our salvation—that attitude of looking to the past, no matter what has happened, as a lesson and not really holding a grudge.

Some Miscellany

We had a Day of Absolution a while ago where everything was forgiven. Once a year, the day before the Green Corn Dance, everybody was forgiven, and we started fresh. There was a lot of thinking like that to maintain balance. That kept feuding and fighting out of the tribe. We like to settle arguments with a ball game, a stickball game. That was the little brother of war. If you ever play, it's like a war with sticks. I'm getting too old and slow to play anymore, but it used to be a lot of fun.

I get most of my stories from different people whom I have talked to here in the village. My grandfather, my mother's father, told me a lot of stories. We lived with them until I was ten years old, and I was always out in the woods with him or on a creek bank. Later in life, he became a Baptist preacher, but most of his life, he made moonshine. He was half Cherokee and half Chippewa. His mother was from Wisconsin. She was a Chippewa and met his father at Carlisle, [which is] up in Pennsylvania. Used to, if you wanted more than an eighth-grade education, you had to go to Carlisle or Dartmouth, or someplace like that. They had hooked up at Carlisle, so we're part Chippewa.

Spear Finger

One of the most popular stories in our culture is about Spear Finger. She was an evil deity who roamed these mountains. She could shape-shift. Some people called her Stone Coat. She had the ability to move boulders with her mind. Her heart was in her hand. When we would attack her, she had almost like a force field around her. Our weapons wouldn't penetrate her coat. That's why they called her Stone Coat.

She loved to eat the livers of children. She would disguise herself as an old lady, and when children were around, she would beg them to come help her. When they would get close enough, she had a big fingernail on one of her fingers that she would use to stab them and steal their livers. I've heard stories that she wouldn't kill the child, but they would turn into almost like a zombie.

One night, she was dancing around her fire and bragging that if only the Cherokee knew where her heart was, we would be able to kill her. The chickadee [a truth-telling bird in the Cherokee culture] heard her and came and told us what he heard. So, the next time we encountered Spear Finger, one of the warriors shot her in the hand and killed her. They threw her into a pit and burned her to get rid of her body.

They claim a lot of the medicine songs came from that fire when she was being burned. Over around Looking Glass Mountain and Brevard, around over there is where she used to hang out. They claim that she is the one who moved those boulders around into place on some of those mountains up there.

Lloyd Arneach

As a professional Cherokee storyteller, Lloyd Arneach performed throughout the state of Georgia and beyond, from the Kennedy Center to the High Museum of Art in Atlanta. Arneach's interview includes a few wonderful examples of the Cherokee-storytelling tradition but is primarily a very in-depth treatise on the life of a storyteller and the role of storytelling within the Cherokee community and beyond.

There's a Story in Your Heart

In a story that I write down, the words are going to be the same every time. When I tell aloud that same story, my words may change as I tell it. It may just be a simple one- or two-word change. Even though I've read it on paper many times, the actual telling is a little different each time. Every teller will add. Even though it's their story, it will change. This also depends on the audience. The more experienced tellers may find out that certain words evoke more feelings from an audience than other words. I know I do in one of the stories I tell. If I share that particular story, I have to be aware of the audience. If I say, "She was gathering food to share with her man," some of these audiences take offense at that. They really get upset because I said, "Her man," but if I change it to say, "She was gathering food to share with her husband," it's more acceptable. I have to be aware of the audience enough to know when a group may be upset with this or that. Even though they wanted me to come and share my stories, I have to tell them in a certain way to keep from offending someone.

Lloyd Arneach

I have to take a very quick reading on the crowd at the very beginning. None of my programs say what stories I will be telling, so I may have a person that says, "I would like to have a specific story," and I can do that story. I have no preset program prior to walking on to the stage. Not all storytellers do this, but I find this is better. I may have a group of stories I want to share with an audience, but when I get there, I realize that this is not where their interests lie, so I'm not able to keep their attention with those types of stories. I change my program, and they never realize that I've changed the stories that I planned to share with them.

I have some [storyteller] friends who are very rigid. They have a schedule that they will work on for days before their program, and I always wonder how they feel when the audience didn't respond to those stories. They had a preset notion that was "This is what I'm going to share regardless of what they think, and this is what I'm going to work on." Even though they find that the audience doesn't respond to it, they continue on with their program because they are not prepared for that aspect. That's how they feel comfortable onstage. They're familiar with that, and it works for them. I ask people to use what works for them. If you're comfortable with the schedule you have, use it. If you're able to change and select a different type of story, go with that. The main thing is that when you get onstage, you have to feel comfortable.

I have stories that will interest certain people; I can be sharing about Sequoyah or the Trail of Tears, and when I have a certain group of kids, I may try to make it more interesting. If I'm storytelling to third graders, they will get bits and parts of it that are funny, but they're just like, "Okay, what's the next story?" They're already waiting for the next story. Those in high school who are studying US history may find it interesting how the Cherokee written language came to be, and if I'm telling them about the museum, they're very interested in that. Even if it's a good story, it depends on the audience and whether or not it's going to hold their interest. A lot of people say a story has to have a beginning, middle, and an end, but some of my stories just stop and leave the people finishing the story in their mind. I don't have many of those that don't have a recognized ending, so I kind of step out of the norm as far as storytelling goes. I find whatever works for me and leave them wanting more. I always want to leave an audience wanting more rather than having them think, "When is he going to shut up?"

A person who can hold interest makes a good storyteller. If they can take the dullest story in the world and make it interesting to people, that's a good storyteller. Several years ago, I heard of a storyteller who took a good traditional story, but he made it hilarious and interesting for these kids with an updated version. I've tried to get hold of this fella and say, "You need to get these down on CDs or some kind of media that we can share with other people because it's hilarious!" He did it right off the top of his head; I couldn't begin to make that right off the top of my head. I can make a story up, but I couldn't use the words that he did right off the top of my head because I don't know the vocabulary. It's just an individual that can hold your attention that makes a good storyteller, regardless of the story.

The Cherokee traditionally did not tell stories until after the harvest had ended. We did not tell stories after we put the plants in the ground in the spring because we felt that if you started telling stories while the plants were growing, they would start listening to you, and they would forget to grow. In the harvest time, you would have virtually no harvest to take. We would tell the stories after the harvest had been gathered. During the winter months is basically when we'd tell the stories. We would do this at night; they would sit around fires or fireplaces in the cabins. The dad may be doing some wood carving or making a new tool, and the mother may be doing some beadwork or working with leather, and they'd just start telling stories. They had what they called family stories—stories that the family had heard and had been passed down but that were never told in public, not because it's forbidden or anything, but just because none of the family would go out and tell stories in the public. When those who are telling the stories pass away, if the younger people didn't keep that going, the stories were gone.

I know a number of families that had traditional stories. The kids can only remember bits and pieces of the stories, but they don't remember the entire story. That is a shame because there are so many unique stories that have been lost simply because this tradition has not been continued. Now, we have video and Xbox, and we have powerful and very digital phones.

There are tellers that use a lot of music in their stories. They may use a dulcimer in telling a story about a lady who was always depressed and was walking through the forest. *Suddenly she heard this music, and she followed it. She found this old man sitting on the porch of his cabin playing a dulcimer and singing. There was no one around; he was just doing it for his own pleasure. She sat in the yard and listened to him and asked him if he could teach her how to play. She started coming over on a regular basis. Finally, she was telling her own stories and singing her own songs, and it sounded like this*, and then the teller would put the dulcimer up on their lap and start playing and singing with the dulcimer.

There are so many ways to use musical instruments. I use one in one of the stories I have been working on, but I still do not feel like I'm accomplished enough yet. It's about Little People, much like the leprechauns of Ireland. The adults can hear them, but they can't see them. Young people can see them and hear them. It was said that if you went into the forest, you could hear singing and drumming in the forest ahead of you. If it was an adult going into the forest, as they got closer, suddenly the music stopped, and if the adult kept walking, he would hear it start up behind him. He realized he had heard the Little People singing and dancing. They stopped when he got close, and they wouldn't let the adults see them. You would just keep walking because you would know what happened. It was said that if you pleased the Little People, they would play their flute for you.

Listening for the Little People

One young man decided he was going to do a good deed. He would get the Little People to play their flute for him. So, he helped a neighbor bring in the harvest, and when he finished, he went into the forest, waited, and built a fire. He said, "Maybe that deed wasn't big enough." So, he started going and helping more and more people, and when he finished, he would always go into the forest, build a fire, sit down, and wait while listening for the Little People. He did this for years, and people knew that if you needed help, all you had to do was send for him, and he would come and help you. Each time he finished helping someone, he would go into the forest, sit, and wait for the Little People.

One cold winter day he was going into the forest, and he heard children screaming in the forest ahead of him; he started running through the forest. He came to the edge of a large river, and he looked up the river. There on the bank were kids running down the bank, pointing to the water. He saw there in the ice that a small boy was floating down the river, and he was just going under again. The man went down to the edge of the bank and broke the ice and waded out until he was chest-deep. As the young boy came by, he grabbed him, picked him up, and held him to his chest, and struggled back to the bottom of the bank and told the children standing at the top to go get robes and make a fire as he struggled up the bank with the boy.

By the time he got to the top of the bank, the children had a fire started and others had gone to get robes. He held the young boy up; he was conscious, but he couldn't stand on his own. He held him up and started walking with him around the fire in one direction to warm that side, and then he would turn and walk the other way to warm the other side of him.

Then, suddenly, warriors appeared out of the forest. They grabbed the young boy from him and put robes over the young boy's shoulders. They built a second fire and started working with the young boy between the two fires. The young man went over and sat down on a log. Finally, the young boy was able to stand up on his own, and when he did, a warrior came over to the young man. The young man stood up, and the warrior said, "He is my only child. You have given me my life back. Wherever my lodge fire burns, there will be a place for you."

The young man knew the warrior had given him the greatest honor he could—he made him a member of his family. The warrior said, "Come and spend this night in my lodge," and the young man said, "No, I will stay here." The warrior told him, "There are robes, and there is food. Take what you will."

Finally, the warriors and the children disappeared back into the woods. Night had fallen, and the young man sat there beside the fire. He heard the winds as they brushed through the treetops, and he

*heard the call of a distant owl as he began to search for food. Then he
heard the flute of the Little People.*

The young man was trying to do good deeds, but he stopped
thinking about what his reward would be and went out and
helped someone with no thought for himself.

The Little People would say, "Now you have done a good
deed, and we will play for you." That's when I would play the
flute. That's the story, but I have never gotten confident enough
on the flute to play that in public yet. That is the story that I
really want to share because it brings out that you shouldn't do
good deeds for yourself. You should do good deeds for other
people. When you do good deeds with no thought of yourself,
that's when you really get rewarded. It is good deeds without
any kind of benefit to yourself that are the best—just you doing
something good.

There is a difference between acting on the stage and storytelling. I can always tell when someone has had acting train-
ing first and then gone into storytelling. It's difficult for them
to make that transition because so many things change in the
storytelling venue. I've known those who have gone from storytelling to acting, and that's an easier transition because what
you do is expand on what you already do as a storyteller. If you
come from the acting field to storytelling, you have to learn to
tone it down. You never turn your back on an audience as an
actor, but in storytelling, some of the stories require that you
do turn your back on the audience. So right away, you're going
against what an actor is trained to do. Some people say they
have trouble doing that. In storytelling, it's a part of the story.

With storytelling, the ego is very fragile because you're up
there onstage by yourself. There is no one to lean on, no one to
tell you what line comes next, and there's no one you can turn
to onstage. You're totally alone on the stage, and you have to be
able to deal with it. There are a lot of little techniques you can
learn about dealing with that situation. I've got a basic story-

telling technique, and if you use this and have an open mind, I can take someone who has never done public speaking of any kind, and in twenty minutes, I can have them telling a story off the top of their head. I can tell them, "I want you to include these four, five, or six elements in that story," and they will do it without stuttering. It's just amazing. I'd like to say that I came up with it, but I didn't. For a storytelling group, the main thing is to have an enjoyment for stories. Whether you're scared of the stage or not, that shouldn't be related to it. If you enjoy being onstage, that's a plus already, but if you enjoy the stories and you think you would like to do storytelling, that's the attitude you want for someone coming in. It may be someone who enjoyed being the class clown. That's wonderful because you're already over the fear of being in front of people. There are a wide variety of attitudes that will come into this group, and it's nurturing.

In Atlanta, they have one of the largest storytelling groups in the Southeast. It's called the Southern Order of Storytellers, and it's so large that they are divided into what they call cluster groups. They meet at different times and different days all around Atlanta because the group is so huge. I think they have some members near Dahlonega. We have group members here in Asheville. I used to be the president of that group.

If you want to make a storytelling group in your acting class, you could contact some of these groups, tell them what you're doing, and ask them if someone would be able to come and give you some basic guidelines for getting the group started. That would be the biggest asset. The drama coach would be an excellent person to have over for this group, but to have a storyteller come would be great because there are certain things that you can do as a storyteller that you don't want to do as an actor.

Everybody has a story. You may not realize it, but everybody has a story to tell—and not just one story, a number of stories. I met a young girl who was a Cree Indian from Canada. I was talking to a group of people, and I turned to her and asked if she knew any of the old legends or stories of her people, and she said she didn't know them. She didn't have any stories to tell. I thought for a moment, and I said, "What is your most memorable experience?" She said, "Well, some friends and I were coming back from the settlement." She lived in Canada at the time. She said to her friends, "Let's go to the top of the ridge and see if we can see any moose in the lake on the other side."

So, they went up to the top of the ridge, and as they sat there looking at this huge lake, over on the far side they saw a moose walk out of the forest. It waded out into the water and slowly started swimming across the lake. The sun was setting on the far side of the lake, and she said it looked like the moose was swimming into the setting sun. We were all quiet for a while, and then I said, "You have stories to tell, but you don't realize it." One of the teenage boys in the group, with his eyes wide, said, "I've only seen a moose in a picture, and you saw one swimming into the setting sun." I was just so pleased that everything had come together. Anything you hear about, what happened that Saturday night or what you did over the summer, if you tell someone about it, you're a storyteller.

I had never really thought about it, but when I was young, I had two uncles who were great storytellers. We would have family gatherings, and my uncle George would tell a story, and then Uncle Dave would tell a story. They would go back and forth. There were a lot of stories. It was like a tennis match; one would tell a story, then the other would tell a story. I didn't realize it, but I was learning the old stories of my people. I never thought anything about it; I never tell any of those stories.

We had a lady come in from Alabama—she became the librarian here at the high school—and she realized the young Cherokee were not learning the old stories of our people. She got about six or eight of us together, and she had us learn a story well enough for us to tell it. Usually, one Saturday of the winter months, we would go out to youth groups and churches, and we would each share a story. Afterwards, we would meet the people there. She just wanted us to tell the stories and meet people off of the reservation. I enjoyed that, but I never told anything until 1970. I was working at a computer programmer place. My babysitter had a Girl Scout troop, and she couldn't find a book on Indians in the entire county library system. This was in Georgia. She said, "Wait a minute, I babysit for an Indian!" She called me up and asked me if I could help her. She told me the requirements, and I said, "Sure, I can do that. I will just have to come straight from work. Is that going to be a problem? I won't have time to change." She said it was no problem at all.

I went straight from work and went into the house. They were having a meeting in her basement. As I sat down, I heard one of the girls say, "The Indian's going to be here soon. I just don't know what he's going to look like." I was wearing a three-piece suit, and when I got up to tell my story, you could hear the jaws hitting the floor. When the meeting was over, Mrs. West [my babysitter] told other scout leaders in the county about me because they all had the same problem. They couldn't find books on Indians, so she used me as a resource. I started getting calls at night, and I started going to Girl Scout and Boy Scout meetings. Museums and schools started calling, and then universities started calling. All the people from the museums and universities heard about me purely from word of mouth; I didn't do any advertising whatsoever. There were people who heard about me from people who had heard me tell stories. I told stories at Emory University, Georgia Tech, Georgia State, the High Museum of Art in Atlanta, the Carter Presidential Center, and the Martin Luther King Center.

Then I got a call from a student at Georgia State. She had an assignment to record stories from the original tellers. She asked if she could come and record some of my stories, and I said, "Well, if you want some original tellers, you're going to need to go back and talk to our elders on the Reservation." She said, "No, no. You're fine. I could record yours." So, she came and recorded stories from me. I didn't think anything of it. The night came in the '80s that I got a call from Dr. John Burrison at Georgia State. He said, "I teach the folklore class here at Georgia State, and one of our students recorded you back in 1971. We have been using those recordings as resource material in my class. I'm going to gather all of these stories and put them in a book, and I'm asking all the tellers if they would be willing to come in for a book signing." I said, "Sure, I'd be delighted; just let me know." I didn't think anything about it.

In November of 1988, we discovered that my wife, Charlotte, had a terminal brain tumor. No one had lasted more than twenty-four months with that diagnosis. She was totally bedridden. She couldn't feed herself; she couldn't walk. She did still have her mental capabilities, and she was able to communicate with no problem. My son and I, along with my father-in-law, had her at home. There was someone twenty-four hours a day that would sit in the room with her. We had a nurse that would come by once a week that would check on her condition and report back to the doctors. The doctors would tell us, "All right now, this is what's going to start happening."

Dr. Burrison called me back in the spring of 1989 and he said, "We're going to do a book signing in September. Would you be able to come?" I said, "Well, let me ask Charlotte." So, I talked to her and she said, "Oh yeah, go ahead. You need to get out of the house. Tell him you'll go." I called him back and told him that I was going to be there. Charlotte passed away at the end of August in 1989, and I went to the book signing in September. I did everything I could to fill my time. While I was taking a break from the book signing, a lady came up to me and said, "I'm Betty Ann Wylie. I'm a member of the Southern Order of Storytellers. We have a storytelling festival in January. Would you be willing to come and share your stories with us?" I said that I would. So, in January, I started telling stories. Until that time, I had been sharing Cherokee culture and history. In January of 1990, I started storytelling. In 1993, I moved back to the reservation and became a full-time storyteller. Shortly afterward, I moved back here. I literally backed into telling Cherokee stories and history, and if I hadn't been doing that, I wouldn't have backed into storytelling.

I never thought about making storytelling a career; I didn't even realize that you could do that. Suddenly, bam! Everything was right there. My only regret is that Charlotte didn't get to see where storytelling has taken me. I was a very introverted individual. When there was a party, I would grab a chair, sit in the corner, and be happy watching all these people do different things. Charlotte was always the center of attention. She was always easygoing; people loved her. She had wonderful friends, and she taught me to enjoy people. People are a lot of fun, but . . . to find out, you have to talk to them. So, I learned to talk to people. By the time I started speaking about the history and culture, I was very comfortable being in front of a group, and I had twenty years of experiencing that before moving into storytelling. Storytelling has taken me places that I never thought I would go, and I have never thought of going. That was how I got into storytelling.

After one event, I was talking to a lady, and we had basically gotten into storytelling about the same time. She was part of the center for storytellers. I was saying, "You know, I couldn't get this one person to pay attention to the story." She said, "Lloyd, if you have a hundred people in the room, and one of them is not paying attention, and the other ninety-nine are hanging on every word, share with the ninety-nine, and don't worry about that one. They will come around." So, I started doing that. Then people told me that you have to have an audience respond. If they don't respond, they either like it or they don't. That's a response. If you don't pay attention to them, you will not be asked back because you have to keep their interest one way or another.

A number of people have contributed to where I am today. I also learned from my own mistakes by the school of hard knocks. There was no storytelling school that you could go to back then. There were people sitting and listening to you and advising you, but these were other storytellers. It was a long and rocky road, but fortunately, I had the experience with the Cherokee culture and history. I made a tremendous amount of mistakes. I started refining my storytelling over the years from different people sharing with me.

I find people are interested in Native American stories, so I am pigeon-holed. I have a lot of stories that are not Native American stories. The audience will say, "Well, we don't hear a lot of Native American stories from Native Americans." So, I say, "Yeah, okay. I'll share those, but I have all these other stories, if you want to hear them." It has been the love of my culture and other people's cultures that has taught me tolerance. There are people that don't know about Indians and have eighteenth-century ideas about Indians riding horseback, hunting game, and living in tepees. I used to let that bother me quite a bit, but it was simply out of ignorance.

I go back to how I was raised. We would have a meeting, and everyone was allowed to speak. There wasn't anyone that didn't want to speak in the meeting, and no one would shut them down or shout at them. No one would get up and walk out, because that was being disrespectful. You knew that everyone had their own rightful opinion. They were able to say what they wanted, whether you agreed with it or not.

With storytelling, I enjoy getting up and sharing the stories, sharing the culture, the way we used to live, and bits and pieces of the story. I don't do it all at once because if you want a piece of candy, I don't want to give you the whole bar. If I give you a little bit here and there, you appreciate that one little bit. It means more. So, through the course of the program, I will sprinkle in little bits of things, like how my people never lived in cabins. We made cabins, but we built them a little bit differently. We put logs vertically into the ground, put mud on the inside and on the outside. These homes were very cool during the summer and very warm during the winter. Then I would move on with the story. I spent less than two minutes sharing a little bit of our history, and [listeners] would walk away with that information in between stories.

I would tell them, "We used to have elk and buffalo in the mountains of Western North Carolina." A strange note on that would be that the buffalo was the largest animal that the Cherokee had. I couldn't find stories about the buffalo. We also had elk here in the mountains, and I have found stories about elk. The Cherokee don't have a word for elk, so they called the elk a big deer. If you think about it, elk are larger versions of the deer.

There are a lot of things we don't have names for. We don't have a word for plane. I was talking to an elder and asked, "How would you describe a plane to another Cherokee?" He said, "That would be a canoe that flies." I said, "Okay, what about a submarine?" He said, "That would be a canoe that sinks." I asked, "What about a television?" He said, "That would be a stump that talks." There are a lot of things in our culture that does not translate into English, but through storytelling, I can share that part of our culture.

It's a gradual process. I don't jump into some of the more intense things at first. I do the stories to judge what kind of audience I have. My culture has had an influence on storytelling, the way I share them and where I share them. I tell people that I'm not a traditional storyteller because I would tell stories at the drop of a hat, as you have discovered in this conversation.

I enjoy telling stories that have a moral. Sometimes I will point out how a lesson is carried throughout that story. Without pointing it out, you would not think of it; you wouldn't connect the dots in the story. When I bring out that this is one of the lessons in the story, the audience can connect the dots for themselves. Those stories I enjoy.

The stories that tell of how much nature means to us are some of my favorites as well. All the living creatures, the trees, and the shrubs are our brothers and sisters. Before a Cherokee hunter would cut a tree down, they would ask for the forgiveness of the tree because they were going to kill a living thing. Before they would kill a deer, they would ask for the forgiveness of the deer because they were going to kill a brother or sister. He would then bring the body home. He would use all parts of the body, and nothing would be thrown away. In doing this, he honors the life that had been given up so that he might live. This aspect of our culture is something I like to bring out in the stories, and I like to do it on a gradual basis.

A specific story that I enjoying telling the most is the one I tell the least. It's Chief Joseph and the Flight of the Nez Perce. It's about trying to get to Canada for freedom. That affects me more than any story I tell, and I don't know why. I have never been able to understand. I heard his story as a teenager, and now I'm able to go out and share the story. But, I need a special audience. I need an audience that when I talk about a hawk soaring over the valley and then floating across to the next ridge, sees that hawk as I'm talking about it. Those audiences have made a connection. I will start to share kids' stories, and I will finish with Chief Joseph. I need about forty-five minutes to prepare that audience with a different series of stories and also my emotions with each story because it brings up very, very deep meanings within me. I also like sharing the Trail of Tears, and the story of Junaluska, and the story of Wounded Knee and what happened there. Chief Joseph is my favorite to tell, but the circumstances have not always come together, I guess. I have told that story in the past twenty years fewer than thirty times.

I have to primarily understand that not everybody is going to appreciate the stories that I share, and there are some that have been resentful towards the Indians. They feel like the Indians have gotten handouts from the government and have lived on it for years. They come in with a chip on their shoulder. I'm just an Indian who enjoys telling stories; I'm not here to have a political agenda or a political platform. I'm just here sharing stories as a Native American. It's important to understand that it's not personal because they don't know me. It's about what I stand for. The objective is that I can't let that bother me. It doesn't happen very often, but it happens enough. I would like to say it only happens a few times, but it still happens every year. I don't let that bother me.

That's been one of the most difficult things to do—to not take the things that they're saying personally. I have been called names, but as I said, they don't know me. They're, for whatever reason, wanting to beat me down or degrade me, and that's not going to happen. My self-esteem is not based on another person's opinion of me. I carry my own opinion of myself. Some people say, "If you can't wear your traditional clothes, your self-esteem must be very low!" And I say, "No, I love wearing traditional clothes." But if I can't wear them, it doesn't take down my self-esteem. It is contained within me, and I carry it with me everywhere. I don't beat people over the head with my culture. If they want to learn, I will be glad to share, but if they don't want to learn, that's fine also. There's no problem either way.

I enjoy the questions people ask, and I love getting to sit and talk with people. I feel they may never meet another Native American in their life. I try to present them with an image of myself that they will always remember, no matter what type of environment I'm in. I am always aware of the image that I am projecting and the image that they will take away from me.

It is fine to get up onstage and share stories. For too many people, young people especially, getting up onstage in front of people is nerve-racking. For example, when they're doing a book report in front of the class, they are like, "Oh my gosh," only to find out that it is a lot of fun when you get up onstage. One of the things I try to teach when I do my storytelling classes is that if you make a mistake, don't try to hide it. The audience will be aware that you are trying to hide the mistake. They will become embarrassed for you, and you'll lose that moment. When I make a mistake, like when I lead into the introduction of the wrong story, I say, "Sorry, I got carried away, listening to my-self! I started the wrong story." Then I start again. Admit that you made a mistake, instead of trying to correct it after the fact. You can tell that the tempo's changed, the cadence has changed, the rhythm has changed, and it's broken. They realize some-thing is wrong. Share with the audience—that's what you're there for. You will find out that you become more relaxed.

I have had instances where I forgot to turn my cell phone off and someone called me right in the middle of storytelling. I said, "I am so sorry; we didn't have this problem in the old days!" The crowd just started laughing. Again, that's a stupid mistake that I made. I would ask them to turn their cell phones off, but I totally forgot about mine. That was a mistake on my part that should have never happened, but it did. That was how I handled it—the audience was like, "Okay, he made a mistake, and he shared it with us." Then we continued.

Storytelling is so much fun. That's what I want to give to the younger generation. If you have stories to tell, it's fun to get out there and share the story. We want more storytellers be-cause when people are sitting and listening to the story, they're learning to communicate. A storyteller communicates with the audience, and the audience communicates with their facial ex-pressions, their voices, and their sounds. They communicate with the storyteller. Storytelling is communication.

You can learn more about Lloyd Arneach by visiting www.arneach.com.

Don Patterson

By the mid-1980s, Foxfire had blossomed into a world-renowned program for teaching and learning, and as such, it attracted a number of scholars and educators from a variety of disciplines. Along with its strong focus on educational pedagogy, Foxfire was also coming into its own as a program steeped in the study of American folklore. This discipline-centric approach attracted folklorist Barbara R. Duncan, who also headed up Foxfire's North Carolina Teachers' Network, headquartered at Western Carolina University.

During those years, Barbara contributed her knowledge as a folklorist to a number of the students' articles in *The Foxfire Magazine* and served as a consultant and editor on a few of the *Foxfire* books, most notably *Foxfire 10*. It was at this time in Foxfire's history that a group of students interviewed Don Patterson, who was born in the Burton Community prior to its being flooded to create Lake Burton in 1919. Don was raised in Rabun County around Tallulah River on what was known as Bullard Mountain and came to learn a great many stories, primarily those focused on the supernatural and on witches.

A portion of this interview was featured in *Foxfire 10*, which contains a significant section on the Lake Burton project and a good deal of the folklore surrounding that community both before and after the creation of the lake. Don was an amazing storyteller and really captured the imagination of our students. This interview contains a great deal of local legends and anecdotes from this area and, as an added bonus, also features some insightful commentary from Barbara Duncan, which is the italicized text found throughout the article.

Stories from Burton

I was born at Burton. Richard and Rebecca Patterson were my parents. They mostly farmed. I had two sisters and five brothers, but one died when he was a baby. [My brothers were] Will, John, Lamar, Jesse, and Ralph. I was the next-to-the-last one to be born. [My sisters were] Della and Dollye Mae.

Clayton didn't even exist at that time. The town of Burton was just a general store and a post office, and they had a place where they built caskets. You know, back then they built their caskets. They go in there, slap them in there, and slap them in the ground.

The Derricks, the Philyaws, the Englishes, the Fradys, the Lovells, and all that bunch lived in that vicinity. That's about all there was over there.

Back in those days, see, witches came from England. You know the story on what happened in England. In those years, they burned them at the stake and [did other] things like that. There were some who escaped and came to the United States. [Hiley Bullard] got in with that bunch of people who came when my granddaddy and his folks came to the United States. They came as immigrants that come through [Ellis Island] where the Statue of Liberty is. They came through there, and then they came into the United States, and the government dispersed them out and everything. The government would sell sections of land to different people. That's how it all got started.

My granddaddy, Lee Frady, owned all of that [land] down in

there from Burton bridge and all that you see down in there was his fields. He told me Hiley Bullard and her daddy lived across Tallulah River from him on Bullard Mountain.

Back then it rained more that it does now. It had been raining for at least a week, and that river was level with the banks, and there were no bridges across it or anything. [So,] they had to ford the rivers then with wagons and things like that. [Hiley] crossed that river when it was level with the banks, and she'd come over to his house. She'd come over to his house to buy milk and eggs and stuff like that.

He said he [first found out that] she was a witch when she came up there, and it had been raining for over a week and the river was out of the banks. After a few minutes, she went on in to get her buttermilk. He [wondered] how in the world she came across that river. [And] when she came out, he said, "Hiley, how in the world did you come across that river?" She said, "Oh, I made me a horse." He just let it go at that.

The next day, after the river went down, he went down to look to see how bad it damaged his fields down in there. I believe it was Philyaw that [had land] joined to my granddaddy's land across that river. Well, [granddaddy] was checking his fields and this here Philyaw fellow was also checking his fields. They run into each other and got to talking. That fellow said to my granddaddy, "I got up this morning, and I was never in such a fix in my life." He said, "I want you to look at my hands." Granddaddy said he looked at his hands, and they looked like they'd been dragged across rocks and things. He said, "I feel just like I been rode to death." [And] that was who [Hiley] made a horse out of to come across that river. They know pretty well that's what took place.

Stories of witches "riding" someone, usually in a nightmare, appear in many European traditions and have been documented by David Hufford in The Terror That Comes in the Night.
Stories of witches spoiling cows' milk is common in Appalachian

*traditions, from New England through Pennsylvania Dutch country
and in the South. The belief is also common that if you give a witch
something, she (or he) has power over you.*

*The belief that giving a witch something gives him or her power
over you reflects the idea of transference: that a part can represent
the whole. (In poetry we call it metonymy.) This is common in Appalachian traditions of healing and witchcraft. In witchcraft beliefs, the
idea that if a witch has something of yours, he or she can act on that
object and those acts will affect you. This is a universal belief—from
ancient traditional beliefs in Africa (stereotyped as "voodoo dolls") to
modern "psychics" doing readings or finding lost persons by holding an
object that once was theirs.*

*Witches are also believed, in Appalachian tradition, to be able to
act on a person at a distance.*

Then one time his sow had ten pigs. They were nice. Hiley
seen 'em and told him, "I want two of those." He said, "Hiley,
I can't let you have them." Back then in the 1800s they had to
have stuff for their winter food. They couldn't just let it all go
like they do now and sell all their hogs and everything. He said,
"I got to keep them for my own meat to go through till next
year."

She said, "If you don't let me have them, they won't do you
any good." Sure enough, he said he went out the next morning,
and every one of those pigs were out running around the edge
of the pen with their backs bowed up. He said it went on for
several hours, and every one of them dropped dead. She killed
them all. See, she didn't have to be there [to kill them. However,] if he had let her have them two hogs, he never would have
had any meat. He could have went ahead and killed the ones he
kept and cured it and everything. It [would have] disappeared,
though. That's the way a witch operates. [For example], if you
ever let a witch have milk, just like I was telling you before, . . .
as long as they keep it sweet, they can get all your milk. You
can't get any milk. In other words, if they got something that

you let them have or sold it to them, as long as that's intact and good, they can clean your plow on other stuff. As long as you have it, they can clean you out.

Long down in years, Hiley died. She just died. When she died, all of the community around there, which was very few, would have nothing to do [with her]. She was laying there dead. All of them said, "No, you're not burying her in my graveyard." So, my granddaddy, he's like myself. He likes to try to help anybody and do anything for anybody else if he can. He said, "Well, we can't just let her lay there. I'll let 'em bury her in my cemetery." That's where she's buried now.

Special events are often remarked surrounding a witch's death and burial place.

I got a little story about what happened to her daddy. The Bullard place was up above the Burton bridge on Bullard Mountain. They had a house up there, she and her daddy.

My great-uncle bought land on up toward the upper end of Tallulah River, at the upper end of the lake. They were out one Sunday, about a week after Hiley had died. They got to talking, and they said, "I wonder how old man Bullard is doing since Hiley died. Let's just walk over to his house and see how he's comin' on."

They walked over there, and a couple of dogs were there, and chickens in the yard and everything. They hollered, and nobody answered. So, they went on up on the porch and knocked on the door. He said the door was standing open—that's right. The door was standing open, and they hollered and nobody answered. They got to looking around and said, "You reckon he died. Let's go in and check." So, they went in the house. All of his clothes were hanging there. Everything was intact. Nothing had been disturbed. They couldn't figure out where he was at. I'll tell you the reason why. Him and her were one and the same. He was her, or she was him.

[There were no] heirs, just her and her daddy supposedly. They never seen both of them at one time together, either. They could see him in the field or come by or something like that, but they never would see him with her.

I believe she was a witch. [By hearing] the things [that grand-daddy] told me she done, I know she was a witch.

People often connect witchcraft, and even some kinds of faith healing—removing warts and so on—with the persecution of witches in medieval Europe. Recent studies have shown that many of the "witches" burned at the stake were often herbalists, midwives, and faith healers whose methods were not approved by the powers that be of the time. In many instances, witches were wealthy widows whose property, on their conviction of witchcraft, became part of government or church property. During the Reformation (circa 1400–1600), many people were burned as witches because they were Catholic in a Protestant community or vice versa. Other, more radical theories suggest that belief in witches and witch persecutions may have been induced by village-wide ergot poisoning from moldy rye; or that witches' confessions or "rides" and "covens" were actually datura-induced hallucinations.

The fact remains that in many small communities in the country during the 1800s, from New England through Pennsylvania Dutch country to the South, an isolated individual (man or woman) was often held responsible for strange occurrences in a community or group or neighbors, including the spoiling of milk, the crying of babies, various kinds of sickness, and problems with crops and livestock. Motivation of these witches was usually considered to be jealousy or meanness.

Often, stories were told about these witches being able to take the shape of black cats, black dogs, or other creatures. The idea of a witch [taking the form of] another person is not as commonly found as the belief that the witch may appear in the form of an animal. This belief in "shape-shifting" has been common in European cultures, in Native American cultures, and around the world.

You see, back then it was natural for deer and bear and stuff to be in here. People hunted them for meat. Back then they did something that's against the law now. They hunted deer with dogs. [Now, if] they catch you dogging a deer, you're gone. The dogs would run 'em up on a high ridge and they'd shoot 'em. Anyway, one afternoon my great-uncle went hunting, and he [was] going to get him a deer. He went up to Devil's Race Pass to see about getting a deer.

He said his dogs struck one down in the cove over there, and he was up on the high ridge that they call Devil's Race Pass waiting on him. He had a muzzle-loader, and all of a sudden, this great big buck came right down toward him. He waited till he got pretty close, and then he threw that rifle up and BAM! He knowed he hit it right between the eyes, but it didn't run off. It just kicked up its heels and turned around and snorted like it was saying, "Come on, buddy, come on again."

He said he loaded that muzzle-loader again right quick and pulled down and BAM! He said he knew he hit it that time. He said it'd just kick up its heels and snort and wouldn't pay him any attention. Well, those people were up on things like witch stuff, and they knew silver would kill [a witch]. He reached in his pocket, took out a dime, like that, and said, "I'll get you." He just scraped that silver off that dime with his knife, put it down in the barrel, loaded it, throwed it up, and he said when he did, here's this man standing there saying, "You wouldn't shoot me, would you?" He didn't shoot him because he knew him. I believe I'd have shot him. He said, "I was just teasing with you." He said he knew he was a witch then.

Though considered dangerous and frightening, witches were fairly easily stopped by a variety of means known to individuals within any community. These means included special prayers using the "three highest names" (the Father, the Son, and the Holy Spirit); shooting with silver in various forms—a dime, or a specially made silver bullet; and the withholding of gifts.

Witches were often considered to have an inappropriate sense of humor.

There are three kinds of spirits. There are evil spirits, unrest spirits, and the Holy Spirit. The evil spirit will always appear to you in black. An unrest spirit will always appear in white. Then you know what the Holy Spirit is. Now, you can ask these spirits, if you encounter one, say, "In the name of the Father, the Son, and the Holy Spirit, what do you want?" The evil spirit will not answer you. It will leave and never return. It will not answer you. An unrest spirit will answer you. It will tell you what is keeping it from being at rest, and then it will leave and never return because it's out of its unrest then. That's your spirits. A lot of people don't believe in that kind of stuff, but it does exist. There could be a reason [why they appear], but I don't know why.

This here lady from Commerce, Georgia, was talking [to me]. It was around Halloween, I guess. I had a fuel company in Rabun County, and I carried this fuel out to her house. She lived up at Mountain City. She [was the one who] told me about the spirits. She said if you encounter something, if you'll ask what it wants, it will leave and never return.

She was telling me that when she was a little girl, her sister had a boyfriend. Back then you didn't go [on a date] unless you had chaperones with you, and he was coming to carry her to the church. He was in a well-to-do family and he had a surrey. It was a two-seated buggy with fringe around it. It had two big horses and a fancy harness, and he carried her sister and her to church. [She went as the chaperone.] Well, they started back— she said she was riding on the outside—and she just happened to look over and this here lady dressed in a wedding gown was walking along the side.

She said she punched her sister [in the side], and [her sister] looked over there, and she punched her boyfriend. He said, "Whoa," and said, "lady, you can get in back and ride if you like. We're going on down toward Commerce." [The lady] just stood there. He said, "Okay," and started the horse up, and she kept going along with them. He just took that whip and went, "Backoww!" and the horse let out. That thing stayed right to [near them]. He was running his horses to death, and [when] he slowed down, she stayed right there. Back then they didn't have bridges or nothing, so he stopped and let his horses drink. When he done that, this thing turned loose and walked straight down the [side of the] river. See, a spirit won't cross over water.

Now, when I was a kid, before my baby brother was born, we had this old Model-T Ford, and we turned off—now I seen this myself—and we passed this bank, and this white horse jumped off this bank right in front of us. My oldest brother, Will, was driving, and when he slammed his brakes on, he killed the motor.

I remember him saying, "Who in the world has a big white horse like that? I've never seen one around here." [None of us knew of one.] He had to get out to crank that thing, and [then he] got back in and turned the lights on, and they wouldn't shine out in front of him. He said, "What in the world is wrong with my lights?" He got out there, and you know sometimes they're not grounded good, the lights aren't, and I can remember him banging on the fender. They were burning, but they weren't shining. It was like there was a sheet in front of them.

He said, "They just don't shine. Well," he says, "I know the road's good, so I'll take it easy and go on down." I remember us taking off, and we went on down the hill, and the lights went "Whish!" Just like that and [they started] shining out just as pretty as you ever did see. Now, I seen that one myself. It was a spirit. I don't know what it was doing, but the lights wouldn't shine out [on the road].

Stories of ghosts have combined easily with technological develop-ments. For example, flight attendants and pilots tell stories of seeing ghosts on airliners, warning of impending disaster.

The last instance I know of is when some [folks] were over there fishing. They were right this side of the cemetery where the lake comes up here. The two wives were sitting over here on this bank, and the men had gone around on the other side away from their wives to a small hollow up there. All of a sudden, one of [the wives] started screaming like everything, and [the men] came running back and said, "What happened?"

One of the women was pregnant and she was sitting there. The other one was fishing, and she turned around and looked, and she said right up over the top of [the pregnant woman] was a huge black image, coming right down on her like this. When she screamed, it looked just like it went into her. So, Hiley may be walking around here since that baby's been born. It may be walking around here somewhere. Ain't that weird?

The idea of babies being marked by their mothers' experience is common; and the idea of spirits being reincarnated is found worldwide.

Now, Will's wife still lives over on the lake. Quite a few years ago, they were setting down there camping not too far from where this other took place. They'd done eat supper and everything. They'd done quit fishing and had a fire built up. All of a sudden, she heared something; all of them heared it. They seen this man dressed in a white shirt and everything walk right below where they were at. An unrest spirit will always appear in white.

My daddy built Dr. Childs a log cabin out there on the point. Dr. Childs was coming in one morning and said that when he came in—he had just passed the cemetery there—he hit something. BAM! Just like he'd run into a tree.

He said he knew he didn't run into a tree. He got out and looked and said he thought, "Somebody's cow's been laying in the road, and I've run [over] it." He got out there, and there wasn't nothing around, nothing. He said he drove on out to the house.

He come over to our house the next day. He had seen some things before. That was the reason he came over to our house. He asked my mother, "Do you believe in ghosts?"

My mother just laughed. She said, "Well, I've heard a lot of tales about them. I don't think they'd hurt you or anything like that."

He said, "Well, I experienced something last night that's got me kind of puzzled. I was sitting on my porch before this, and I seen a man. Twice I seen him come down below my house in those ivy bushes dressed and come across my walkway to my boathouse." He said, "I thought it was somebody hiding some whiskey or something. He came down below my house, started out on this side, come around the ridge like that, crossed my walkway between my boathouse and my house, and went out this way. That was the last I seen him. Then [I hit] this thing." He said, "I'm beginning to wonder about these spirit things. I didn't see it. It was like hitting a dead wall."

Seeing spirits going about their business, as though "hiding whiskey" makes older generations (and other cultures) seem to live closer to the spirit world than we do today.

I was dating this girl, Gerthy Thomson—Joe Thomson's sister—over at Clayton. She was staying with Roy Stevens who had a Chevrolet place, and I was dating her. I carried her to the movies.

Back then you walked. You didn't drive a car much, and it was one of those dark nights. I'm telling you, you couldn't see [a foot] in front of your face. I had carried her over to the walk-in theater [which was] over there above Reeves's before you got to where the Bank of Clayton was.

Anyway, I was coming back, and I was coming through Shady Side [in the] dark. I know I wasn't looking for no boogers or nothing, and all of a sudden, I run smack into something. "Kabam!" I knowed it wasn't a tree or nothing 'cause I was in the road. I said, "Woop!" and nobody says nothing, and I says, "Hey!" . . . nothing. Then I thought it was somebody's cow. I had some kitchen matches with me, and I struck one on the road. There wasn't nothing. I knowed they didn't run off, or I would have heard them run. I started peeling off. I told myself if I kept running, I was going to run myself to death. If you ever run into anything, don't run—you'll run yourself to death.

I walked on down to the Cannons that lived there, and they had a lamp on, and it was shining out. So, when I walked by, I looked back. There wasn't nothing. I never did encounter it again. I didn't see anything, but I sure did feel it.

When we left Rabun County, we bought a farm down between Toccoa and Clarkesville. We lived there a while, and all of a sudden, one Friday night, it was raining, and something walked up and knocked three times on the door. Then it'd knock three times again and three times again. It'd knock three times, three times [again], and then it wouldn't exist. We had a dog that'd eat the seat of your pants out, and it was just laying on the porch. It wasn't the dog scratching either, because it was on the door. This went on, and we noticed after a year that it had to be a-raining on a Friday night. So, for a couple of years we put up with that stuff of knocking on the door on rainy Friday nights.

One night, my older sister, younger brother, and myself were studying. My daddy was at work. He was a night watchman when they were building that road between Hollywood and Toccoa, and my mother said, "What do you say we sit up?" So, we all agreed we'd sit up till eleven o'clock.

It always happened at eleven o'clock at night. Of course, back on the farm like that, you go to bed with the chickens, but [the spirit rapping would] wake you up. I guess I must have been in fourth or fifth grade. [I was] young enough to get scared real good.

So, we just sat by the fireplace. I was back as far as I could get over. It came on getting up toward eleven o'clock, I looked at that big eight-day clock, and I got scared. It seemed like that thing said, "Zoom," just like that. I can remember seeing my mother and what she did when that thing knocked on that door. It knocked on that door, and she said, "Don't nobody say nothing." She eased up, and she went over to that door and she asked it, "In the name of the Father, the Son, and the Holy Spirit, what do you want?"

It only knocked one time. After that, it could be storming on Friday night and it'd never knock. I knew it was an evil spirit because it didn't answer her.

The idea of different kinds of spirits is common in folklore around the world. The power of the "three highest names" is believed in for healing and for dealing with witches and spirits throughout Appalachia and elsewhere in this country.

The "unrest spirit," as Don Patterson calls it, is found often in ghost stories in the Appalachians and elsewhere. These stories date back hundreds, if not thousands, of years in European traditions. When the returning ghost (or revenant) has his or her request fulfilled and appears no more, these ghosts (and their stories) are referred to by folklorists as the grateful dead. (From which the rock 'n' roll group took its name.)

This fellow lived almost up at the end of Persimmon, and the only corn mill they had was at Rocky Branch over there. He'd work on the farm all day, and down in the afternoon he'd take his corn to mill. He had to walk, you know. The road came down the river and then come out down by my granddaddy's house, and on down around over to Rocky Branch to what used to be the old highway. He'd go to the corn mill, and it always started when he came and crossed the branch. The first time, he heared something in the bushes above him. He said he turned around and looked and didn't see anything and kept walking. He said directly he heared something behind him, and he looked around. He said [it was a] large black dog. It was black—you know evil spirits always appear in black.

He said it was extremely large for a dog. At first, he thought it was a bear, but then he saw that it was a dog. It wasn't dark yet. He turned around and hollered at it, "Get out of here," or something like that. He said it just stood there. So, when he went on, the dog would stay a certain distance from him. It went on [like that] until he got down there to Acorn Creek. When he got to that creek and crossed it, this black dog turned and went up the creek. He went on around here to Rocky Branch to the mill, got his corn ground, came back, crossed Acorn Creek, and he heard something behind him. He looked back, and that black dog was behind him again. He said that every time he'd stop, it'd stop.

He went on around there past my granddaddy's house where this other little branch was. He said he turned around and told it, "Next time I come to mill, I'm gonna bring my gun and if you follow me, I'm gonna shoot you."

Next time he come to the mill, the thing did the same thing. He didn't shoot it as he went to the corn mill, but he told it right before he crossed Acorn Creek, "You follow me when I come back and I'll shoot you." He went on to the corn mill, and he come back, and it followed him almost right above my granddaddy's house.

So, the guy said [when he started back from the mill], "I told you that if you followed me again, I was going to shoot you." He just pulled out his gun and *Bang! Bang!* Twice.

[Granddaddy] says he heared a gun fire, and he wondered what all that was about, so he stepped off the porch and went out there. It was a little after dark then because [the guy had] done been to the mill and come back. Granddaddy said all he found was a sack of meal in there. He just picked it up and carried it down and set it on his porch.

Then the next day this guy that lived way up at Persimmon

came to the house, and [the guy] said, "Did you find a sack of meal that I dropped up there when I shot last night at that thing?"

Granddaddy said, "What thing?"

And the guy said, "That thing that's been following me." He said, "I shot at it. When I shot at it, balls of fire as big as a wash pot started making a big roaring sound around me just like this. I run—like to run myself to death. I run all the way and fell on my porch."

In most stories, the spirit or witch does not actually hurt the person who sees it. In stories from Appalachian communities in the 1800s, witches or evil spirits often appear as black dogs, black cats, and occasionally panthers or other animals who behave strangely. But panthers have their own folklore as well. If we wanted to find a scientific explanation for this story, our late-twentieth-century perspective on ecology might lead us to speculate whether one of the last wolves in the area was following the fellow who lived at the end of Persimmon for some company. Wolves, of course, have social behaviors that might seem strange and threatening to a lone nineteenth-century traveler. As for the roaring balls of fire big as wash pots—well, science can't explain everything.

Jesse Elliott was staying at our house over on the lake, and he was dating a girl over at Towns County. He had a Model-A Roadster. It was like a convertible. Well, one weekend he was coming back home—it took a long time because they were dirt roads back then—and he got about to Burton bridge and said just as he started onto the old bridge, he saw this big white horse coming. The bridge was narrow and you couldn't pass two cars on it, and it was going full blast. He pulled over and stopped, and he said he looked up at it, and there was a man on it with no head. It scared old Jesse to death, and talk about burning them roads up! He come in there and woke us all up. He said, "If you seen what I did, you'd be up in the air, too!" It was about two or three in the morning.

Way back years ago, a lot of people buried their people in their yard, but they passed a law that all people had to be moved to a certified cemetery [if they weren't already]. So, they got the orders from the government or whatever, and they were digging this grave that was out in that yard. They got down the casket, and the guy took the spade, and as soon as it touched the casket there was the bloodcurdling-est scream come out of that grave. Everybody left and run—that was in the morning part—and before they could even get anybody talked into finishing the job, it was late in the afternoon.

A recent article in the Journal of American Folklore *suggests that traditions of vampires in eastern Europe can be traced to the physical events that happen for scientifically explainable reasons when bodies are disinterred. Various stages of decomposition can result in noises and phenomena which could be interpreted as "the living dead."*

Grady Stonecypher got drowned over there below Burton bridge. They were making whiskey, so they quit the next morning, and they says, "Let's go down there to the lake and let's take us a bath."

Well, my mother was watching for them, and Grady parked his Model-A touring car in the yard. Him and my daddy and my uncle went down there, and they was going to jump in the lake and wash off. So, they took their clothes off—going skinny-dipping—and they jumped in the water. Grady dove into the lake off this rock, and my daddy and my uncle were already in the lake washing off. It was time, they figured, he should come back up, you know, [and so] my daddy dove around. It was pretty deep down in there, and he couldn't see nothing. So, they got out, put their clothes on, and started for the house.

In the meantime, my mother said she went to look out the window—said you could see way out yonder—and she said all of a sudden, she seen Grady walk up to his car. It looked like he got something out of the car, and she went back and started getting breakfast ready. She seen Grady [at his car, but] he was up at the lake up there drowning.

When they come in, she said, "Is Grady coming in?" and Daddy said, "I'm afraid not." When they found him, he had a hold of one of those bushes down there, and when they pulled him out, they pulled out the bush, too!

This McClure feller came up from Atlanta, and he was going to pay C. M., my first cousin, and me a dollar apiece—which was like a wagon wheel back then, or about a hundred dollars—to take him on a fishing trip. Well, I didn't know there was a graveyard down there at Burton, and there is an island there, you know, and he says, "Let's go to that one right there and fish." Anyway, we caught a bunch of fish. We fried fish and had the biggest time. Then we went to bed.

My first cousin was always trying to play tricks on me, and he was on my right and old McClure was on my left side. I had drifted off to sleep, and all of a sudden, this here blanket started going down off of us like someone was pulling it off of us, and I thought it was C. M. taking his foot and pushing it, trying to scare us. So, I reached down there and elbowed him and said, "What are you trying to do, scare us?" and he was done asleep. He said, "What are you doing hitting me like that?" [The blanket] had been pulled down to [our waists], you know. McClure was sleeping, and he was snoring. So, we pulled it back up, and C. M. said, "What do you mean the blanket was pulled down?" So, in a few minutes it goes down off us again and he accused me.

Then we woke McClure up, arguing. He said, "What's a-matter with you boys, scared?" I said, "No. Something keeps pulling the cover off." He said, "No, y'all are just imagining things." I told him to just pull that cover up there and see if it don't start coming off. In a few minutes it did. We pulled it back up and let it go. It went all the way down to the bushes from us, and I said, "You think my leg is long enough to push that blanket down that far?" and he said, "I'm getting out of here."

We got all the stuff together and got in the boat. He says, "Let's go across the lake." We went across the lake, built a big fire, and stayed awake the rest of the night. We had army blankets— they are made out of wool—you know. There may have been a magnetic field in that mountain there that pulled them off us. There wasn't no wind or nothing, though. The next day McClure says, "Let's go over there where we were last night." You can't really see anything now, but back then when they dug up those graves, they just left them open, but they've filled up since then. When we went back over there, we went over all those graves, and McClure started saying, "What is that? What is that? What is that?" We figured out what it was. It was those graves they didn't fill in. They just left them that way. He said, "No wonder we had such a hard time last night. We were sleepin' in a graveyard."

[Once] these two teachers, [who were sisters, lived there next to the school]. It was a two-room country school, and they had these woodstoves. They taught school, and they rented this big house up on the hill up there. [It was a] big two-story house, and one day one of the teachers told one of the boys, "How about you going out and getting some wood to bring in to put in the stove?"

He says, "Okay," goes out to get the wood, and when he happens to look up, there was this woman standing on the porch. He went back in there with the wood, and he told the teacher, "There's a lady standing on your porch." She thought at that time that it was a friend of hers and her sister's—a lady from up in Virginia. [The lady] had promised to come to spend a few days with them.

She told the class, "Y'all just go ahead and study, and I'll go up and get her settled in." So, she just went on up to the house, and she walked in and hollered the girl's name, and nobody answered. Nothing.

She wondered where in the world she went. She said, "Well, maybe she went on upstairs." She went up, and the stairway was built up, then a landing, and turned up left to the next set of stairs. She said she went upstairs and hollered her name and everything, and nobody, nothing answered. Said she came back down, and when she came down to the landing, she heard something behind her on the stairway. This woman was coming down the first flight down to the landing. It came on the landing and stopped. She didn't recognize her; she didn't know who she was. So, she just eased on down to the floor, down the last of the steps.

She said that she looked and seen the lady standing on the first flight of stairs, and she had just disappeared. She thought she was getting ill or something. So, she just went on down and told her sister about it. She said that night she was in bed grading papers. That old house didn't have doors to the bedrooms; it had drapes. She said she heard a rasping sound and looked up from grading papers. She looked and seen them curtains come open. [Well, in her room] they had what they called a quilt press. It's a shelf, and they pack the quilts on top of it. She said she seen the curtains come apart, and the woman walked in. It was the same woman. She knew it wasn't real because it walked by the quilt press, and she could see the quilts through it. She said it walked on over to the bed, and instead of sitting down and getting in the bed like a person, it floated up and was in the bed with her.

She said she tried to move and couldn't. She said, "I thought I was dreaming this," and she pinched herself. She pinched a blue place on her arm, trying to figure out if she was dreaming. She said that thing was like a block of ice against her. She said it may have stayed there five minutes, but it seemed like eternity. That's how she phrased it, "It seemed like an eternity."

She said that then it got up and got out of the bed and walked out the door. She said until it walked out the door, she couldn't move.

She said that another occasion, one night she was in the bed and had dozed off to sleep, and all of a sudden, the shutters on the windows were going BANG! BANG! BANG! She thought a storm must be coming up, so she got up, walked over to shut them, and there wasn't a breeze at all. She fastened them and went back and got on the bed, and they tore loose again. After she'd done fastened them, they went to flopping again.

Many ghost stories, whether true or not, include the elements of seeing a ghost return to their house. The experience of seeing (or hearing) a spirit in the room and then not being able to move for what seems like "an eternity" has been documented around the world. This experience is probably based on an unusual sleep state [now known as sleep paralysis] where one's conscious mind seems to wake while one's body stays in a sleeping state. Out of this state, which seems to have been experienced by about twenty percent of the population, have risen traditions of being "hag ridden," of nightmares, and of other interactions with the spirit world.

[My granddaddy] and this other feller had some whiskey they were making—back then the Tallulah River ran next to the road, and the store was on the other side of the road—[and they] walked across the road over there and was standing on the bank of the river. [Granddaddy] said there were old laurel bushes swaying in the river, and he was looking at that. All of a sudden, this man's leg and foot come up out of the water and went back down. So, he waited again until he seen it again [so he would know he wasn't seeing things], and in a few moments, here come that foot out of the water. He says, "I want you to look over at that old laurel bush and tell me what you see." So, he looked and up comes this foot again, you know, and he says, "My goodness, that's somebody's foot coming up out of there." So, they went across and told everybody, and they all come to see it.

Well, the river was pretty deep up there. It was up under your arms, and it was swift. So, what they did, there's a bridge coming down from Timpson way and the road joined into that, so they all went over there [to the store] and got a roll of plow line. They called it plow line back then. It was rope they used for plowing to guide the horses with. [Granddaddy] had a whole roll of it over in his store, so he just got it, and one of the fellers took one end of it, and he took it across the bridge, come back down and tied it to a tree over where the leg was coming up, and they stretched it across the river. Then two men got down in there and went across over there to pull him out, and when they pulled him out, he didn't have no head. His head was gone. Well, I asked [Granddaddy] what they did about it, and he said, "If they find somebody dead, back then, they buried him. They didn't have no big investigation or nothing like that." He didn't have a thing in his pockets to identify him, and so they just went up there and built a casket and buried him in Burton cemetery.

If somebody gets missing and gets killed or something, they'll always show up. Maybe it'll be ten years, but it will *always* turn up. Well, my brother was a heavy equipment operator, and back in the '50s, they started grading this road between here and Clayton. So, one afternoon he was right this side of Burton bridge making this big cut right before you get to the bridge, and he said [he saw] what he thought was the prettiest white rock he had ever seen. He just stopped the dozer, you know, and he said [to himself], "I'm going to take it with me." Well, when he picked it up, it was a man's skull.

They stopped work—all of them did, you know—and they called the sheriff out there. They asked him about where [my brother] picked it up at, [and he said], "Back there where it first rolled out at." They eased around, and they never found another bone at all. That was that man's head. They did have it at the jail for a long time.

My uncle helped dig up [Burton] cemetery. What they'd do was dig up those people and put them in new caskets. They said they dug up this one, and he had been dead for twenty years. The casket had done decayed, and he said there wasn't nothing in there. When they got to that, they knew that was the body.

So, they'd shovel it up and put it in the casket. This guy was over in there shoveling it up in there, and when he picked his shovel up, there was a gold chain hanging down. He reached and got it. It was a gold watch, and he said, "Oh, I found me a watch." There were guards that would stand there with guns to make sure everything was carried out right. He wound it up and it run, you know. Gold doesn't rust, so it had just run down, and the guard said, "Put it in the casket. You can't take it." [He did put it in the casket.]

Then there was this other lady that died, and back then they didn't embalm them or nothing. They just buried them. Back then they didn't have no undertakers. The neighbors would just go dress them, put them in a casket, and they'd bury 'em. My grandmother helped dress her. They'd bury 'em, at least, by the next day. You couldn't wait any length of time.

She said they had her laying up on a table—one of those big eating tables—and they was dressing her. Well, they got her ready, and my grandmother said she caught her up under the arms to lay her in the casket. She was sweating, and, well, a dead person don't sweat. So, they put her on in the casket after they had checked her out.

Then it had only been a little while [before] they dug the grave up. Well, for some crazy idea, when they started digging that grave up, the husband says, "When you dig my wife up, I want to see her just one more time." They says, "You can't do that." Well, he went to the State of Georgia and got a order from the governor so that he could open her up and look at her.

When they opened her up to look at her, it took three men to hold him. I mean he just went wild, and I reckon why is because his wife was laying on her face with both hands full of hair. She was in a coma, and when she come to in that grave, she pulled all of her hair out and turned over on her face.

Kimsey Hampton

We don't have much biographical information on Kimsey Hampton. We know that he was interviewed by his grandson, Foxfire student Tommy Lamb. Tommy noted that he had always looked forward to visiting his grandfather and that this interview took place around Christmas in 1976. According to Tommy, his grandfather loved to tell pranks and tales anytime he got the opportunity. "Every time I would visit him, he would keep all the family and everyone else amused with his stories about himself or his friends," Tommy wrote.

Here, we share some of Kimsey's anecdotes. Nearly every one takes on the formula of a jest or joke, with a punch line at the end. No doubt, these stories about his life and experiences were fixed in Kimsey's repertoire. He would have told these stories time and time again, but, as Tommy suggests, the stories were great entertainment to those who interacted with Kimsey.

A Clumsy Tale

My father was as awkward as he could be—he'd fall down in the middle of a public road. One time we was up on McClures Creek in North Carolina. Snow was about one inch deep on the ground, and the ground was frozen. We was snaking logs on the side of the mountain. We came to some kind of a flat. We got ready to turn down over the hill. We had a thing we called a jay grab. That was a grab with a long bar of iron; it had kind of a crook up on top of it that you could hook the spread in, and when the log started to run, you could pull the horse out the one side, and the spread hook'd come off of that, and the log'd go on. The horse could stay on the side of the road. We got right to th'top of the hill where I had to run the horse a little piece to outrun the logs to go on what they call a jay-hole. I stopped the horse, and m'daddy he had a peavey on his shoulder. He was cold anyhow, and blowin' his hands, with his arm up around the peavey handle. He come down where I was at and said, "What'd you stop for? Is the logs hung?"

I said, "No, I just stopped to let the horse rest before running into that jay-hole down there."

He said, "They must be hung." And he took the peavey off his shoulder, jumped at that log with that peavey, and the log was froze. He jumped full speed up on the log and rared back against the peavey handle, and the peavey hook plowed a little ditch around that log, and he looked around my way and grunted as he fell flat on his face.

Whok!

One time me an' my father was making molasses on an old cane mill with an' old horse a-pullin' it around an' around. [My father] built a kind of a hog pen of a-lookin' thing, and set the cane mill on top of it, and he left a spike stickin' up about three inches high, right at the side of his head where he fed the cane into the mill, and that sweep would come right over the top of his head as the horse came around. I told him he'd better bend that thing down or drive it down one. He said, "Do you think I don't know what I'm a-doing?"

Well, I'uz out there a little piece, and I heard a little racket say, "Whok!" And I looked around and that spike had caught him in the side of the head and just swept him around. He started to holler, "Whoa!" That's how come him to say "Whok!"

A Real 'Owler!

I was going down the railroad one night and there was an old store that set down below the road, a big old store. The windows were all broke out of it and there was nothing in it. There was a screech owl flew up on the railing right in front of me and I just tried to pick it up. It would fly on down the road five or six feet in front of me and I just kept trying to pick it up and every time I would bend over to get it, it would fly a little further. It flew off the railroad down in that store. I went down there and it was setting in the window and I tried to catch it. It flew inside that old store onto one of the counters. I walked in the door. The moon was shining in one of the windows. It was setting on the counter and I just decided I was gonna catch it. When I reached to get it, it went to crying just like a baby. You talk about somebody getting out of there in high gear! Brother, I got out of there. As far as I know, that owl is still there.

Ghost Steed

Me and my daddy was going up the railroad one time. We heard a horse a-running down the track. Sounded like it had hornets on it. My daddy and I got out of the way. We heard the horse pass us, but we never did see nothing. Whenever it passed, we struck matches to see if we could see the hoofprints and we couldn't find a one. There wasn't any tracks.

Ghost Lamp

My sister and her husband was going down the same place there, when they were going together. There was a light come up right in front of them. It just looked like a match had been struck and it stayed three hundred or four hundred yards ahead of them moving as they moved. Then it just disappeared. Lots of people seen and heard different things.

Ghost Bantam

My daddy was going up the road about eleven o'clock one night. He was coming home from preaching at church (he was a Baptist preacher), and a little old banny rooster got to fighting him on the britches leg. My daddy never did see nothing.

Ghost Baby

My daddy and four or five more went up there to a place above Burnett Siding, North Carolina, up above what they call Lake Logan now. We could hear a baby crying nearly any night we would go there. But you can't find out where it is at. You go hunting for it and it sounds like it is somewhere else. We hunted for it lots of times, but we never did find nothing.

Groundhog Huntin'

I had two brothers. We was all the time a-gettin' in a row over somethin' r'nother, didn't make no difference what it was, they'd quarrel. They went groundhog huntin' one time, and I went with 'em, and both of 'em would talk to me, but they wouldn't talk to each other. We got up on the side of a hill, and there was a groundhog hole went in under a rock. My brother that was named Sad, me and him was down there a-diggin' under the edge of the rock. The other brother named Jess (his name was Jesse Garner Staton Rhodes Patton Rhodes Curt McDonald San Moore Jake Moore—named hisself after seven preachers—he was about sixteen year old 'fore he had any name at all—before that they just called him Boy) took a mattock and went way up on the side of the hill above the rock. He started diggin'. Just doin' that for spite for Sad. Directly, Sad looked up there, looked back down, and dug a while, looked back up and said, "Jess, what are you a-doin' up there? There's a hog down here!"

We finally caught that groundhog under that rock, but up where Jess was digging, it would have taken three groundhogs to dig a hole that far up the mountain.

Don't Harass a Man about Being Married

One time in North Carolina, Suncrest Lumber Company had a railroad, went a way back in the mountains twenty or twenty-five miles. Had about five or six Shay engines, weighed seventy-two tons a piece. At that time, Salem Collins was the engineer and Hobert Rogers was a-firin'. Me an' my brother Mitch was a-settin' out on a carload of logs while we was goin' down the mountain. Paul Sims had just married about three, four days before then. My brother was ridin' back'erds, I was ridin' for'erds, and Paul was settin' a-straddle of the logs, and we was devilin' him about bein' married. As we went around a curve, the carload of logs turned over. We went off down in below the road, but we jumped fer enough so we went in below some trees, and the logs just poured in against them trees. I looked around at Paul Sims, and his mouth was wide open, his teeth just a-jumpin' up and down, just skeered to death. None of us got hurt, but it sort of taught us a lesson—we never did devil Paul no more *that* day about being married.

Fire-yer!

There was an old man up on Big East Fork was about eighty years old and used a walkin' stick all the time. They cleared up a new ground and had big old piles of brush piled up and it was real dry, and he told his wife he was goin' up on that hill and set one of those brush piles afire. She said, "You'd better not; if you do, you'll get the whole woods on fire."

He said, "I know what I'm a-doin'." He hobbled up there with the walkin' stick, set a pile on fire, wind got t'blowin'. It blowed the fire out into another pile, and into another'un, until after a while the whole side of the mountain was on fire an' he got up on a stump wavin' his walkin' stick hollerin', "Fire-yer. Fire-yer. God dang it, fire-yer!"

Showin' Out

One time, me an' my sister's boy by the name of Carl Stacy went to the swimming hole—it was about seventeen feet deep. (I learned how deep it was after I learned to swim.) Neither of us could swim.

We were settin' on a big old rock on the fer side of the creek, and some girls come up the road and said, "Let's see you boys jump in and swim some." We hollered an' told 'em we couldn't swim, and they said, "Aw, don't tell us stuff like that—big boys like you can't swim?"

I told Carl, "I'll try it across there if you will."

He said, "All right."

So, we was gonna show out in front of the girls. I jumped just as fer out as I could jump. And about the time I hit the water, I heard him comin', too. I went plumb to the bottom back'erds a-tryin' t'swim. The more I tried to swim for'erds, the further back'erds I'd go. I went plumb to the bottom of that hole of water and hit on a big ol' rock with m'feet and I'd give a big kick and come up in about four foot of the bank, and finally got out, and I looked back, and I see'd Carl Stacey with his mouth open goin' back'erds the same way as I went. I got a-hold of a pole and he got a-hold of it and I drug him out. It's a wonder that both of us hadn't a-drowned.

C-O-A-T!

There's a feller in North Carolina one time by the name of Rufus Jarnett, and his wife was named Iola. He was a kind of old man—fifty-five to sixty year old—and his wife couldn't hear good. He started out one mornin', got a little piece away from the house, decided he wanted his coat, and shouted out, "Hey, Iola, bring me my coat!"

She said, "What'd you say, Rufus?"

He said, "Bring me my coat!"

She said, "I can't understand you, Rufus."

He said, "Bring me my C-O-A-T. A garment to wear on your back, you old witch, you!"

Dog Races

Me and Carl Stacy, we'uz way up on the side of the mountain, and had his old dog with us. The old dog was named Tows. There was a snakin' road where they snaked logs off the mountain down to our house. That's the first dog I ever see'd with a runnin' fit on him. So, old Tows took a-runnin' fit an' we thought he'uz gone mad. Me an' Carl started runnin' down that snakin' road—Carl was in front, I'uz behind, and the dog right next to me. I'uz tryin' my best to get in front of him. I couldn't outrun him to save my life. We'uz goin' down the mountains as hard as we could run. There was a forked limb a-layin' in the road with the fork turned up the hill toward us. Somehow Carl stepped with one foot in the fork of that limb, and as he started to step again, that limb upset, and he went up in the air about five foot high and while he'uz up in the air, I run under him and got him between me an' the dog. I'd a-died before I'd a-let him in front of me no more. It never did hurt him; he just hit the ground a-runnin'. We finally did outrun the old dog.

"To Hell with You and That Peavey, Too!"

One time, me an' a feller by the name of John Reese was a-cuttin' acid wood and pulpwood, stuff like that. It'd snowed one night about two feet deep. He come over to the house the next mornin' a-wantin' t'go t'work. I told him, "Mr. Reese, the snow's s'deep, we can't work a time like this."

He said, "Lord, I got t'work. I got a family t'feed."

My daddy told him, "Just go down to the store, get all the stuff you want, and have it put on my ticket till the snow melts off. We can't work at a time like this."

"No, I got t'work. I can't go in debt like that."

Well, I decided if he could stand it, I could. So, I got ready and me and him went on to work, and it took us about three hours to walk five miles. They was some blocks o'wood layin' way up on the side of the hill. We'uz gonna roll 'em down into the hollow and bust 'em up and rick 'em up down next to what they call a flume. (That was a thing made like a hog trough; had water in it you could put the wood up in, and it'd take it plumb on out to the railroad.)

We got up on the hill an' got t'rollin' them blocks down, and one was froze up against the upper side of a tree and [John Reese] got to liftin' with a peavey, and the old hook just barely did catch in it, and he put his shoulder in under it and give a big jerk to turn the block over. 'Bout that time, the peavey hook busted a big hunk out of the side of the block, and he went right over the block on his belly and went out of sight and under the snow. He raised up and said, "I wish the world'd come to a end."

I said, "John, what'd you do with that peavey if it was to?"

He said, "To hell with you and the peavey, too!"

Land Swap

We lived up 'ere just above Lake Logan. We lived on one side of Pigeon River, and Burnett's Siding Church was over on the other side up the road about two miles. We owned about two acres of land over there, wasn't fit 'raise rabbits on, the land was so poor. So, Poppy decided to swap the land for a one-horse wagon. So, me an' him got up one mornin' right early in the wintertime. The creek was froze about half over—it was cold. We went to the edge of the creek, and it was half a mile down to where you cross the bridge, and then come back up the road on the other side. You could just ford across the creek and be in the road right there, save that half a mile circle. So, I stopped the horse right at the bank and told my daddy to get on behind me. He says, "Wait a minute. Let's go on down to the creek." He jumped on one or two rocks and got out about the middle of the creek on a big old rock. I got the horse right up next th'side of this rock, and he put one leg up on the horse's back and give a great big jump to come up on the horse and never jumped far enough, and had to go back. And that rock was froze where his foot hit it and his foot slipped out from under him and he went plumb out of sight in that cold water. I see'd his hat go floatin' down Pigeon River. He got up an' I commenced laughin' at him an' he never said a word in the world. Just waded out and headed back to the house. He never did swap that land for that one-horse wagon.

Ronda Reno

Students and Foxfire staff interviewed Ronda Reno in 2018 for an article on folk medicine and its continued relevance in today's hypermodern age. Ronda is the owner-operator of Cross & Thistle Apothecary in Royston, Georgia, and was raised in the Warwoman Community in eastern Rabun County, Georgia. Much of what she learned about folk medicine came from her great-grandmother Vera MacPherson Forrester, who served primarily as a midwife to the community but who also possessed a good deal of knowledge about native medicinal plants.

Aside from her work as an herbalist, Ronda is also quite the storyteller. She carries a great deal of folk history, legends, and anecdotes in her repertoire. During one of our interviews, Ronda provided us with some history about her family, the concept of the "granny witch," and a version of the Warwoman legend.

In the conversation that follows her story, we get a glimpse into how fluid oral tradition can be. Even in this book, we see how different versions of the same story coexist within small communities. Oral tradition, like folk music or foodways, has room for improvisation and reimagining. Often, storytellers will take the foundation of a story and embellish it with details more relevant to the audience or the teller's local community. A storyteller's own worldview also comes into play as well as that of his or her shared community. Other variables such as a particular agenda must also be considered when analyzing how stories change from teller to teller.

The interviewers identified in this piece are Foxfire facilitator Kaye Collins and students Willow Fisher and Sara Abernathy.

Ronda Reno

Kaye Collins: So how far back can you find granny witches in your family?

Ronda: All the way back to William the Conqueror.

Kaye: Wow.

Ronda: Yep.

Willow Fisher: How long ago was that?

Ronda: Before 1066.

Sara Abernathy: Oh.

Willow: Oh my goodness. That's a really long time.

Ronda: Mmm-hmm.

Kaye: A lot of wisdom there.

Ronda: Yep. Uh, we had family that actually came down through Salem that didn't leave Salem. [Laughs.]

Kaye: Wow.

Ronda: They were burned at the stake as witches.

Kaye: Seriously?

Ronda: A lot of midwives were killed during the, the witch trials. And you know actually a lot of healing women left England and Scotland and places like that 'cause they were in fear of their lives 'cause King James kinda went off his rocker a little bit and started killing anything that looked like they were gonna pick up an herb, and a lot of, a lot of tradition was lost during his reign during what they called the Witch Inquisition. So I know, from what we can document, we know that there was at least one that was burned at the stake in Salem. But we also know that there were four burned in Scotland, um, back during the first reign back in 1629, 1630. . . . When it, when it first, the witch outbreak as they called it. So, they were all burnt. So just for simply bein' poor and healin' with herbs and 'cause you know, some, you know I was always brought up you want to get your aboveground plants before the sun comes up 'cause that you know is still nutrient rich, the sun hasn't dried it out for the day. You know, it's had all night to replenish itself and rehydrate itself, so early in the morning before the sun comes up that's gonna be the best time to get you anything aboveground, and anything below the ground you wanna get it durin' the heat of the day when everything runs back into the ground.

Kaye: Ah. I've never heard that.

Ronda: So it wouldn't have been unusual to see women like that out at night harvesting stuff, and of course they would mistake it for [laughs] whatever else kind a lunacy they were dealin' with, their own demons, I reckon. But a lot of women were arrested, tried, killed, hung, drowned, burnt for just, simply, tryin' to help somebody. And I know there were cases that they attended a birth, and of course the baby was born with a birthmark. And of course they were . . .

Kaye: Blamed?

Ronda: Yeah. [Laughs.] Just it was such a funny time back then, I guess, you know, anything.

Kaye: A lot of superstition.

Ronda: Yeah. Anything that couldn't be explained it was automatically assumed [whispering] *that was the devil's doing so* kill it! You know, and children were put to death and like that. They would actually kill the children because they believed that if they were born with a witch's mark that it was believed that either the mother or the birther, the midwife, was in cahoots with the devil, so there was no help for the child, so they would actually drown the children or cut their umbilical cords too little, too short, and let em bleed out. Mmm-hmm.

Willow: Oh my goodness.

Ronda: Oh yeah. There have been, um, scripts found, um, where you know, women of aristocracy, talked about where their children being killed or havin' their head bashed up against a wall or somethin'. Yeah, it's, it's pitiful just to listen. Um, if y'all ever get a chance to go to England, UK, whatever they want to call it now, go into some of the, like Newgate Prison and stuff like that, and listen to some of the stories that they tell because women tend to define themselves there because they were the ones that birthed the noble ones, and the noble one's baby was born dead and she was to blame because of something she should have done or did do, and she didn't had, and I mean women were put in Newgate for just the simplest of things.

You know, working-class women and poor-class women didn't tend to fare well, especially women like us. So it's, you know, and when we came over here escaping the Jacobite slaughter. Um, they were killing women, children, and of course the men. Uh, they were sending men to basically, like, concentration camps, and they were just lining up and shootin' 'em because they were sympathizers, Jacobites. So and, the women and some of the older men actually escaped on ships. They actually escaped to Ireland, and that's where the Scots-Irish come from. Everybody thinks it's a bloodline, and it's not. The Scots people escaped to Ireland and came from Ireland to the colonies and they were called Scots-Irish. It's not a bloodline. It's um, it's an order of migration. Had to get that out. Yes, it's an order of migration. But you know the Scots people are actually Irish anyway.

Kaye: Yeah, I'm Scots-Irish.

Ronda: Yeah. That means that your family came from Scotland into Ireland and came from Ireland to here. A lot of 'em, a lot of us are like that. So . . .

Kaye: I think a lot of people in Appalachia are.

Ronda: Yeah. You know, that's why it was called "the High-lands" because when the first Scottish and Scots-Irish people came, it reminded them so much of the Highlands that they had to flee that they called it Highlands. And there was one, I cain't remember what part it was. They actually called it Aberdeen for the, for part of the coastal mountains in Scotland 'cause that's where my family's from is Aberdeen. And they called it Aberdeen, but I think later it changed to something else. But that's, like I think that's like it's up above Pine Mountain goin' into . . . It's between Pine Mountain and Highlands before you go in there. But it was called Aber, and now they call it some-thin' else, but now it's just a small little community between Pine Mountain and Highlands. Cain't think of what the name is of it now.

Kaye: Yeah, I know people who live there, but I couldn't think of the name of it.

Ronda: Yeah it's just, it's like a little unincorporated commu-nity between the two.

Kaye: Yeah.

Ronda: The little town, for the life of me I cain't remember what the name of it is now, then you go on to the Highlands and of course you've got Franklin and all that.

Kaye: Did any of your ancestors get information from the In-dians that lived here?

Ronda: Oh Lord, yes. It probably went from the Native Amer-icans to any of the Scots-Irish people or they probably would a perished the first year. I don't, uh, we don't have any handwritten accounts, but I know for a fact, well, I cain't say fact, just I guess.

Kaye: Family legend?

Ronda: Oral history. You know, talks about when they come here. As a matter a fact, it has to do with this story right here. What I heard the original story of Warwoman was, and that ain't it, that's what they say. [Laughs.] When all the Scots-Irish people were comin' over here, and of course they were comin' ta here with English settlers, too, there was a Mitchum family that moved in up on near Sara's Creek. As a matter a fact that's where I've always heard Sara's Creek was named after was Sara Mitchum. Um, they moved in. It was our family, the Mitchum family, um, the David family, which is another part of my family, as a matter a fact, is David, who built the cabins, Henry David. Um, and there was another one, I cain't remember the other one was, but anyway, they all tended to acclimate with the Native Americans, but for some reason the Mitchum family wanted to move past the Indian boundary line, and they were not supposed to be; they had been told to stay on this side of the line; you cain't go over there; you know this is to help Native American land. And of course you couldn't be out after dark or any of that stuff.

But, anyway, apparently being the little snotty English family they was [laughs], they figured they could just move anywhere they wanted to. Well, from what we were always told that the Cherokee people attacked the Mitchum family and killed what they thought was the whole family. They killed Mr. Mitchum, both 'a the kids, who they had thought they had killed Sara Mitchum. And from what we were told, Sara Mitchum managed to drag herself to my granny's house. Two miles across the mountain. She had been partially scalped, she had been stabbed a couple a times, she had been . . . I heard a few other things had been done to her, but I really don't believe that because Native Americans wouldn't have touched a white woman in that way. It would have been considered beneath them, filthy. So I don't think she was . . .

Um, but anyway, they said Granny healed her. Healed her body anyway, but they said her mind completely left her. And they said Granny just woke up one morning and she was gone. And they went back to the cabin and of course no one, they never could find her. And of course Native Americans believed you don't kill nobody crazy, you know, because they, Native Americans, believed that if you killed somebody that was crazy, you absorb their spirit, their powers and of course nobody wanted to be crazy, so [laughs] so you know, they wouldn't touch her, they wouldn't kill her. Well as more settlers begin to come into the mountain, more white settlers were interminglin' with the Native Americans of course, you know the result of that was blended children. And the way our legend has always told that a widowed Scotswoman had married into the Cherokee family, and of course that produced a son. The son had no qualms about offin' this woman, and they were out um, gatherin', pickin', gettin' water, doin' somethin', and [Sara Mitchum] come up on him and tried to kill the boy, and of course the boy ended up killing her and they say she's buried up on this mountain somewhere. They don't know where, but that's where I've always heard the real legend of Warwoman come from. They called her "War Woman."

Kaye: Sara? They called Sara "War Woman"?

Ronda: They called Sara "War Woman." But I've always heard that. To be honest, I've never heard it anywhere else, so . . .

Kaye: Well, I've heard lots of rumors about how it started, but I haven't heard that one.

Ronda: Yeah, so I mean, and I haven't, like I said, I've heard several, you know, and it all has to do with a crazy white woman. [Laughs.] Yeah. But that's just one of the legends. You know, I had never heard that one that they got up here before in my life until we seen that plaque.

Kaye: Really?

Ronda: I'd never heard it. I never grew up hearing anything like that. Ever.

. . .

Kaye: The sanitized version?

Ronda: And you know, that's what my husband said. He goes, "Oh that's the tourist version." [Laughs.] I'm like I bet it is.

Kaye: Oh, that's funny.

Kip Ramey

Kip Ramey is an outsider artist from the Warwoman Community in Northeast Georgia. His work primarily uses found objects that he manipulates into mixed-media pieces. Most recognizable are mixed-media paintings that use the tops of drink cans reimagined as faces. The found object aspect of his work, as well as his motivation to combat littering, sends him often into the local national forests to collect materials.

Kip is also someone who loves telling stories. His life as an artist has provided him a great deal of experiences that make for great narratives. Additionally, his upbringing in a community with a rich oral tradition has put Kip in front of some of the best storytellers in Southern Appalachia. As part of an interview with Kip, Foxfire students became interested in his fascination with the North American mythical creature Bigfoot.

Bigfoot is generally associated with the Pacific Northwest, though legends about the bipedal humanoid have also made recent appearances in the oral tradition of West Virginia. Kip's firsthand anecdote about this particular legendary creature fits in well with the larger body of fantastical firsthand account narratives that have grown in popularity since around the 1970s, including those about UFO encounters and abductions as well as

interactions with regional phenomena such as the chupacabra
(Southwest), Mothman (West Virginia), Rougaru (Louisiana),
and others.

Kip Ramey and his now-deceased art truck

Bigfoot

To me as a kid I was obsessed with the unknown. Bigfoot,
Nessie [the Loch Ness Monster], and just monsters in general.
I never wanted them to find him [Bigfoot]. They would always
say, "Maybe next time we can see him." Now everything is
about finding Bigfoot.

When I was a kid, you just heard about Bigfoot. You know,
your grandma would tell you stories, you know. My great-
grandmother was a great storyteller. She told scary stories,
though, just to scare us as kids, you know. God bless her, but
she, she was something else, you know. Her favorite thing was
just to scare the children; her favorite story was about when she

went to the state of Washington and seeing Bigfoot while she was there. There could be a Bigfoot.

I myself have seen something to where I believe was Bigfoot. He did not walk up to me and [say], "Hey! Look at me! I'm Bigfoot," but I really think it was Bigfoot. It was down by Warwoman . . . well, I won't say where because he [Bigfoot] might beat me up if I say where. Anyways, we got a little dog named Darcie. She's a small little dog. We went down to find this cave because my dad said there used to be Indians that lived there, so there might be Indian relics and blah, blah, blah so on and so forth. Anyways, we were at the cave. We had to walk across the ridge to find it and walk so far, then you come to it. Now, there is another way you can go—you walk past the blocked gate; you can see it directly across the road from it.

So, I had a bunch of kids with me. I also had my wife, my dog, and myself. It was about thirty degrees outside. So, we were walking and walking and walking, and we didn't see nothing. I'm thinking these kids are getting antsy, it is getting dark, we have been there two or three hours, so I was like, "Let's go home." When we were walking back—well, before all of this, I was carrying a .22 pistol with me just in case, you know. You never know what will or could happen, so we were walking back to the car, and I see an abandoned bees' nest in a tree. I'm thinking, "Wow, this looks really cool! I want to take this home with me." I shot it out, and it scared the dog, so she ran back in the truck. I had my brother's truck, which is a big jacked-up Chevrolet, so you know a dog this big [holds his hand about one foot or so off the ground] can't jump into it.

We eventually get back to the truck, and there Darcie is in the back of the huge pickup truck [in the bed of the truck]. In my mind, I was thinking, "What! How did she get in the back of the truck?," you know, but whatever. I took her out, but I was more worried of those kids, you know. The kids said, "I want to play in the culvert." [They] went down and played in the culvert a little bit. Then I said, "It is time to go, y'all," and it was fixing to get dark.

It was supposed to be minus degrees outside, so I wanted to go home, too. I got them all rounded up, [and] I started calling for Darcie. No Darcie. She was gone. We stayed there an hour just calling her and looking for her. No Darcie. She was just gone. So, I said, "We have got to get these kids. . . ." They were starting to whine and cry, the kids were. I said, "Okay, we are going to get y'all home and as soon as we get you home, we are going to come right back." And we . . . it was about an hour and a half into the woods, so we come back to the house, drop the kids off, got my dad. We went back. Drove in there. It was pitch-black dark, probably about ten o'clock when we got back there. It was really cold. It was probably about five degrees out.

One of Kip's favorite subject matters for his art is Bigfoot

We came to the end of the road, where the gate is, and I got this little flashlight, and I am whistling and was calling her. "Darcie, Darcie, come on, Darcie, come on." I turned around to face the other way and shine the light, and I see these giant arms. I can't explain it. They was like hairy black, brown, arms and they come out like this [stretches out his arms]. That was all I could see with a flashlight. Then [Darcie] fell out of them, and she came running toward me. Just out of the shock of it, I am thinking, "Holy cow, there is Darcie!" I didn't process what was happening. I picked her up, and she was warm, and she had been petted so much, her fur was slick. I have lost my sense of smell, so when I got in the truck, my wife said, "She smells, and it is something I have never smelt before!" [My wife] is one of those people, you can mix Clorox and raspberries and Ajax, and she will [tell] you that it is Ajax, Clorox, and raspberries. But, she couldn't identify the smell. It was the weirdest thing, because it was five degrees, and [Darcie] was warm. I still can't, to this day, really enter into my head what happened. We got in the truck and left. And I am thinking I am just happy to see her. I am like, "What in the world just happened?" But, that is the only thing I have ever seen that it could have been. There wouldn't nobody there to mess with me, so . . .

[Neither my dad nor my wife saw anything] because they were in the truck. I just turned around, and I'm like, "I am losing my mind!" I was just so happy to see [Darcie]. So, till this day I don't know. I don't know what it was, but I got my dog back. That is all. Thank God, I got my dog back. That just made me realize that we don't have a clue. We don't know what it is. I mean, we have hope, and faith, and whether we believe in God or whatever we believe in. You can have hope and faith and if it makes you a good person in whatever you are doing. But, I just thanked God she was back and whatever was looking out for her, was looking out for her and us. 'Cause it could have got us. It wouldn't have wanted me either. It would have thrown me back. I don't know what it was. It was something. There is just some things that don't have answers like a UFO. It would come right here, land in the middle of the Universal Joint, and talk to us, but I would still be like, "I wonder if that was a government thing," you know. The things that happen to us shape us and shape other people around us, you know. . . .

CONTRIBUTORS

Sarah Abernathy

Brooks Adams

Robbie Bailey

Kim Baldwin

Perry Barrett

Bobby Bass

Russell Bauman

Amy Beck

Scott Beck

Clark Bowen

Jan Brown

Judy Brown

Laurie Brunson

Andrea Burrell

Melanie Burrell

Kevin Cannon

Lee Carpenter

Lester Carpenter

Maybelle Carpenter

Bit Carver

Kaye Carver

Stephanie Cash

Dickie Chastain

Joanna Chieves

Mike Cook

Leah Crumley

Lee Darnell

Lori Darnell

Melanie Deitz

Scott Dick

Melissa Easter

Al Edwards

Nicole Edwards	Kim Hendricks	Kaleb Love
Elena Ellis	Lisa Henry	Katie Lunsfor
Audrey Eubank	McKaylin Hensley	Kelli Marcus
Willow Fisher	Frank Hill	Jason Maxwell
Lacy Forester	Rebecca Hill	Ray McBride
Shay Foster	Cailey Horn	Scott McKay
Kevin Fountain	Lacy Hunter	Marie Mellinger
George Freemon	Suzanne James	John Nichols
Stephen Gant	Richard Jones	Susie Nichols
Linda Garland	Mickey Justice	Ethel Page
Lori Gillespie	Michelle Keener	Kirk Patterson
Teresia Gravely	Tonia Kelly	Linda Phillips
Cynthia Green	Kara Kennedy	Alleson Queen
Gina Hamby	Lauren Korte	Mary Sue Raaf
Richard Harmon	Tommy Lamb	Annette Reems
Erin Harrison	Annemarie Lee	Renee Richard
Lee Heimrich	Lori Lee	Cristie Rickman
Tim Henderson	Hope Loudermilk	Sabrina Ritchie

Julia Roane	Greg Strickland	Marty Veal
Brandie Rushing	Annette Sutherland	Sheila Vinson
Bill Selph	Barbara Taylor	Lawanda Wall
Susan Shirley	Mary Thomas	Sarah Wallace
Jenni Shoemaker	Sheri Thurmond	Curtis Weaver
Becky Smith	Teresa Thurmond	Kenny Whitmire
Dewey Smith		Fred Willard
Leigh Ann Smith	Mario Trujillo	David Wilson
Tina Smith	Donna Turpin	Billy Wooten
Amanda Speed	Samantha Tyler	

ABOUT THE EDITOR

T. J. Smith is the president and executive director of The Foxfire Fund, Inc., and holds a PhD in folklore from the University of Louisiana at Lafayette.

For more information about Foxfire, be sure to visit
www.foxfire.org.